A Home for the Heart

Other Books by Charlotte Kasl

◆ ◆ ◆

Women, Sex, and Addiction: A Search for Love and Power

Many Roads, One Journey: Moving Beyond the 12 Steps

Finding Joy: 101 Ways to Free Your Spirit and Dance with Life

Yes, You Can! A Guide to Empowerment Groups

A Home for the Heart

A Practical Guide to
Intimate and
Social Relationships

• • •

Charlotte Sophia Kasl, Ph.D.

HarperPerennial
A Division of HarperCollins Publishers

Designed by Interrobang Design Studio

The Library of Congress has catalogued the hardcover edition as follows:

Kasl, Charlotte Davis.
    A home for the heart : creating intimacy and community with
loved ones, neighbors, and friends / Charlotte Sophia Kasl. — 1st ed.
        p.   cm.
    Includes bibliographical references.
    ISBN 0-06-017255-X
    1. Intimacy (Psychology). 2. Love. 3. Interpersonal relations. I. Title.
BF575.I5K37   1997
158' .2—dc20   96-33605

ISBN 0-06-092919-7 (pbk.)

98 99 00 01 02 ❖/RRD 10 9 8 7 6 5 4 3 2 1

Bright blessings . . .

To the reader seeking
greater love, intimacy, and compassion

To all people who give of themselves to create
healthy communities, preserve land and habitat, and
foster peace and understanding in the world

To Cathy and Jack who loved well

CONTENTS

IV   MANY SMALL STEPS

V JUST BETWEEN YOU AND ME: SENDING AND RECEIVING MESSAGES

VI "STAYING CONSTANT THROUGH CONFLICT"

ACKNOWLEDGMENTS

*H*eartfelt thanks to the many people who helped me with this book.

To both of my editors, Terry Karten and Janet Goldstein, heartfelt thanks for faith and support. To assistant editor, Kera Bolonik, I send appreciation for friendly help with the numerous details involved in putting this book together. A special thanks to Edite Kroll, my literary agent, for unending support, humor, and helpful input throughout the evolution of this book. Many thanks to Michelle Moellis for designing the graphics.

During the process of writing, I called on many people for ideas or to read parts of the manuscript. I thank you all for your generosity: Gertrude Laskechewitz, Marylee Hardenbergh, Sarah and Mollie Mitchell-Olds, Janet England, Jeanine Walker, Ron Erickson, Jean Templeton, Sigurd Hoppe, Leslie Ojala, Hugh Martinson, David Kester, Helen Watkins, Christine Sullivan, Arnelle Dow, Sue Ivison, and members of the neighboring Smith family—Carla, Nate, and Matt—who gave interviews on friendship. A special thanks to Ruth Singer for reading parts of the manuscript and helping me find quotations to use at the beginning of some of the chapters. Another special thanks to Carla Smith for kind help with biblical references.

I also give thanks to my Quaker meeting and the dear people of Missoula who are wonderfully dedicated to creating and maintaining a sense of community—not only among the people but by protecting the land, rivers, forests, wildlife, wilderness, and parks. To live among people who love the land so dearly gives me a true home for my heart.

With all best wishes,

Charlotte Sophia Kasl
Lolo/Missoula, Montana
July 1996

INTRODUCTION

*T*his book is for people wanting deeper intimacy, more love, and less fear. It operates at many levels, by looking at our relationship to self, spirit and others, not as separate entities, but as an integrated whole, an evolutionary process that is embedded in community. In *Finding Joy*, I talked about the path from loneliness and depression to self-acceptance and inner peace. This book provides a next step by exploring intimacy and the role of community in helping people deepen their ability to find nurture and pleasure in relationships of all kinds.

Intimacy and community are deeply intertwined. The values that permeate cultures and societies lay the foundation for personal relationships. When community is built on a life-loving spirituality that tolerates differences and supports people in their personal evolution, we are likely to see a deeper capacity for love and intimacy than societies where conformity, status, position and material possessions are a fundamental value. Even so, each of us has the capacity to make changes in our lives that increase our ability for intimacy. When we do this collectively, we affect the nature of our community.

The American dream of happiness was once described by Franklin Roosevelt as a chicken in every pot. The longing for basic comfort and a full belly seemed like the ultimate joy. But it didn't work. While most people now have a chicken in the pot, not to mention televisions, computers and other technological wonders, happiness over the years has not increased. Various studies suggest that people are more stressed and less happy on the whole than forty years ago when they had far fewer possessions. The unrequited longing many of us feel can only be filled with intimacy, spirit and community. Contentment and happiness come from the ability to appreciate and enjoy more deeply a few things of meaning, rather than having more things and more stimulation.

A Home for the Heart is a journey that starts by considering the meaning of love, intimacy, and community, and ends with a ride on a hand-carved carousel—created by people in community. In between, we look at the intricacies of relationships with friends, family, neighbors, primary partners, and the natural world—all of which are seen as pieces of an interconnected whole. We also look at the relationship metaphors found in our connections to money, sex, food, and drugs, as well as in our giving and receiving. Each section in *A Home for the Heart* can be seen as a building block for community; in a way, it is also circular: The skills in any one area affect our skills in all the others.

Writing this book has been like having a constant mirror in front of me, helping me be more conscious of my relationships. While it's easy to observe others, the ultimate challenge in forming relationships is to observe ourselves. This book invites self-exploration. It also encourages the reader to have compassion for oneself and others, remembering that most of our blocks to intimacy come from lack of good models or fear that overlays childhood wounds and oppression in the culture.

My ultimate hope in writing this book is for people to find well-being through connection and intimacy so we will live more in harmony with each other and the natural world. When we feel satisfied inside, we naturally move toward simplicity and greater care for each other. As we find a home for our heart, we come to value that which nurtures life—love, connection, air, water, earth—and let go of wanting that which is scarce or depletes the earth. We come to value love as the manifestation of spirit expressed through our connections to all sentient life.

A few words about terminology in the book: Because many people in committed relationships are not married or are of the same sex, I rarely use the term husband, wife, or spouse, except in specific examples. I use partner, mate, dear one, or beloved. The examples are frequently a composite of several similar examples. They come from clients I've worked with over the years, observations, and personal experience. If they seem familiar, it's because they are common to many people. With pronouns, I use "they," "s/he," or "he or she." Sometimes I use "she" in one sentence and "he" in the next. I use the term "marriage" not in the legal sense of the word, but rather in the spiritual sense of the word to mean a bonded, committed relationship.

PART I

...

THE SACRED SONG
OF LONGING

1

LOVE—A HOME FOR THE HEART

Love is the only satisfactory answer to the problem of human existence.

—Erich Fromm

*L*ove is the energy at the center of all life. It is the reality beneath our fears, the breath within the breath, the seed of all that grows. Loving ourselves, loving others, and loving spirit/God are inseparable, for all life is interconnected and sacred. Love is an energy force like the air you breathe; if you withdraw your love from anyone, you take your breath away.

We become increasingly able to love as we integrate ourselves and become whole. Our wholeness is expressed in a lust for life and a capacity for joy, delight, and adventure. Our wholeness gives birth to compassion, which Ram Dass describes in *Compassion in Action* as "the tender opening of our hearts to pain and suffering." For most people, the journey toward love requires that we penetrate the armor around our hearts, feel our grief, and open ourselves to all our feelings. In doing so we become more truly alive, deepen our self-acceptance, and become less and less dependent on others to validate our worth. This frees us to stand in the center of our power and to give generously of ourselves from a sense of inner safety, potency, and vitality. The ability to give generously of ourselves without feeling we are giving up something or being controlled is at the heart of intimacy because it reflects our individual strength and development.

We reach for words to describe love, but, ultimately, love is an experience of unity, peace, or ecstasy that goes beyond words. Too often people mistake love for fancy presents, sentimental greeting cards, or lavish praise. But love is not sentimental; love takes discipline, awareness, and a willingness to step into the fire of transformation. It is born of the minute-to-minute choices we make throughout our days as we bring honesty, integrity, and compassion to all we do and say.

People often treat love like a commodity that you can turn on for some people and off for others. But you can't truly love your partner and hate your neighbor, or exploit the people who work for you. Love can't be compartmentalized because it is central to your being. You can't turn on half a lightbulb. You can dim it or make it brighter, but when it's on, the light shines equally in all directions.

Disconnection and separateness, nearly always stemming from fear, are the opposite of love. To be disconnected can be a dull anxious feeling of inner detachment that makes life seem mundane, superficial, and routine. We feel controlled by external events and lack an inner core that allows us to be spontaneous, fluid, and flexible. We see people as bodies, but not as souls—they have form and shape and even beauty, but we don't feel their essence. When we are disconnected from our inner core, we are unable to absorb and be moved by beauty, wonder, and kindness. We hear music, but it doesn't make our heart sing. We see flowers, but they might as well be plastic. We touch someone, but there is no connection. When we feel separated, it's hard to trust that anyone cares, or could possibly love us if they were to see our hidden, shameful side.

We can bring ourselves back to love—to the home of our heart—by remembering that we are all children of our Creator, sacred because we are alive. If we accept our intrinsic worth, we can give up the futile search for external validation and put our energy into developing our ability to develop our talents and strengths. We can also remember that we have free will. Because we are pure potential, we are not locked into our past, but have the ability to recreate ourselves moment to moment by our thoughts, actions, and willingness to experiment with new behavior and give up old rigid patterns that no longer serve our growth. We also become willing to dive deep below the surface into our buried wounds. We have an amazing ability to heal and transform as we tap the powerful energy source underlying all our feelings and emotions. Instead of labeling our feelings as good or bad we see them as energy that can be redirected for our growth. The inward journey becomes easier as we tap into our heart's capacity for humor, compassion, and mercy. We become able to take ourselves into our heart, embracing all that we are and all that we have been. It becomes a mystical, humorous, fascinating show as we learn to observe ourselves, yet immerse ourselves in life.

From this point of self-acceptance and compassion we develop the willingness to share our feelings in their raw, vulnerable state, not after we've figured them out or gotten them under control. This doesn't mean that we unload our emotions on others, it means that we stop hiding, faking a smile, or presenting ourselves as we wish to be seen. We accept our humanness and allow it to be seen.

One of my favorite phrases from one of the dances of universal peace is "God is love, lover, and Beloved." If we break "Beloved" in two, we have "be loved": Be loved by spirit, be loved by yourself, be loved by others. If we remove the last letter of "Beloved," we have "be love." Don't seek love or lover, simply *be love*. Be at peace with All That Is, and know you *are* the Beloved. And when you find a lover, know that the journey is to dance together in the circle of love, growing, playing, struggling, and accepting with a smile the incredible predicament of being human. When we can do this, even for a few moments, we will feel a flow of energy like the current of a river dissolving our separateness and bringing us to greater unity.

To become love, lover, and Beloved means making love your highest priority. It doesn't necessarily mean you quit your job or change the external situation of your life, although that might be part of the process. It means giving yourself to the daily practice of bringing love and awareness to everything you do. It also means stretching, reaching, growing, and stepping through fear again and again. This usually involves some form of daily spiritual practice or a daily plan to go deeper into yourself and break old patterns that sit like ice jams inside, blocking your ability to reach out and love generously or be reached by those who would love you.

Love involves a fundamental change in consciousness of realizing there are no "others" out there, rather, we are all inter-twined in a single web that is the miracle of life, a cosmic energy field. On a concrete level this means internalizing in the deepest part of yourself the thought, "There but for the grace of God go I," or, more accurately, "There go I." When you feel scorn or contempt for someone, a part of you can remember that given different circumstances, you could be like that person or in that person's situation. Likewise, when you see someone show greatness, you can know that you too have a great nature within you.

In Nepal, where many religions and customs meet, it is customary to greet people by saying *"Namaste,"* which can be translated as "I salute the divinity in you," or, "To the light in you," or, "To the God in you." It is like taking a breath of life and combining it with the knowledge that we are all children of creation and are sending this energy out to everyone we meet. *Namaste.* I salute the divinity in you. This is where we begin.

2

ALLOW YOURSELF YOUR LONGING

In your longing for your giant self lies your goodness: and that longing is in all of you.

—Kahlil Gibran

Reach down inside, past the worries of the day, the thoughts of tomorrow, and listen to the deepest part of yourself. Tap into your longing for love, connection, and understanding. Can you hear it? What does it say? When I listen deeply, I think of the relationships and community I have, and I feel good. Then, as I listen longer, I crack open to a deeper layer that longs for closer connections with more honesty, passion, consciousness, and a greater ability to give and receive love. I want to know love in all of my being, to feel free to experience a deeper sense of unity with people, animals, and the earth.

Many of us bury our longing for greater love and intimacy because we believe it is out of reach—it is not for ordinary people. We might tell ourselves it is too painful to long for passionate, intimate connections because we have been hurt, rejected, or betrayed. Maybe it's hard to have faith in our worthiness because we have internalized the notion of a judgmental, fearsome God, or have been taught that we are inferior. Maybe we've hid out so long in a role, it seems unimaginable to let it slip away and feel the nakedness of our longing. So we put on a protective coating that keeps us from ourselves and others. We dissociate from our true selves in a myriad of ways. We put on a mask, we drink, smoke, eat too much, or get busy and productive. Yet what do we produce? Even if we rush through the day obsessed with tasks to accomplish, read a ton of books, or exercise compulsively, we can only mask the longing for connection because it is natural to human existence. We are all tribal people and our health, joy, and happiness are intricately tied to interconnecting with others and with spirit.

Take a look at the motivation underlying all the things you do. If you look deep enough, you will realize that many of your actions are motivated by a desire for love and connection—to find it, maintain it, or keep from losing it. Remember the miles you have traveled, the money you have spent, the heartaches you have survived, the times you stayed up all night, worried about your looks, or sought wealth, status, and fame. Wasn't much of that all about a great longing to feel special so that someone would love you or say, "Good for you"?

Think for a moment of how you spend your time. What are you truly seeking? What do you want to have accomplished when you finish this life? Go as deep as you can. Is there a place that simply wants to slow down, tune into life, know yourself, and feel close to others? A turning point in my life came at the age of forty-four when I saw my father die a very lonely man. He had waited until retirement at age sixty-eight to travel, but it was too late, he had Alzheimer's disease. He had written books, been admired, and had received numerous awards, yet he was profoundly lonely. It jolted my complacency about work and relationships. I resolved to make a priority of friendships and spiritual growth along with doing work I loved.

If you are seeking greater love and intimacy in your life, you might ask yourself how much time you give to growing, reaching out to others, and nurturing your relationships. How deep is your capacity for stillness and quiet, which allows the wisdom within you to emerge? How honest are you with yourself and others?

Your longing is your connection to your soul, the part of you that cries out for spirit and for love. To hear this inner cry is to touch the earth, reach for the sky, and open yourself to your awakening heart, the source of compassion and understanding. To feel your longing creates a thirst and hunger for the true nourishment of life. Dare to feel it and immerse yourself in a passionate journey for all that will truly fill you and bring peace.

3

MAKE FRIENDS WITH YOUR EMPTY PLACES

Let a streaming beauty flow through you . . . Opening into that gives peace, a song of being empty, pure silence.

—Rumi

When we allow ourselves our longing, we sometimes find a big, empty place inside. It makes us uncomfortable and anxious. We want to run. If this is your experience, instead of running away, you might take a few deep breaths and slide down into that scary place inside. Stay with it. The empty place won't swallow you up. Notice how you feel—sweaty, jumpy, scared, or fascinated, excited, and curious? If it's frightening, breathe, soften your belly, and elicit compassion for this wounded part of you that has been ignored for so long. Feel it. Embrace this part of you. Remember, it is out of the womb, the emptiness, that life is created. In this place of anxiety or emptiness you will come to know your rejected self and your fears. It is from this scary place that you will free yourself and open the door to love and intimacy.

One way people become more at peace with their empty place is to visit it daily. Every time you want to detach, numb out, or run away, stop, go inside, and make friends with your fears. Stay with the terror of silence, of nothingness. One woman I knew drew her empty place. It started as a frightening dark hole. Then a day or so later she drew the hole with herself sitting at the bottom with a ray of light shining in. Over time, as she drew pictures of her empty place, she added flowers and books and a comfortable chair. She was increasingly able to breathe and relax in her empty place without wanting to eat or get busy—her usual escapes. Then she drew a ladder on the wall of the empty place and saw someone peering over the rim. She invited him to come sit with her. They both talked about their empty places, and as they did, they felt a sense of happiness and warmth coming over them. Like everything, the empty place is energy. When we meet it with consciousness and simply breathe into it and stop labeling it as bad, it begins to dissolve into a peaceful stillness.

Denying our empty place creates fear and anxiety. So long as we run away, the dark hole seems bigger and bigger, scarier and scarier, like a villain or a big dragon chasing us in a bad dream. If we stop and face the dragon, we begin the process of knowing and integrating ourselves. When we hide from parts of ourselves—our fears, anger, grief, power, and joy—we feel split inside. It's like locking up parts of ourselves in little boxes and using a lot of energy to keep the boxes from flying open. The distance we keep from our buried selves is reflected in the distance we keep from others. In a hundred ways we transmit the message, stay away, you might see me. Stay away, I might see myself. In this state of self-absorption we have little ability to see or empathize with others.

The more we heal the split-off places within us, the more our fears dissolve and the more we feel centered in ourselves. This allows us to take the armor off our heart and say, come close, I want to know you and be known by you. Another way to start the process of making friends with your empty places is to talk with a friend about the parts of you that seem shameful and unlovable. You might find that your friend understands you very well.

4

CONTEMPLATE INTIMACY

The river that flows in you also flows in me.
—Kabir

When a friend was asked to describe her primary relationship, she paused for a moment, allowing the words to come from inside: "There's a rhythm and flow. A sense of ease. I feel invited to be honest. There's attraction . . . electricity between us. There's a way we understand each other and a willingness to struggle with each other through the hard times." You notice that she didn't describe characteristics of her mate. Intimacy is often felt in the spaces in between us—a sense of familiarity, knowing, and care that flows between the two people. Martin

Buber writes in *I and Thou* that "Spirit is not in the *I* but between the *I* and *Thou*. It is not like the blood that circulates in you, but like the air in which you breathe."

Dictionary synonyms of intimacy are "familiar," "warm," "affectionate," "close," "aware," "conscious," "deep." Often, the experience of intimacy is beyond words—it is the milk and honey of existence. When we experience it, we know it—there's a sense of time stopping, of simply being at one with who we are, authentically connected to another being. Yet, intimacy is not idyllic and easy. Having disputes and resolving conflict are intrinsic to intimacy when done with integrity.

Intimacy, including sexual intimacy, has a mystical quality because through our union with another person we begin to feel a greater oneness with All That Is. The river that flows in *us* flows through all things. Intimacy carries the seeds of transformation because it expands our hearts, allowing us to see life from the big perspective of compassion and understanding. Intimacy brings the music and the words together, allowing us to dissolve into one another while remaining conscious of our separate journeys.

True intimacy requires a willingness to be vulnerable and to be affected by another—to be known, loved, and transformed. We speak and make love with our eyes open to each other. We live with the possibility of loss of each other through death or separation. Intimacy also requires surrender to our inner truths. It's like making a covenant with ourselves: *I will not perform for you, exaggerate for you, or fake it to please you. I will let you know me as I am without trying to control your response. Likewise, I do not want you to perform for me, fake it, take on a role, or worry about my responses. I want to know you as you are.* To give up all pretense is scary. Yet only through this level of honesty and integrity do we develop the core sense of self that allows us to risk closeness—to open our hearts and allow ourselves to be known.

We can only connect with people when we can see them as distinct from us. In *The Art of Loving*, Erich Fromm writes, "*Love is union under the condition of preserving one's integrity, one's individuality.*" Part of becoming intimate is to ask in a hundred ways,

"Who am I?" Likewise, we need to open ourselves to the other and be able to ask, "Who are you?" Then we need to dance with the differences, to allow the discomfort and fascination simply to exist. We can come together like a song in two-part harmony, but we are not one melody together. If we try to modulate the differences, we dull the spark of intimacy. We distort our perceptions of others, assuming they want what we want or that they perceive situations as we do. We never truly know them for who they are. When we see people as distinct, we bring them into sharp focus. This is beautifully illustrated in *The Little Prince*, by Antoine de Saint-Exupéry. In this journey of awakening, the Fox asks the Little Prince to "tame him."

> "What does that mean—tame," asks the Little Prince.
> "It is an act too often neglected," says the Fox. "It means to establish ties. To me, you are still nothing more than a little boy who is just like a hundred thousand other little boys. And I have no need of you. And you, on your part, have no need of me. To you I am nothing more than a fox like a hundred thousand other foxes. But if you tame me, then we shall need each other. To me, you will be unique in all the world. To you, I shall be unique in all the world . . . "

It is this profound sense of knowing and cherishing someone—foibles and all—that lies at the heart of intimacy. It is in this connection we find the answer to the challenge of human existence and the anxiety that comes from separation. The richness of an intimate, authentic human bond can never be taken away, even if the other person leaves. The memories we had with them are ready to be kindled by the associations we've made with them—their smell, laughter, warmth, the songs we knew and the places we've been together. They live on in our heart. In *The Little Prince*, the Fox tells the Little Prince, ". . . You have hair the color of gold. Think how wonderful that will be when you have tamed me! The grain, which is also golden, will bring me back the thought of you."

When the Little Prince says he doesn't have much time to be tamed because he has friends to discover, and "a great many things to understand," the Fox replies, "*One only understands the things that one tames.*" Think of the experience of seeing a dear one who has been away for a time. When his or her face appears, your heart jumps because you have come home to yourself and to connection. Your whole history together is felt throughout your body in a single moment.

HOW DO WE CREATE INTIMACY?

The foundation involves developing our self-identity, our spirituality, and the ability to tolerate discomfort and anxiety. Without a well-defined center within us, intimacy carries the threat of annihilation or being swallowed up in another person's reality. We fear being infiltrated with their values, beliefs, feelings, and anxieties. We might experience constant confusion trying to decipher our own will and beliefs. We get tangled up inside trying to do the "right" thing or please, which triggers feelings of resentment or anger. We handle our anxiety—the fear of being swallowed up—by either keeping distance, living in constant drama, or lunging into dependent relationships and then running in terror when we feel overwhelmed.

To develop a sense of self we can look at the constant demands we place on others to do our bidding, then embark on a path of relinquishing these attachments. The Buddhist notion of nonattachment offers us a helpful perspective on intimacy. The belief that we create our suffering by our attachments puts the responsibility for our feelings directly on us. If we are *attached* to someone giving us praise, telling us we are lovable or doing things our way, we are likely to create feelings of anger, hurt, or judgment when they don't conform to our wishes. Our self-esteem will depend on their praise or agreement with our beliefs.

From the perspective of nonattachment, our job is to let go of our attachments, develop a deep and abiding faith in the power of being honest in relationships and encourage others to do likewise. We need to realize that maintaining our integrity in relationships is the only path toward intimacy. When this knowledge rests deeply in the center of our being, we are not easily shaken by what others say and do. Our self-esteem stands fast in the face of differences, heated discussions, or anger from those we love. We learn to say what's true and not personalize what others say by feeling hurt, running away, or feeling victimized. Rather, we are able to hear their words as *their* thoughts, *their* programming, and *their* frustrations, which are part of *their* journey. We may not like what they say or may not agree with them, but we do not need to become entangled in their feelings. This does not mean we don't care, rather, that we are able to step back and see from a broader perspective as a loving witness to both of our unfolding journeys. It's a stance of loving compassion.

From this centered place of loving compassion, we feel safe enough to reveal deeper levels of self. We speak our truths as they are revealed to us or when the time feels right because we feel led to do so, not to elicit sympathy or to "get the other person to talk." The challenge is always to look inward and explore our reactions, hurts, anger, and the impulse to throw someone out of our heart. We can explore the demands and expectations we're placing on another person and see how we are creating our unhappiness.

Returning to Kabir's words, "The river that flows in you also flows in me," we can allow ourslves to feel the river of each other's passion when we are deeply rooted in our own identity. Our capacity for experiencing powerful energy within us expands, and we can experience the realm of oneness without losing ourselves. As Kahlil Gibran says in *The Prophet*, "Love one another, but make not a bond of love: Let it rather be a moving sea between the shores of your souls. Fill each other's cup but drink not from one cup."

5

FIND INTIMACY THROUGH CREATIVITY AND NATURE

Let me feel thy embrace, Beloved, on all planes of existence.
                                        —Hayrat Inayat Khan

*I*ntimacy is not just something we have with other people, it's something we have with art, music, dance, writing, athletics, and nature. When we draw, play, write, engage in sports, make music, sing, drum, or dance we relinquish control and allow the muses to guide us. It's like both getting out of ourselves and getting into ourselves more deeply. It takes discipline, yet it cracks our ego boundaries, allowing us to fly into the spontaneous world of be-ing—living in the moment, feeling creation bubbling through us. It's a form of both making love and meditating because we merge heart and mind and exist in pure connection with the present. The challenge for many is to bring creativity into relationships—to allow spontaneity, playfulness, and originality to change old, hackneyed patterns so the connection stays alive and moving.

Our creative passions can enrich our lives. They can also become a hideout and take us away from human intimacy. When I was young, my sanctuary was playing the piano. I could leave the world, make beautiful sounds, and for a while there was no loneliness. As I got older, I noticed that men fell in love with me after hearing me play the piano. While on one level this had a tremendous appeal, it also led to frustration and emptiness. People would expect me to be a sensitive, creative person, and I was—but I couldn't manifest my inner experience with other people. I often felt at a loss for words or wondered how to be—what was I supposed to do? Eventually I realized I had to meet people without the piano in between us. So I stopped teaching and performing. It was terrifying because I felt wobbly and unsure of myself. It was like giving up a crutch and learning to walk all over again. Ultimately, I learned that there is nothing so creative as being intimate with another human being—but it has not been an easy journey and, of course, I am still learning. I have also gone back to playing the piano, but with a different consciousness. I play to experience the music, to feel the genius and beauty of these great composers in my hands and in my body. The concern is not to do it right or perform, rather to immerse myself in it, to feel the joy inside of me. It is the same kind of consciousness that allows lovemaking to come alive.

Along with the arts, our connection with nature helps us feel the presence of the Beloved. The greatest legacy my father gave me was sharing his love of adventure, hiking and being in the forest. Sitting on a rock by a river, canoeing, camping, or walking through the woods is a sure source of renewal and joy for me. It takes me out of myself and reminds me of the bigger picture of life.

Like the arts, intimacy with nature brings us in touch with beauty and spirit, but cannot replace human connections. Ideally, we become able to have both loves, or to have them merge together: We experience the wondrous feeling of lying on soft, mossy earth as being cradled in the arms of both Mother Earth and our lover. The soft breeze on a spring day feels like the lightness in our heart when we feel love for someone. As we merge our relationships to nature and creativity, we heighten the wonder and power of both.

I remember a recent hike in the mountains with a dear friend. Our talking faded as we became mesmerized by the beauty around us. I felt my feet connecting with the ground and the rapid beating of my heart as the path got steeper. I could see the snow on the mountaintop and the larches turning gold and feel the crisp fall air on my skin. There was a sense of being fused with my companion and with nature all at once. These moments of bliss are powerful medicine, a true home for the heart that sustains us through the struggles and difficulties in life.

6

NOTICE WHEN PEOPLE SEEM LIKE OBJECTS

True beings are lived in the present, the life of objects is in the past.
—Martin Buber

*T*he opposite of intimacy is seeing people as separate or as objects. One way to become aware of this is to distinguish the different feelings in your body as you relate to others. In *I and Thou*, Martin Buber refers to "I-It" relationships. They reflect a narcissistic stance, a bit like toddlers playing with toys. They pick them up, look at them, put them in their mouths, shake them, and when they are bored, put them down. Sometimes, if they are broken, the child will discard them unceremoniously. It is a one-way relationship—child to object. The energy doesn't flow back and forth.

I-It relationships lack empathy or compassion. We look at people only with thoughts of how they can serve us or enhance our lives. We have little concept of our impact on others. As you scan your history of relationships, you might recall being treated like an object or having treated someone else like an object. You might also remember the feelings in your body.

Objectifying others keeps us disconnected and lonely. Being

objectified leaves us feeling used, resentful, and confused. Objectification of others precludes intimacy, especially sexual intimacy. I remember going to a party during my college days with an old friend, Al. We had walked into the room and were standing on a landing above the crowd. He looked around the room and said, "I could have her, or her, or her in bed with me tonight." His approach was definitely an I-It approach. Instead of trying to know the women as people, he was "reading" them so he could tap into their vulnerability and seduce them for his pleasure. At the time, he wasn't aware that he was doing anything wrong. He was acting out of male cultural conditioning. But in relating to the women as sexual conquests he became an *It* himself, the natural consequence of objectifying others.

I-It relationships can take the form of a chess game of moves and countermoves, with each person having a covert plan that is often unconscious. In the example with Al, the women who were his willing bed partners also had an unconscious need that they were longing to have filled, possibly the need to feel loved, appreciated, and held in someone's arms. Unfortunately, like Al, until their needs became conscious and could be voiced, they could never be directly fulfilled.

In I-It relationships there is often a presumption of ownership, which can lead to control and domination. "She's *my* wife" is easily extended to "You're *my* wife so you *must* have sex with me when I want." "Because you are *my* husband, you must support me." "Because you are *my* employee, you must work the hours I say." To get away from the language of ownership, one couple I knew stopped using the terms "my wife," "my child," "my husband" and simply said each other's names—"This is Torry." If someone asked, "Is that your wife?", he would say, "We're married to each other."

To become conscious of objectifying others you could notice the times you refer to someone in a possessive way or feel *entitled* to being waited on, taken care of, or validated for your opinion. Notice when you want to be with someone because of their status or because they are so needy you will never be confronted with looking at yourself. Think of the things you take for granted from your friends, loved ones, fellow workers or employees, or people who serve you in stores and businesses. Do you ever think of how cheaply you can "get" someone to work for you?

Everyone starts life viewing the world from an I-It perspective: "Mommy is here to give me what I need. The world revolves around me." This is natural and healthy when we are infants, but we need to shift as we grow up to a more integrated stance in which we both give and receive. One reason the terrible twos are terrible is because we start learning (hopefully) that we are not the center of the universe. Our mother loves other people—how could she! Our father is sometimes nice and sometimes distant. We have to start sharing, waiting, and possibly putting up with a baby brother or sister. Getting through this period of self-centeredness, or narcissism, is crucial to forming intimate ties and becoming a contributing member of community.

One of the ways to move away from I-It thinking is to notice your objectifying language or automatic expectations and ask yourself, Who gives me this right? Where am I coming from? Having money, status, rank, or being male or white are not acceptable answers in the world of intimate relationships. Neither are childhood wounds or oppression. *No matter what the reason, whenever we attempt to exploit or use someone, we perpetuate the use-and-abuse cycle that wounds us all.*

I-It relationships are at the core of all violence. The thinking goes like this: If I am superior to you or you exist for my use, if you do not do my bidding I have the right to use force. Even though we may not like what someone does, when we retaliate in a violent way, we are objectifying ourselves and the other person. Only by moving to a level of mercy and compassion do we break this cycle. A remarkable story in *Life Magazine*, August 1966, tells of a woman's mercy at a Ku Klux Klan rally. According to the story, Keshia Thomas, an eighteen-year-old African American woman, wanted to ask one of her adversaries, "What did I ever do to you?" Before she had a chance, the protesters threw a man on the ground and began to physically assault him. She threw herself on him to protect him from harm and the crowd immediately withdrew. As the story said, "Thomas had performed an alchemy more miraculous than turning lead into gold. She had transformed violence into peace."

As you appraise your I-It relationships, it's important to be gentle with yourself. We objectify people because we were objectified and not encouraged to develop an autonomous self. We often had a parent who covertly threatened us with a withdrawal of love or imminent collapse if we spoke up. Underlying I-It relationships is fear—the fear of difference, being known, having our shame exposed, or being rejected. To change means to summon the courage to be known in your wholeness, including your needy, scared parts—this decreases our fear. As you come to regard yourself in a humane, caring way, you will increasingly see the humanity in others and develop the capacity for mercy and kindness.

7

DO YOU FEEL SOMETHING IS MISSING? I-YOU RELATIONSHIPS

*H*ave you ever had the feeling that a relationship was pleasant and okay but that something important was missing? Between objectified and intimate relationships many people have what I call I-You relationships. While there is no conscious intent to use or exploit the other person, there is a lack of intimacy. These relationships are probably the norm of this culture. When I think of my parents, their marriage strikes me as primarily an I-You relationship. They cooperated, planned the budget, and shared the work. They read us stories and took us to church. They were good, hard-working people who wished the best for their children. Yet, as a child observing them, it never occurred to me that married people loved each other. I never saw a charge of energy between them. They didn't deal with conflict openly, get angry, express emotions, or show their pain. My father seemed real to me when he was in the woods and I adored my mother when she played her violin—it gave me a glimpse into her inner world. But when they were together there was little sense of intimacy. I believe they wanted to know each other but didn't know how. Their disconnection lived in me as I experienced a longing for a nameless something I never saw in their marriage or felt in our own interactions.

I was profoundly lonely living in this I-You household. I rarely spoke to either of my parents about hurts, fears, or the longing of my heart. I never told my parents that my second-grade teacher was hitting kids in the face with a ruler. In all the years together as a family there were only a few moments of an I-Thou connection between us. Those are the moments I treasure—when my mother told me of a dream she had before going into surgery for a possible cancer, when my father told me (when I was fifteen) that he hated the way he got in fights with me and swore every morning that he wouldn't do it, but just seemed to lose control. These moments gave me a window into the inner workings of these people, these semi-strangers called my parents.

As a result of my childhood, I spent my early adulthood somewhat dissociated from feelings and emotions that led to having I-It and I-You relationships of my own. While I appeared competent and intelligent on the surface—due largely to playing the piano—I felt distant from most people and emotional events passed me by with a sense of unreality. Looking back, I'm floored by some of my behavior. In my late twenties, I lived in a music club in London run by a grand old Englishwoman usually accompanied by her two large bulldogs. Even though I admired and liked her enormously, when she became sick and went to the hospital, I couldn't motivate myself to go visit her even though a part of me wanted to. When I heard she had died, I was sad, but I didn't go to the memorial service. It wasn't that I didn't care, it was like being cloaked in a veil of unreality that I couldn't shake off. Everything passed by in a semi-daze.

Many people go through life feeling a veil of disconnection that leads to I-You relationships. They live out roles, have comfortable routines, but are left spiritually hungry. They have physical comfort, but somewhere deep within lies an unrequited longing, a sense that something is missing. If this applies to you, trust the feeling. Reach deep inside and create an image of it—the size, shape, color, tone, feeling. See if you can discern between a longing that comes from a sense of neediness or dependency and a longing that is your soul seeking life, passion, and joy. Talk about your longing with your friends and loved ones: If your friend or partner disavows a concern—"I think everything is fine"—don't invalidate your longing and don't be discouraged. Keep listening to yourself, keep asking the universe to lead you on the path of being fully alive, connected and powerful.

8

OBSERVE YOUR CONNECTIONS TO OTHERS

*T*o increase intimacy in your life, start becoming aware of how you connect—or don't connect—with others. Imagine a connection meter ranging from intimately connected to boring and distant. If that doesn't work for you, think of adjectives that come to mind in various exchanges with people: "vital," "sparkling," "stimulating," "dull," "routine," "predictable."

We are all energy fields, somewhat like radio transmitters. In transactions with others—both verbal and nonverbal—we transmit vibrations of energy that have both a frequency and a tone. We can have a high vibration that is either frenetic or peaceful and smooth. The sense of attraction to another person has a great deal to do with our perception of their energy vibrations—whether they match ours or we perceive that they can fill in some of our own missing gaps. For example, if a person is feeling down and dreary and spends some time with a person sending a high vibration of loving energy, they might feel themselves being lifted up. Likewise if we are feeling a high vibration of energy, but spend a lot of time with people transmitting a dull low vibration, we might start to feel our energy dropping, almost as if it's being sucked out of us.

The sense of having met a kindred spirit comes when our energy vibrations connect both in tone and vitality. We are literally tuned in on the same wavelength. The fusion creates a sense of excitement. It's something more than one plus one equals two. It's one plus one equals us, something bigger that either one of us could experience alone. It's the synergistic combination of two energy fields creating a new entity.

As you observe the nature of your conversations, tune into their energy level, texture, and tone. In general, high clear vibrations of energy come from being connected to oneself—speaking genuinely from personal experience, including expressing feelings, listening well, and responding directly to each other. Low vibrations come from making distance, pontificating, righteousness, the lack of expressing feeling, constantly shifting the focus back on oneself, and not really listening.

We can observe our connections with others from a place of fascination and interest, without judgment. It can be an eloquent means to self-discovery. Hmm, that's interesting, this conversation just went flat. What was said? Did I get scared? Did one of us interrupt, suddenly change the subject, or launch into heavy political rhetoric?

Tuning into energy isn't about "getting it right." It's about observing ourselves and others and being conscious of the messages we are sending and receiving. Eventually it's about finding a good fit with other people.

Trying to force a connection creates an inner split—I want to want to be with this person but they sap my energy and leave me with a churning gut or confusion in the brain. This happened to me in a work situation. In theory, it was what I thought I wanted. In truth, I got a stomachache daily when I went there and started getting depressed. I didn't want to admit to myself that I didn't fit in and that I didn't really like it there. If I had trusted my gut-level energy reading, I would have left sooner—and saved myself a year of therapy trying to make it work.

If we didn't get good training in connecting intimately with others, we're likely to write scripts for our times together—tonight we'll eat at a beautiful restaurant, have a walk together in the sunset, and then make passionate love. Yet it's only when we tear up the script and let ourselves be open to the relationship as it unfolds that we start to create authentic connections. We become a witness to the process instead of trying to force something to happen.

Sometimes we engage deeply with someone, other times we move on. As you allow yourself to feel the different qualities of connections in your life, you tap into your inner perceptual world. While we can learn skills that will make a profound difference in our relationships, we also need to accept that we will never connect equally with all people and that that's perfectly all right. The important step is to become honest with whatever happens so that we stay centered on our own journey.

9

NOTICE WHEN YOU FEEL REAL

We become real to ourselves as we become connected to our inner world and spend time with people who are also honest and authentic. It's like a circular flow of energy that helps us come alive to ourselves. Feeling real with someone evolves as we become familiar with the details of each other's lives— habits, tender spots, and strengths. There is a gently humorous sense of cherishing each other's foibles and fears. Through loving each other you both become real. In the children's book *The Velveteen Rabbit*, Margery Williams tells about a little boy and his toys that become "Real." Real toys assume an important place in the child's inner fantasy world. They are members of his family or community.

> "What is REAL?" asked the Rabbit one day . . . "Does it mean having things that buzz inside you and a stick-out handle?"
>
> "Real isn't how you are made," said the Skin Horse. "It's a thing that happens to you. When a child loves you for a long long time, not just to play with, but REALLY loves you, then you become Real."
>
> "Does it happen all at once, like being wound up," he asked, "or bit by bit?"
>
> "It doesn't happen all at once," said the Skin Horse. "You become. It takes a long time. That's why it doesn't often happen to people who break easily, or have sharp edges or who have to be carefully kept."

Think of a time you felt "Real" with someone. Was it with friends, in nature, with animals? Bring that feeling into your heart and keep it close to you. It will help you have the experience more often. Think of your sharp edges or fragility or need to be carefully kept. Do you blow up easily, get scared, or expect people to do things your way? One way to transform these behaviors is to talk about them. We can apologize when our sharp edges are abrasive to someone. We can say, "I'm feeling fragile and sensitive. It's not really about you." We don't have to be perfect; rather, by acknowledging our behavior we become real and create intimacy.

When people are real to us, we see beyond superficial appearances.

. . . the Rabbit was left out on the lawn until long after dusk . . . He was wet through with the dew and quite earthy from diving into the burrows the Boy had made for him in the flower bed, and Nana grumbled as she rubbed him off with a corner of her apron.

"You must have your old Bunny!" she said. "Fancy all that fuss for a toy!"

The Boy sat up in bed and stretched out his hands.

"Give me my Bunny!" he said. "You mustn't say that. He isn't a toy. He's REAL!"

When the little Rabbit heard that he was happy . . . The nursery magic had happened to him, and he was a toy no longer. He was Real. The Boy himself had said it.

Our beloved may look very ordinary to others, just as the rabbit was nothing but a dirty toy to Nana, but to us, he or she is beautiful and special. As we become real, we see the soul beneath the surface and stop worrying about age, appearance, hip size, and thinning hair. When this happens, we see beauty of spirit and are fed by the warmth of intimacy.

PART II

• • •

A TAPESTRY OF CONNECTIONS

10

FEEL THE CIRCLE OF
ALL YOUR RELATIONSHIPS

I am often annoyed at forms asking if I'm single, married, divorced, or separated. I often check none of them, or all of them, because I dislike my circle of relationships being reduced to marital status. All our relationships—past, present, and future—can be seen as a mosaic forming a whole. The care we give to any one of them affects the quality of them all. It's not so much that we *have* relationships, it's the nature of how we relate to others, and how we allow others to live in us. Our well-being relates to the quality of the whole circle, not any one relationship. While there are dimensions of our lives that grow best in a primary relationship, it is not crucial for being happy and feeling valued.

We tend to think of ourselves as a fixed entity with skin as our boundary. In reality we are a permeable energy field—fluid and porous—always changing, always being impacted by people and places. Think of a time when you were feeling down and a few kind words from a friend lifted your spirits. You drew their energy into you and allowed it to ignite your lighter side. On the other hand, if you recall thoughts that taunt you—Who do you think you are, you can't do that—you are hearing how some authority figure or teaching still lives in your mind. They may be thousands of miles away, but you carry them with you wherever you go. *Part of the journey to intimacy is to sift through all the internalized voices that live in us, releasing the negative teachings that do not serve our well-being, and retaining what is useful.* We'll talk more about that later.

We live in relationship to hundreds of people, each affecting our relationship to others. For example, if you have good buddies to play with, you will have more energy for your work and other friends. If there's someone to call when you are upset, you might be more patient with your friends, children, or partner. If you have a good relationship with a primary partner, you will not burden your friends with tales of woe. They, in turn, will be happier to see you.

In the big picture of our relationships, there may be people we connect with every year or two, possibly through cards or letters associated with a particular holiday. There are people we see quite often at a friendly level—the mail carrier, the neighbor, people on the elevator at work, or someone in a class we attend. We have golf buddies, people we call for support, work relationships that may or may not cross into the realm of close friendship. There are also friendships where there is little contact but where there exists an abiding feeling of care and connection. Some friends may live far away, but simply thinking about them delights us and reminds us that we are valued and loved, and that we could count on them for support.

One way to explore the whole of your relationship circle— past and present—might be to close your eyes for a minute, take a deep breath, and let your mind scan the panorama of people who have touched your life. Tune into your body. Let the memories flow through your mind and feel the waves of emotions and feelings associated with each one. This is all living in you.

As I close my eyes and let the images pass through, I think of my childhood piano teacher and feel a sense of warmth. I think of my Grandma Davis reading to me as a young child, and I feel happy. I think of a brother who is estranged from me and I feel a sharp pain. I think of my mother and I feel a sense of kindness. Scanning our relationships and tuning into the accompanying feelings can give us a clear sense of our unfinished business. For example, ten years ago, thinking of my mother brought pain and sadness. Now, mercifully, those feelings are resolved and she no longer lives in me as a source of unhappiness.

Another way to get a sense of the picture of your relationship circle is to draw it, starting with yourself in the center. You can symbolize people with a shape and put them at whatever distance from you that feels right. As you draw it, note when you have an instinct to put a person in one place but a part of you says, *That's not nice* or *They should be closer . . . or farther away.* After drawing people in, you can denote the nature of the relationship with a colored line between the two of you. It might be solid, dotted, irregular, jagged, or squiggly. If you are doing your lifelong circle, the people can be dead or alive. Follow your instincts and let yourself be surprised. Include places and pets if they come to mind.

People are often amazed at the number of relationships that have impacted their lives. I was amazed recently at my fortieth high school reunion by the memories that came back as we reminisced. When they played familiar songs from the fifties, it was as if forty years had evaporated and I was dancing cheek to cheek with a "cute guy" to "The Little White Cloud That Cried." All these people still live in me although I may not have thought of them in years.

When you are done, sit back and take in what you have drawn. Note any judgments in your head and let them go. This is your life at the moment, it's where you are on your journey. Whether you drew it or not, you can reflect on the follow questions:

How do you feel about your relationship circle?

What are you glad about?

What seems to be missing?

How has it changed over the years?

What do you wish were different right now?

How do these different people still live inside you in positive and negative ways? How are their voices still controlling you, or helping you?

How much unfinished business is there with other people (hurt, anger, grief)?

How is your circle of connection today?

Who would you like to shift in your circle—closer or more distant—and how could you do this?

Now, look at the whole drawing, taking it in as one big unit—the totality of your connections. It's like looking outside yourself and inside yourself at the same time, because what you have drawn lives *in* you and is affecting you in hundreds of ways. Allow yourself to feel the empty places and to know what you might like to change. Do you want more connections, or to deepen the relationships you have? Or both? The ability to enrich your circle often relates to the balance you have between knowing yourself, understanding others, and creating a bond between you and other people. In other words, it's a balance between I, you, and us.

11

LEARN THE DANCE OF I, YOU, AND US

I, you, he, she, we.
In the garden of mystic lovers, these are not true distinctions.

—*Rumi*

*O*ne of the questions that permeates life is, Who am I? Am I this body, these thoughts, these funny habits, a spirit, a mind?

We are all of these things. Being in touch with all of who you are is the starting point for being in touch with others. We can only know others as deeply as we know ourselves.

Throughout life we need to engage in the artful dance of juggling these three entities—I, you, and us. They are all intertwined with growth in any area affecting the other aspects of I, you, and us. If I have an inflated sense of I—*My* needs and wants are the most important, *my* opinions are the right opinions—I will have great trouble knowing or understanding others and will be unable to create intimate relationships. On the other hand, if I lack internal definition, and take the stance, *"Whatever you want, honey, is just great with me, I'm not important,"* I won't be present in a relationship and will be prone to depression. My relationships will have more of a parent-child nature than two equal adults who have chosen each other. If I take the concept of "us" to an extreme—*I've got to have our relationship, it means everything to me*—I will make you more important than me, will live in fear of losing our relationship, and will not evolve as a person.

A starting point for exploring the I, you, and us balance in your life is to make some drawings representing their relative proportions in various relationships. Think of a relationship—whatever comes to mind—and draw a circle to represent the size of each segment—I, you, and us. You can do lots of circles, including immediate family, children, parents, friends, or anyone who pops into your mind. Notice if your hand starts to draw one way, and your mind interrupts and wants to draw it based on *how you want it to be.* This suggests that we feel shame for being the way we are. But, remember, the starting point for all growth is to accept ourselves exactly as we are this moment, no matter what. We can't change what we don't acknowledge. As you draw, identify the person you are representing in the circles. After you draw some, turn the page and see what other people have drawn.

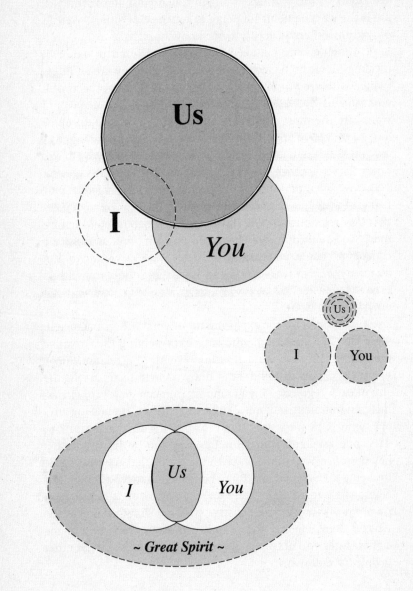

If you did the drawings, or can imagine them, what do they look like? Are they different with different people? Is there a pattern? Does the me get bigger or smaller when you are with a man? A woman? Children? A spouse? A partner, or certain friends? How do you feel about the results? What would you like to change?

Now draw the relationships as you would like to see them.

Here's my sense of a healthy balance as it fluctuates in our lives:

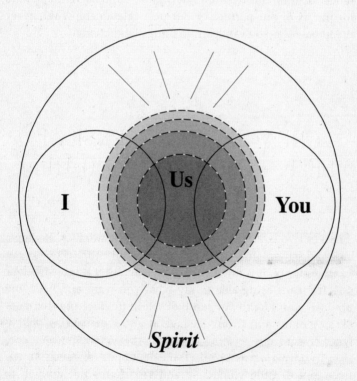

The greater the strength of self—the I—the greater our ability to create a sense of us. This enables us to give to each other from a sense of abundance, and merge together knowing we can return to our separate selves.

Without a strong sense of self, we tend to merge and get enmeshed, or keep great distance in order to feel safe.

Balancing I, you, and us is a challenge for most people. The first step is to look at what aspects of I, you, or us need strengthening. It can vary in different relationships. The sense of self—the I—might be inflated at home with our partner or children, yet weak at work or school, where we negate our thoughts in order to fit in or please others. We may put too much focus on our children's needs and not make enough time for the us of our partner or our peer relationships. Whatever the imbalance, you can learn to bring about change.

12

CREATING MORE SENSE OF SELF—STRENGTHENING THE *I*

*I*t takes two equal, visible people to create intimacy. Having a sense of self means finding that core within that echoes your heart and soul. It is not an arrogant self, rather it is a conscious self. It means being able to say what you want and need and not lose your identity or sense of self in the face of other people's opinions and strong feelings. It also means being able to listen to someone without absorbing their anxieties and worries. To develop a sense of self means to put our cards on the table and become vulnerable and visible. It's not enough to always say "Whatever you want is fine with me." First of all, it's not really true—you *do* have ideas and wants. And second, you won't create intimacy because you are staying invisible and placing yourself below the other person—a one-down position. People can't love you if you're not there.

For many people, and women in particular, asserting their authentic Self feels like committing a crime against the powers that be. It's heresy, cause for witch burning. Keep reminding yourself that it's a good crime, the crime of being true to yourself and opening up your power and potential. You are going against thousands of years of conditioning that say be passive and compliant. If someone calls you a bitch in the process of learning to stand up for yourself, take it as a compliment and say thanks. It means you are being real and taking care of yourself.

A starting place for strengthening your sense of self is to internalize the beliefs: *I'm worthy, I count, I get to say what I believe or want . . . No one can speak for me.* You can make up other phrases to counteract negative messages in your head. Repeating these phrases may flush out all the inner voices from the past that silenced you. *I get to speak up* may be countered with *Be quiet, don't make waves, you don't count.* You can explore where they came from and talk back to them: *I do matter. If I want an equal relationship, I have to show who I am. It's all right to be imperfect. I get to make mistakes. Better a mistake than always being controlled by fear.* The anxiety of affirming the I is often intense, particularly if we had narcissistic parents who saw us as being on earth to fulfill their needs. It can feel like a huge rip inside as we break the symbiotic loyalty ties and dare to speak from our own internal center and give birth to ourSelves.

A good question to ask yourself is: What do I have to gain and what do I have to lose by giving birth to mySelf? If you assert yourself and people put you down, there wasn't much basis for a relationship in the first place, so you haven't lost much at all—except your illusion of what might have been. If you reveal yourself and take a stand, you have everything to gain—self-respect, energy, and growth. It's not a bad trade-off when you think about it. Making your voice heard may lead to differences or conflict, but a strong sense of I enables you to stay rooted in yourself when others differ from you. Most of all, your fear will diminish and you will feel more centered in your life.

Another way to increase the sense of I is by asking yourself the following questions throughout the day. Sometimes people set their wristwatches to ring every couple of hours so they can take a break, take a deep breath, and check in with themselves, asking:

What do *I* feel?

What do *I* think?

What do *I* want?

What do *I* like?

What is *my* opinion?

To tune into your center, start with the details of daily life: What shoes do I *really* want to wear? What are *my* priorities for the day? What movie do *I* want to see? These inner-directed decisions are the basic food of I. You may hear old voices in your head chiding you, "You're being selfish. You're being so self centered," but think of it as being centered in your self—the heart of your being.

The next step is to be loyal to yourself in situations with other people. Allow yourself to know what you want. This doesn't mean you demand to have your way, it means you are visible to yourself and others. You don't accommodate or give up a part of yourself to "keep peace" or avoid a conflict. You stay firmly rooted in your own reality. Taking the initiative in relationships takes you one step farther. If you reach out your hand and invite someone to join you for dinner, or to talk over a concern, you are honoring yourself. Another way to affirm yourself is learning to be able to end a conversation when it rambles on or you are feeling used as an emotions dumping ground. Ultimately, it's a matter of knowing that you have choices.

As you increase your inner awareness, tune into your conversations with others. Be aware of how often you wait for cues from others as to the "right" thing to say or do. While being sensitive to others is appropriate and good, people with little sense of self do it as a matter of course and forget to listen to themselves. At first it might be difficult to push through your fear and say what's true for you. But as you do, you become a contributing member of the relationship who is able to enter into the spirit realm of intimacy.

To develop a sense of I, you also need to pay attention to your feelings when giving and receiving. People with a weak sense of self often keep people from giving to them, yet covertly depend on others to take care of them without acknowledging it. Overtly the message is, I won't ask for anything directly and I don't want you to give me anything so I won't owe you anything. Covertly the message is, I'm weak and fragile, you should take care of me, give to me, and do not expect much from me in return.

In terms of giving, the person with a fragile sense of I needs to be aware of the motivation behind giving to others. If you are giving with an agenda to get something back, if you are giving out of guilt, if you are giving to look like a "good" person, then it is better not to give. Indeed you are not giving, you are creating the appearance of giving. On the other hand, when you feel an inner desire from the heart to give to someone, you may have to nudge yourself to follow through and give. People with a weak sense of self often give to distant friends, or those who won't receive, and fail to give to those who love them and will receive. That's because giving to people who matter to us creates connection and closeness, which is often scary to the person with a weak sense of self. Yet, when we push through this barrier and give to those we love, we grow immeasurably. We shatter the internal belief that we are impotent and impoverished. We dare to be close, to show our love and vulnerability. In giving from the heart we find a richness of spirit.

Another aspect of expanding the sense of self is through developing skills and talents that stimulate your excitement and bring pleasure. You want to get the energy of your life flowing within you. As you spark your creativity, you find your identity at a deep level. Many people have a fear of strong feelings and passion, yet this is the stuff of a powerful person. A related resource for developing a sense of self is through meditation or solitude. The more you slow down your life and experience peace with your inner quiet place, the more you can hear the voice of your spirit.

Some friends and loved ones will be thankful and relieved that you are more passionate and authentic. Other people might get scared and try to manipulate you with guilt to return to your compliant role: "You were nicer before you took that assertiveness course." "You were never so bossy before." If you were always agreeable and listened endlessly, people might get suddenly angry at you or drift away from your life. "You don't care about me anymore." This can be painful, but remember: *Whenever a relationship dissolves because we are growing, we will find a new relationship that is more fulfilling*. The more we define ourselves, the more we attract other people who are well-defined.

To counteract feelings of guilt as you take your rightful place in the world, try flipping the guilt into resentment. Instead of saying, *I feel guilty asking for what I want,* say, *I resent that I was never taught to say what I want.* Instead of saying, *I feel selfish for wanting to stay home and rest,* say, *I resent that I was taught I always have to be productive.* This takes you from the grip of guilt into your power and gives you energy. While you don't want to stay resentful forever, it's important to realize that your fears of expressing yourSelf originated from outside sources. You weren't born with these thoughts in your head, they were put there. They were learned, and they can be unlearned.

Another aspect of affirming one's sense of self comes from listening to others without constantly reacting by trying to fix them, soothe their pain, validate what they're saying, or agree with them. Simply become a witness and hear what they say without making attempts to make it better or ease their pain. Developing a core, a sense of self, is a long-term process that is no easy task. Initially you may state your opinion with a whisper, giggle, or follow your words with, *But it doesn't really matter.*

Your timing may be off and you may be clumsy. That's fine. You've tried. Keep at it, try again. We crawl before we walk. Every time you affirm yourself you feed your spirit, your physical body, and your potential for intimacy. You can let your friends know that you are working to make these changes. I was delighted when a good friend announced to all of us that she didn't want anyone to give her any advice. She had listened to others all her life and she was working to listen to herself. I thought it was great because she was telling us how to be good friends to her.

Becoming visible can feel like stepping out of a fog. It brings a sense of clarity and helps untie the knot of fear in our gut. As we come into our inner power, life takes on a flow and our relationships become more equal, intimate, and fulfilling.

13

MAKING ROOM FOR *YOU*

Bonding is the willingness to simply . . . make room in our heart for our pain so as to have room in our heart for another's.

—Stephen and Ondrea Levine

*T*o experience intimacy we need to make room in our heart for others. If we tend to take center stage, dominate conversations, or be constantly self-absorbed with our pain and worries, we won't have much room for others. For some people, stepping aside and being present for others triggers an old reaction that stems from having been invisible as a child. Perhaps you always had to negate your feelings to survive around self-centered or alcoholic parents. If this was the case, stepping aside to put your focus on someone else can trigger a sense of panic, as if you are disappearing.

To allow others into your heart doesn't mean hiding yourself, being a martyr, or negating your needs, it means making your heart space bigger and allowing yourself to feel your hidden griefs or fears. Usually, we dominate or withdraw when we feel insecure. If we go beneath the surface, we may well find a scared little kid inside who is screaming: See me, notice me, understand me, tell me that I count. We need to start loving that part of ourself.

As we heal our old wounds, we can take the focus off our needs and relinquish our position at center stage. We can also make a concerted effort to change our behavior, which will often trigger buried feelings and memories of past experiences. We need to meet our fears and anxieties and learn to calm ourselves and stop being driven by old programming. It helps to notice when to hold our breath. Conscious breathing and relaxing our bellies helps us drop in our body, quiet ourselves, and be aware of our behavior.

As with all change, start with nonjudgmental observation of yourself. Notice patterns of relating. Do you dominate, withhold, take more than you give, or tend to take center stage? Then ask yourself, Am I afraid? Listen and listen again because fear has a way of hiding. Once you have observed your patterns, try doing something different. Anything different. You don't have to wait until it feels natural or comfortable. Most often, we have to push ourselves to adopt a new behavior, which will feel both awkward and anxiety provoking. But in doing so we precipitate change.

In conversation, you don't need to say much, simply listen. Do not comment, judge, give suggestions or advice. You could say things like, "Hmm. Wow, sounds tough," or you could say almost nothing. Keep noticing the part of you that wants to jump in or change the subject or speak in platitudes. Tell that part of you gently, No, not now, I'll listen to you later. Keep breathing deeply to stay centered in your body. You might throw in a few questions to keep the conversation going: "What other things did you do on your vacation?" or "How are your kids?" If you find yourself taking the focus of the conversation back to yourself, simply say, "Excuse me, I just interrupted you telling me about your mother," and give them the chance to continue. If there are silent spots in the conversation, let them be. You don't have to fill in all the spaces. Just breathe.

Another way to make room for others in your heart is to notice your agenda or scripts for situations. In anticipating or planning a get-together, do you create a scenario in your mind that you want everyone to follow? It's okay to have preferences, but if you expect people to fit into your scheme of things, you are not allowing others to reveal themselves to you or leaving room for spontaneity. Instead of having a script for a situation, try to be part of the event unfolding as opposed to being in control. Again, notice your anxiety when you give up control, shift gears, and allow yourself to enter the flow of people coming together.

Another way to make room for others is to become fascinated by noticing other people—how they walk, their gestures, and their clothes. Notice who moves freely and who looks stiff. Observe people having a conversation or notice the way in which skillful people talk at meetings. Again, remember to notice your breathing and how many times you come back to yourself by comparing or being self-absorbed. Another tactic for change is to think about the people you know and work with. What are their lives like on a daily basis? As you drive through a town or city, think about the people living in all the houses or apartments. What are their lives like?

Remember, you are not a child now. In an equal relationship, you take turns giving empathy and airtime. You are listening now, but you can expect to have your turn in a little while. If you don't get your turn, you can ask for it, and if the other person won't give it to you, you can find other friends who will. You may have to remind yourself of this many times. You also can be aware of how much you truly give of yourself from the heart when you do talk. How personal are you being, how much do you stay in your head opposed to revealing your feelings?

To go to a deeper level, confide in a few friends that you are trying to change your ways of interacting and let them know you are open to feedback. You might ask some trusted friends to touch your arm or say a code word when you interrupt or dominate the conversation or go away and not listen or not make eye contact. It is usually a relief for people to be invited to help. Otherwise, they are very unlikely to be honest with you and will probably withdraw.

An important key to change is to know that *learning to listen to others helps you believe that you matter to other people*. When people don't ask others about themselves, it's often because they see others as above them. "Why would they want to talk to me?" It's not out of arrogance, it's out of insecurity and not feeling that anyone would want to bother to tell about themselves. When we do start listening or giving our attention fully to others we might feel incredibly self-conscious—"Wow, they're talking to me."

Another way to turn your focus to others is to do volunteer service work, take hospice training, or attend a workshop on reevaluation counseling, which teaches basic listening skills. Although the changes feel awkward at first, eventually you will become genuinely fascinated and interested in other people. You will feel the plastic wall between you and others slip away and you will experience genuine intimacy as your heart becomes able to *feel* another's presence.

14

STRENGTHENING THE SENSE OF *US*

The thou meets me through grace—it is not found by seeking.
—Martin Buber

"We or Us thinking" is a state of consciousness, a developmental stage that follows creating a healthy sense of I and learning to include others in our heart. It is a state of grace that comes from walking the spiritual path so that we are able to give and receive love without fear of being swallowed up by another or losing ourselves.

We can become conscious of the language that helps create a sense of us. Us thinking includes phrases like, "Can *we* talk over what *we*'d like to do this weekend?", "Are you noticing some distance between *us*, could *we* talk about it?", "I'd like to talk over *our* sex life." Instead of making unilateral announcements such as "I am going hiking all day tomorrow" you can say, "Hey, my love, can we sit down and talk about the weekend? I want to get some hiking in and see how *we* can work out a schedule." Instead of saying, "I'm going to quit my job," you say, "I'd like to quit my job. Let's sit down and talk over our financial situation to see if it's possible." There may be times when you unilaterally decide on something. If you do, you need to be willing to listen to the emotional response of your friend or loved one who was left out of the decision, without putting them down.

In a true union, both people want the other person to be who they are, to be honest, to enjoy their passions and fulfill themselves. They won't try to squelch each other, rather, they will take pleasure in watching each other grow and expand because it heightens the joy and vitality of the relationship.

Paradoxically, creating a sense of *us* means that we stop depending on the other person to validate our goodness or reality. If I think to myself, "I can't talk until I have reassurance from you that you will agree or sympathize with me," then I am letting you define whether or not I talk. If I am centered in myself, I simply speak from my heart as honestly as I can and don't try to control the outcome. While, over time, we do give equally to each other, we do it in our own way, with our own timing. This creates the true safety net of intimacy that allows the heart to open and give generously of care and understanding.

For some people, it is scary to take on a *we* stance. It feels like losing control, or brings back old feelings of being swallowed up by a possessive, needy parent. That's why creating the sense of us, as opposed to becoming enmeshed, depends on having two well-defined people. Valuing the *us* is different than giving in to someone and negating one's own needs. We surrender our inflated ego, but not our true selves. We stand up for ourselves *and* consider the needs of the other. We remain connected to ourselves *and* connect deeply with others.

Some people resist the unity of us because they consciously or unconsciously want another person to take care of them—to play the role of Big Daddy or the all loving Mommy. They want their friend or partner to be the all wise one who takes control, speaks for them, suggests ideas, makes reservations for dinner, or picks out the new car. Some people want a partner who constantly asks them if they've had enough to eat, worries about them, or reminds them of their appointments. The question is not whether this is right or wrong, it's realizing that coming from a child or parent state will not lead to intimacy. You will constantly reenact scenes from your family of origin and not increase your self-awareness. You will also either have a lot of chaos and drama or the relationship will stagnate.

Creating an us sometimes involves compromise and cooperation. By compromise I mean finding a middle ground that both can live with, not giving up a part of yourself. It's finding the movie that both of you can enjoy. It's having faith that there is a win-win solution. It may be hard to imagine working from the cooperative stance of *we* if situations have usually been defined as win-lose, good-bad, or if you have no faith that anyone would want to meet your needs. You might figure you'd better grab what you can because no one else is ever going to give it to you. *To create intimacy, you need to believe that you can have yourself and the relationship.* Indeed, being true to yourself tests the fabric of the relationship. By speaking your truths you find out if your friend or partner supports you in being whole.

Sometimes it will feel like an act of faith to step aside in the interest of unity or it will take a lot of time to hash out an agreement with someone. While it does take time and effort, the process itself creates intimacy. People often have several parts struggling inside: One part says, "To heck with compromise, I want it my way," another part says, "Oh, I'll just go along and avoid a fight." A third might say, "Relationships are impossible, I give up." Remember that there is a fourth possibility—that you grapple and negotiate until both of you feel satisfied . . . or at least agree to disagree.

Feeling a sense of *us* goes beyond words. We learn to feel someone's essence when we touch their skin. We feel an energy exchange that warms us and fills us up. It opens the way to ecstasy and wonder, which reflects our connection to spirit and a sense of oneness with all.

15

"STRENGTH TO LEAD AND FAITH TO FOLLOW": HOW IS YOUR SUPPORT SYSTEM?

—from *Peace of the River* (Janet Tobitt)

*W*e evolve in relationship to other people. A support system brings us into a web of giving and receiving. We become the changer and the changed, the one who leans and the one who is held up. Creating this balance helps stabilize our very being.

Part of Webster's Unabridged definition of support is "to supply what is needed for sustenance; to keep from yielding, sinking or losing courage or stability; to favor actively in the face of opposition; an act or instance of giving what will benefit or assist." We all need support sometimes. We need a safety net around us just as we needed to be cradled as a child. Support systems are crucial to everyone because relying solely on one's beloved, children, or best friend for intimacy and companionship puts too much stress on the relationship.

When a family or primary relationship is troubled, having a good support system can ease the strain immeasurably. When both people in a close relationship are feeling desperate for empathy and understanding, it's like two people trying to drink out of an empty well. It's easy to start blaming, bickering, criticizing, or hurling past grievances at each other. If both sides of the relationship go to others for support and come back replenished, they are often able to be more generous in giving, listening, and cooperating with their partner.

Giving emotional support is God's love in action. When I think of various traumas in my life, it wasn't the actual experience that left its mark, it was the pain of isolation, the result of having no one present to care or understand. Because of this, the memory carries the scar of loneliness and emptiness. On the other hand, when I have had support through a trauma, the event did not leave an emotional scar. For example, after recovering from surgery and radiation treatments for breast cancer in 1991, I realized with great astonishment that I had not been depressed throughout the process. This was remarkable given that fifteen years of my life had been a struggle with chronic and major depression. Instead of locking up my feelings, I was able to cry, feel my fear, be angry, upset, and celebrate my recovery because the warm embrace of friends encircled me.

This doesn't mean it was perfect. I felt abandoned by members of my family and people in my spiritual community, but my other friends helped me grieve over that loss and appreciate what I did have. When I look back on the experience, it's a quiet memory with little emotional charge because I stayed alive to the experience. I lived it and was not alone. Or, you could say, I lived it *because* I was not alone. By contrast, much earlier in my life when I went though the miscarriage of a dearly longed for child without asking for support—I even walked home from the hospital by myself—I dissociated from my feelings and skipped over the grieving process. As a result, the event haunted me for years.

A support system is not only for aiding each other in times of trouble, it can also be a way of bringing continuity to our lives. We can have quick chats on the phone—"How was your day?"—or take a short walk, or pick up a small gift at a yard sale as part of creating a connection. A friend can provide a means to check out our reality. If we're wondering about our reaction to a conflict or wonder if someone is manipulating us, we can run the scenario past a friend and get a reality check. "Was I acting off base when I said . . ." or "Does that sound fishy to you?" A support person helps us bring light to a situation. When we're stuck in the same tired old conflict with our mate or child, talking to another person can often give us insight or a new perspective. Often, in the very process of talking, we find a new solution. Support is also about using celebration and ritual to mark transitions in our lives. I will talk about this in more detail in the section on rituals.

Our support network provides a crucial arena for personal growth. As we interact with a variety of people, we can practice being authentic and dealing with the stuff of relationships—making plans, setting limits, dealing with conflict, having fun, sharing time and space.

To assess your support system, imagine a troubled time. It might be that you just had a horrible disagreement with someone you love, you just lost your job, or you just heard that a family member/close friend is terminally ill. What is your first instinct? What have you done in the past? Blank out? Pound the wall? Eat? Drink? Scream? Yell at someone close to you? Be rational, say that it must be what's meant to be? Work out? Get busy? Push it out of your mind? Cry all by yourself?

OR

Call someone and ask for support. Would you be able to say what you need, such as: *I'm upset, do you have some time to help me out? Could you come over and be with me? Could you just break* down and cry? Would you also be able to hear that the other person cannot help you at the moment and not take it personally, but simply call someone else?

Scan your life. Who has been there? Who would you call on today? If there are several people you could call, that is a great blessing, one that you had a part in creating.

We create a support system by being supportive of others. Over time, the circle of giving needs to be reciprocal—not in order to keep a scorecard, but because we need both the "strength to lead and faith to follow" to be balanced. If we always give but never show our need, we distance ourselves from others just as our taking without giving back depletes our friends. The exchange of care is a blessing for both people because it opens the heart. Kahlil Gibran writes in *The Prophet*,

> And there are those who have little and give it all. These are the believers in life and the bounty of life, and their coffer is never empty . . . For in truth it is life that gives unto life—while you, who deem yourself a giver are but a witness.

True giving is a selfless, heartfelt act. Our spiritual journey deepens as giving and receiving mingle with the river that flows through us.

If you feel sad or lonely reading this section because you don't have a good support system in your life, or have difficulty giving or receiving, take heart and use your sadness as the motivation to change. There are millions of people yearning for close connections in their lives but afraid to reach out. You can be part of the creative process by doing one thing to initiate a connection with someone. It's the spiritual practice of letting your energy flow—risking connection, risking intimacy.

PART III

◆ ◆ ◆

THE HEART
OF THE JOURNEY

We are all struggling; none of us has gone far.
Let your arrogance go, and look around inside.
                                        —Kabir

16

RELATIONSHIPS ARE
FOR LEARNING

Love brings up anything unlike itself.
—Sondra Rae

*D*eepening our relationships is a path toward softening our hearts and allowing our buried feelings to be felt. When our wounds are touched by love, we become aware of the intense pain we have lived with. When we start to feel connected to others, we become aware of how disconnected we have been. When the love comes in, the tears come out.

Kabir's words—"We are all struggling; none of us has gone far"—invite us to accept our fledgling status on the path. If we can accept that we are beginners in the practice of love, we can embrace the journey from a point of humility that allows us to stay open to the lessons that come our way. It's all right not to know, to grope for guidance and feel totally bewildered. *None of us has gone far*.

"Let your arrogance go and look around inside"—it is a humbling experience to meet our wounded selves, which masquerade in many costumes. When you want to scream at someone, you are likely to be covering your own fear and shame. When you feel disdain for someone, you may have glimpsed a rejected part of yourself. We're always talking about ourselves. All that is disowned and buried within us is being played out in ways that make distance with others. For myself, at an early age I buried a hurt and needy part beneath a competent exterior. It comes out in many forms: being petulant, demanding, self-centered, impatient, or feeling very hurt and left out—all of which I hate to admit. Yet the journey to intimacy means we crack open our ego and admit to these tender spots so we can stop being afraid and stop shielding ourselves from others. People are far more likely to accept us when we acknowledge our not so glorious parts and let them know we are aware and are attempting to change. The less we have hidden inside, the less our shame and fear. As a result, we are able to tolerate deeper levels of intimacy. Revealing our inner world doesn't mean we become perfect, rather, it leads to self-acceptance and a sense of humor—we're just another person slipping and sliding on the path of life.

The path toward intimacy is not for the faint of heart, but for the intrepid traveler, it's a magnificent adventure. As we become the nonjudgmental witness we can smile at our dramas and bring awareness to all we do. "Oh, there I go, being defensive. Stop. Breathe, slow down—what just got triggered in me?" Nothing to be ashamed of. Nothing to hide, simply a part of our humanness being revealed. You can embrace it, heal it. It's just a hurt part, a flush of fear, it's not a monster. I'm not a bad person.

Another step is to realize how much of the time we are detached from the present moment. One time in a therapy group that was stuck—people wouldn't reveal their feelings, they yawned and talked superficially—I asked everyone to keep track for one week of the amount of time they felt connected to the present moment and the amount of time they were disconnected—spacing out, living in a fantasy world, worrying, figuring out someone else, not listening, and so on. The next week people were alert, interested and talkative. Simply by *noticing* their disconnected behavior they felt more alive. Instead of being caught up in it, they could observe it and in doing so break the trance state that had enveloped them. One woman started crying as she said she was present, at best, about 15 percent of the time. Her tears crystalized the pain that had lived in her for so long, manifest in feelings of numbness and fear.

Another step is to take stock of the *ways* in which we hide from ourselves and others—our favorite forms of dissociating. In workshops I'm always amazed at how quickly people generate a list that often goes on for pages: righteousness, arguing, TV, self judgment, setting themselves above or below others, analyzing others, playing the victim, whining, using the computer, talking on the phone, smoking, drinking, being busy, worrying, getting sleepy. In my own life I sometimes find myself playing melodies in the back of my head, tightening my shoulders or breathing in a shallow way.

Most of us feel an inner push-pull as we forge our way toward intimacy. The psychology field uses the term "approach-avoidance." In other words, it feels like a great idea to be close—it's our dream and our longing—yet when met the demands of vulnerability that true intimacy requires, we feel terror and run for cover. Our body may stay present, but our mind and spirit take leave. But then, the loneliness returns and we repeat the cycle.

Our learning happens as we inch closer and closer to others, staying present, paying attention to our fears, suffering the discomfort of seeing and being seen—the wounds, the masks, and the fears. One way to give ourselves the courage to stay engaged is to remember that the feelings we fear will not destroy us. Our fear is not a sign of weakness; our anger is not a bomb that will blow us to bits; our tears are not an endless river that will wash us into the ocean; our hungers are not a bottomless pit. Our feelings loom large because we have locked them in a closet and cloaked them in shame—that ominous feeling of being defective. When brought into the light of day, these fearsome dragons often dissolve into the face of a child who wanted love, was afraid, was lonely, and was doing the best s/he could to survive. This process of unfolding is the greatest act of courage that anyone can undertake. It is the blessing of giving birth to ourselves.

The more we allow relationships to heal us, the more they become a source of adventure, comfort, and joy. We suffer our growing pains in order to forge bonds of caring and compassion. As we accept our fallible status as human beings, we give up the notion of finding a prince or princess, of being the saved or the savior, and join the dance of imperfect people waltzing together, growing, laughing, and finding a home for our hearts.

17

STEP INSIDE THE CIRCLE OF ALL BEINGS

Some one's crying lord, kumbaya
Someone's laughing lord, kumbaya
Someone's singing lord, kumbaya
Oh lord, kumbaya

—Marvin V. Frey

When we were tiny children, we felt completely embodied in our mother. There was no separation. As we developed in the first few years, we gradually learned to experience ourselves separately—we had an identity. This gave us the frightening experience of I and other. It was like being cast out of the Garden of Eden. We grew up and adjusted, at least partially, to our separateness, and worked to define ourselves and create an identity. Yet our longing for oneness remained in the shadows of our consciousness. The only way to assuage the grief of our separateness is to become conscious of the fact that we are intrinsically interwoven with all life. We are not separate after all. We are part of the circle of all beings, all sentient life.

When you sit in a room with other people, you are literally

breathing the same air in and out that has been in their bodies. We are all energy in motion mingling with each other and with the natural world—taking in the air and water, eating, eliminating. We are all variations on a theme—unique and the same. Not one of us looks exactly alike and never will, yet we all have the same basic features and internal organs. We all deal with the impermanence of life and the specter of death, the hope for wholeness and the desire for love. We've all been fools, we've all been brilliant and creative. Whatever we have felt, whatever we have done, someone has felt or done something very similar.

To help yourself feel like a part of the circle of all beings imagine looking down on the earth and seeing that someone's dancing, someone's singing, someone's giving birth, someone's weeping, someone's dying. Hear the cry inside your heart and that of all people, "Oh lord, kumbaya, come by here": Be with us through all of our days as we wander through this mysterious life. Don't leave us to face it alone. As we invite spirit to accompany us on our journey, we touch the spirit of all people, our greatest source of connection.

As we join the circle of all beings, our fear diminishes and we return to the childhood state of wonder and curiosity in which there is no prejudice, no fear of different religions, ethnic groups, races or classes. Our responses become less intellectual and more instinctual, coming from our amazing capacity to "feel" the energy fields of others.

Many people isolate themselves, never revealing their inner world because they think their problems, behaviors and thoughts are unique. I think the gods probably laugh whenever they hear this because from a big mind perspective, we are all cycling through the journey of birth, growth and death. We all want love, connection, purpose and happiness.

To move beyond I and other thinking, we can start thinking in terms of "One of us". I originally heard this concept from Ken Keyes, author of many books on conscious living. "One of us is getting bossy right now"—just as all of us have occasionally been bossy. "One of us is feeling needy right now"—just as all of *us* have felt needy at times. "One of *us* is winning the race right now."

To further connect yourself to the circle you can say, "*Some of us* are having sexual problems," "*Some of us* are sad right now," "*Some of us* are feeling bright and creative." It's more difficult to say "*Some of us* are stealing or beating a child today." You may feel defiant about including violent people in the same circle with you. "I'm not the same as *them*!" Yet, if we want to accept all of who we are, we need to accept that as humans we all have the capacity to do terrible things as well as be kind and loving. Much of it depends on the deck we were handed. If you separate yourself from others by saying, "I can't understand how someone could do that" ask yourself, "What kind of experiences would have led me to do that?"

As you join the circle of "us" and get away from the concept of "them," your inner world will shift in a profound way. You will move from judgment to compassion and understanding. It might also help you appreciate the blessings you have been given. What privilege or love did you receive that kept you from being in desperate relationships, robbing a bank, killing someone or abandoning your children?

To reach a deeper level of compassion, make another switch. After saying "*Some of us* are picking a fight" or "*Some of us* are robbing a bank," say to yourself, "Sometimes, I have picked a fight, sometimes I have stolen." Understand this in spirit, not just in concrete terms. You may not have stolen from a store, but you may have stolen time from someone, or stolen their reputation by gossiping about them.

By using the phrases "One of us" or "Some of us" we also start taking responsibility for a culture that fosters so much violence, prejudice and greed. We can ask why so many of *us* are poor, racist, violent or greedy. What in our system creates this? What in my life contributes to this?

If you have been marginalized in this culture, here's a poem by Edward Markham that gives us the power to include ourselves in the circle even if others push us away. (I have changed the gender pronouns.)

They drew a circle that shut me out:
heretic, rebel, a thing to flout.
But love and I had the wit to win
We drew a circle that put them in.

We are all in the same circle whether we know it or not.
The more our awareness touches this reality, the more whole
we become and the greater our sense of belonging.

18

FINDING YOUR CENTER:
WHAT IS A HEALTHY EGO?

One of the themes of this book could be how to find your
internal center. This is related to ego strength and understanding the workings of our different ego states. We often hear the
ego described in quantitative terms, from big ego to weak ego.
A big ego means you're self-centered and rigid, and a small ego
means you fall apart inside when someone criticizes or dis-
agrees with you. The problem with quantitative description is
that there is no definition of a healthy ego or an understanding
of fluctuations in our ego functioning or different aspects of the
ego. For that reason, it's more useful to look at ego from a *qual-
itative* perspective—the nature of our ego. Is our ego strong
enough to help us stand up for ourselves, flexible enough to be
open to change, porous enough to be infused with compassion?
When we make love, can we let our ego dissolve and merge
with another person? Then can we shore our ego up again to
go off to work? *A healthy ego is flexible, porous, open to input, compassionate, and works in the service of goodness. It is a central core
within us that allows us to rest firmly in the center of our wisdom and
strength.*

To develop a fluid, healthy ego we need to go through a process of examining and evaluating the teachings from our childhood. Instead of being a clone to the beliefs of our parents and educational system, we need to sort through, experiment, and develop an internal sense of what fits for us.

With an underdeveloped ego you can't count on your internal center to stay put for you. It slips and slides. You reach inside to hear your thoughts, but you draw a blank. You say yes when you want to say no, you don't find words to defend yourself when you feel attacked. You act like a chameleon, adapting yourself to different people and different situations.

With a weak ego, we are subject to a paralyzing fear that can feel like having our head disconnected from our body, or can simply result in our going numb. One of the most stunning memories of losing all ego strength was when I was a participant in a supervision group. The supervisor asked me a question that felt hostile and I went totally blank. I disconnected from my body and lost access to my inner world—my center. I tried to say whatever I thought she wanted to hear so she'd take the focus off me—but to no avail. As she persisted, I felt as if I were going into a fog. It was a terrible feeling—paralyzing fear. There was no me inside of me.

In relationships, having a weak ego can leave us feeling split in two or more parts. One part feels like a child in need of a parent, another part wants a lover and a friend, and another part is terrified of getting close to anyone for fear of losing themselves. Sometimes people develop an all-wise teacher part, which is another way of creating distance from other people.

When we have little ego strength or sense of self, we look to rules and roles to hold us together. If we can't speak authentically from our heart, we can follow the rules, speak rhetoric, or play out a role. Unfortunately, when we lock ourselves in a role, we are terrified of authentic contact or conflict because it threatens to shatter the role that holds us together. We don't know how to improvise, set limits, tune into our feelings, or be spontaneous. It's literally as if the soul has not given birth to itself. We have little concept of self and feel fragile and afraid.

Having low ego strength is like being the little piggy with the house of straw. Authenticity feels like the wolf breaking through the walls of the house, exposing our emptiness, fear, and vulnerability. To avoid being authentic and experiencing ourselves fully, we weave a web of fabrications, illusions, or distortions to keep people away and protect our straw house from blowing away or burning down.

HEALTHY EGO

In contrast, a healthy ego integrates seemingly opposite parts of ourselves. Think of a willow tree for a moment. It can bend and not break. It is strong, yet flexible. It draws from the rain, sun and earth, and changes with the seasons. We have a healthy sense of self when we can be strong *and* gentle, generous *and* receptive, assertive *and* passive, sad *and* happy. A healthy ego has porous boundaries that can open and close. We can listen to others, absorb information, process and integrate it. We can also choose not to listen when it doesn't feel right.

I disagree with much of the addiction literature and spiritual writings that urge people to let go of their egos. While I understand the need to get out of the way of our arrogance or narcissistic self, I have worked with many people who don't have much ego to let go of. We need ego to voice our opinions, take care of ourselves, or do our work in the world. I need ego strength to write and believe I have something worth saying. *The real question is, what purpose does the ego serve?* Do I only serve my own self-centered needs, or is my ego merged with compassion, tenderness, and a desire to be of service? Gandhi had a strong ego, but it was given to the service of liberating his people. Mother Teresa is a forthright woman with a strong ego that is merged deeply with compassion, humor, and mercy.

A healthy ego gives us stability so that we are neither defensive nor easily swayed by outside opinion. We can say *Yes, No, I want to,* or *I don't want to* with a sense of quiet confidence. A healthy ego is like a simple, comfortable, sturdy house built on a firm foundation. Inside there is a warm hearth, an enduring fire, and enough food to sustain us.

With a healthy ego, you know you could survive if a loved one were to leave. You would grieve over their loss and miss them terribly, but you wouldn't become desperate. Likewise, we are able to be truthful to others because maintaining our integrity is fundamental to our being. We become capable of sensitivity and compassion, but don't become a chameleon, forever changing colors to please others.

A healthy ego keeps us safe in the world because we learn to trust in our own perceptions and are able to see beneath the surface of political hype, misleading advertisements, or wolves in grandmothers' clothing. We can be both wary and wise, loving and protective. Returning to our image of a willow tree for a moment, it's like saying, I exist, I am here, I can grow, I'm happy to be a willow tree, I don't need to be an oak or an apple tree. This is good enough.

The question remains, How to develop a healthy ego?

19

WHO ARE THESE VOICES IN MY HEAD?: MEETING THE COMMUNITY WITHIN

*I*n the previous essay I spoke of the healthy ego. In reality, the ego is not a fixed entity—strong-weak, big-little. We have many ego states, depending on the situation we are in. As an example, some years back I went for an interview to get a home mortgage when single women were routinely turned down. I walked in with firm resolve and a don't-mess-with-me attitude: "They'd better give me a loan or else I'm going to charge discrimination." I had my facts and figures written down and was friendly, clear and confident in the interview.

Following the interview I returned to my office at the university where I taught piano. As frequently happened, I slipped into a trance, allowing my needs and wants to vacate my being and gave full attention to my students. After that I went home and was swallowed up by fear in trying to ask my roommate to please wash her dishes more often. While this may sound a bit like the three faces of Eve it's really just my different ego states operating in different situations. I operated as an adult in the first, my spirit side took over in the second, and a scared kid state emerged in the third.

The concept of ego states and ego state therapy was pioneered by psychologists John and Helen Watkins. Their book, *Ego State Theory and Therapy* will give the reader a far deeper look at this subject. This section is my approach to working with ego states and can give the reader an idea of the usefulness of this concept, but is by no means an in-depth exploration.

According to Helen Watkins, the central idea is to realize that inner turmoil often signals that different ego states are in conflict. The idea is to find ego states that are able to help us mediate the conflict and guide us to our highest wisdom. There are no fixed ego states that apply to everyone. Rather they present themselves when people explore inner conflict. Everyone is unique and changing, thus it is important not to see our ego states as fixed and concrete, rather as parts of us that have the potential to interact, grow and evolve.

The question to ask at any given time is, What ego state is active? To operate from a healthy ego stance we need to make friends with our less evolved ego states that need help in growing up or becoming integrated. In exploring conflict, people often find several primary ego states, like a committee inside that argues and fights over decisions and sometimes leaves us confused and bewildered. In many ways, it represents what happens in actual committees or in communities.

One way to explore ego state is to think of the ego states we present to the world and the ones we tend to repress or ignore. You might want to think of a conflict and listen inside for the different voices that may represent different ego states. The following is a list of possible ego states you may want to explore for yourself. You may think of others. The point is to recognize the different aspects of yourself. The more aware we are of our ego states and the more we can access our spirit and adult states, the more comfortable our relationships.

Here is a drawing of ego states. In this example, the parts operate in relationships to each other. The rules and directives from the Parent/Church Shoulds part shouts orders that blare through her mind. The Angry part appears to protect the Little Lost Child who feels vulnerable and is prone to getting into dependent relationships with men who promise to take care of her. The Wise Adult Self is present but needs to take center stage and work with the Competent part. Her ego strength will grow as the Parent/Church Shoulds part relinquishes past teachings, reaches inward, finds her own values and gives up being controlled by "the rules." There is almost always depression, anxiety or addictions when the predominate ego states are still being driven by unresolved childhood experiences, or unexamined teachings from cultural institutions.

EXAMPLE OF ONE PERSON'S
· EGO STATES ·

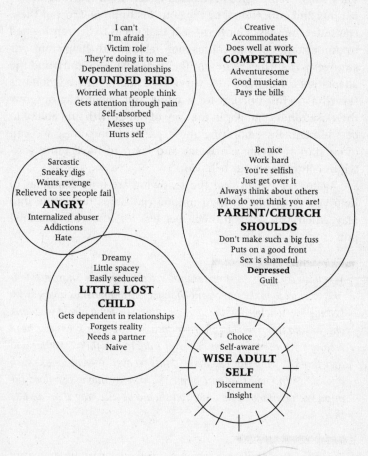

I can't
I'm afraid
Victim role
They're doing it to me
Dependent relationships
WOUNDED BIRD
Worried what people think
Gets attention through pain
Self-absorbed
Messes up
Hurts self

Creative
Accommodates
Does well at work
COMPETENT
Adventuresome
Good musician
Pays the bills

Sarcastic
Sneaky digs
Wants revenge
Relieved to see people fail
ANGRY
Internalized abuser
Addictions
Hate

Be nice
Work hard
You're selfish
Just get over it
Always think about others
Who do you think you are!
**PARENT/CHURCH
SHOULDS**
Don't make such a big fuss
Puts on a good front
Sex is shameful
Depressed
Guilt

Dreamy
Little spacey
Easily seduced
**LITTLE LOST
CHILD**
Gets dependent in relationships
Forgets reality
Needs a partner
Naive

Choice
Self-aware
**WISE ADULT
SELF**
Discernment
Insight

When we recognize these child ego states in ourselves they might trigger shame or feel embarrassing. These wounded parts of ourselves are usually a result of trauma, neglect, or abuse. They might represent internalized beliefs from teaching of our parents and educational or religious institutions. Most of these ego states are masks for fear—fear that needs to be transformed by understanding and compassion, along with help from our stronger parts. They represent the parts that were hurt, and the adaptations we made to survive. Usually, the adaptations served a useful function for a while, but eventually outgrew their usefulness and got in the way of our growth and ability to be intimate. By embracing these parts of ourselves, we can often start resolving old issues and learn to have more conscious control over our behavior.

Again, remember that the following are only examples to help you discern your own unique ego states that come into play when you get confused, feel fear, or lose your personal power.

1. *The scared part/The censor.*

When we try to take a strong stance, voice an opinion, share our feelings or start to make important changes, our center slips away as we become overwhelmed with fear. Sometimes we get so afraid we blank out, or find it extremely difficult to speak. The censor keeps our head reeling with thoughts such as: "Am I doing it right?" "What will they think?" "You can't do that." "Just get over it—don't make such a fuss." "Who will take care of me?" This part might also flood the mind with a litany of shoulds. You should be nice. You shouldn't do that.

2. *The screamer/abuser.*

This part often develops in response to the scared part: We drown out the terror of our emptiness by screaming, getting hysterical or intimidating others to keep them away. We explode with feelings to fill our inner void and keep people away. We might become violent and harm ourselves or others. This part knows how to take revenge, to wound and harm others. This part acts from a primitive, survival level, blames others, unaware of his or her impact on others, and usually sees no reason to apologize to others—who basically deserve what they get.

3. **The pleaser/super competent one.**

This part creates the illusion of self-esteem through validation from others. As a result, one's feelings of worth constantly fluctuate based on external praise and accomplishments. We might be compliant, get the best grades, be charming, delightful, helpful, super achieving and always doing for others in an attempt to gain their approval. In this state we tend to acquiesce to others' demands or wants without paying attention to our own needs.

4. **The needy, dependent one.**

This is the part of us that is deeply dependent on having someone take care of us. This part may have thoughts of wanting to be held, rocked, taken care of, protected, and loved unconditionally. This part can often feel very hurt, little, and abandoned. The underlying cry is often: "Tell me you care about me, take care of me because I feel too little to take care of myself."

5. **The rebel.**

This part often develops to hide the needy part. We react to authority in an attempt to hang on to our sense of self and not feel so needy and vulnerable. While this is still a reactive stance, there is more energy than being compliant and trying to constantly please others. It's more of an adolescent state trying to assert its autonomy.

6. **The all-wise one/seer.**

This part presents him or herself as having it all together. She/he hides vulnerability by playing the authority, wise one or teacher. This protects the person from being vulnerable. It is often a reaction to feeling little and needy and being ashamed to show these parts of ourselves.

7. **The escapist/addict.**

This part overeats, drinks, gets busy, engages in addictive and compulsive behavior—anything to avoid feelings. In this state we fantasize unrealistic scenarios of the perfect love, job or living situation. This part is often dreaming of the perfect prince or princess to rescue us and magically transform our lives.

8. *The victim.*

We see the world as "doing it to us" and we don't want to take responsibility for our lives. Instead of asking to have our needs met directly, we present ourselves as the wounded bird or the wronged one, hoping people will sympathize and commiserate with our poor helpless selves. We lament that "we're afraid" or "it's hard," hoping people will not hold us accountable. We want others to figure out what we need, and give it to us so we don't have to grow up and become vulnerable by asking for what we need. When others challenge our deceits or irresponsibility, we hide from our shame with a diversionary tactic: We tell them they are being mean and uncaring.

These states often develop in relationship to each other. The super competent side evolves to protect the hurt and needy part. The pleaser part evolves to hide the angry part, or the tough part evolves to protect the victim part. We often are conscious of one side—our presented side—and unconscious of the opposing side. Ultimately the buried side wreaks havoc on our lives. For example if we present a competent front to the world (and ourselves), our buried needy side might paralyze us when we want to work. If we present ourselves as charming to get praise, we flip into rage and anger when we are not validated.

Often, if we feel anxious, it's because a part of us, an ego state, is wanting our attention and we need to reckon with that part of ourselves. For example, if we start to stand up for our beliefs and set limits with people, we might feel incredible anxiety and fear. That's because the censor part of us is saying, "Who do you think you are. Don't do that." This part is operating from a childhood belief that you will get put down, punished or banished for voicing your opinions.

The more you can get these parts to dialogue, to understand each other, the less you will feel torn apart inside. It takes courage to look at all these parts, but it can also bring clarity and understanding where there has been confusion and fear. Sometimes you can access these parts of yourself on your own, other times you may need a counselor familiar with ego state therapy to help you.

A FEW THOUGHTS TO CARRY WITH YOU

Nearly any form of anxiety phobia or somatic problem is a buried ego state screaming to be heard.

When our ego-strength collapses into a childlike state it usually signals unfinished business from childhood we need to resolve.

The more you repress a part of yourself, the more it controls your life.

The people who get on our nerves are probably a mirror of a repressed ego state.

The more we are invested in an extreme aspect of our presented self, the more likely there is an opposite part lurking within, e.g., independent-dependent, fearless/afraid.

Addiction and dependency are expressions of buried ego states, particularly our spiritual longing.

When we get depressed or obsessed, we are usually not acknowledging some part of our self—particularly our adult and spirit sides.

The more we bury any aspect of ourself, the more we will attract people with that characteristic into our lives.

THE GOOD NEWS

The more we reveal our hidden parts to ourselves and others, the more ego strength we develop and the more integrated and centered we become.

The more centered we are, the more we live in our adult and spirit parts.

The more we live from our adult and spiritual parts, the more intimacy and love we will have in our lives.

The more intimacy and love we have in our lives, the more we can be of service in the world and feel compassion and joy.

Being able to recognize our ego states is an ongoing process. At one level many people have used this approach in talking about the "inner child." Looking at ego states helps us delineate aspects of all parts of our being, and can be invaluable in healing from childhood trauma and moving on in our lives. As a therapist, I often have marathon sessions using hypnotherapy to help people integrate various ego states that underlie addictions, fear, or self-destructive behavior.

20

IF YOU'RE IN LOVE, SHOW ME! LEARN TO TAKE ENERGY READINGS

*I*n the musical *My Fair Lady*, Eliza Doolittle gets fed up with a lot of high-class romantic talk and sings: "Don't talk of love, beaming above, if you're in love, *show me!*" In other words, deliver the goods, don't just talk about it. Words can lie, mislead, seduce, or put up a wall. We need our ability to perceive beneath the surface, to be wise and wary in the world. In other words, we need to tune into energy and pay attention to behavior, not words.

I started thinking about energy readings after a friend helped me decide to leave a job where I often felt afraid and had a chronic knot in my gut. I had tried to work it out, but to no avail. After I explained the situation to my friend, she said with ease, "I'd stop working there."

"Just like that!" I said with amazement.

"Yes. If it's not working, why drain your energy?"

It seemed too simple. Yet I felt a sense of relief. "You mean, if something drains your energy, you leave."

"Yes. I try to work things out, but if it doesn't work, then I leave."

What started to penetrate was that I didn't have to know why, I didn't have to have reasons, I only had to know it wasn't working. Instead of consuming my time and energy trying to figure it out, I could leave. This was incredibly freeing for me and made a huge shift in my life.

By tuning into our bodies, we can tap a source of infinite wisdom. The little moment of doubt, the sudden stomachache, the sense of dread or sudden drop of energy are all forms of energy readings. They signal that we're afraid, uneasy, or possibly in the presence of danger. We need to stop and pay attention.

To take an energy reading, imagine a meter that goes from energy drain to energy charge. Think of being on a certain committee, taking a class, changing jobs, seeing a movie, being with a particular person—anything—and take an energy reading on a scale of one to ten, with ten being high energy. If there is one simple guideline to energy readings, it's this: *Whatever leads to light, clarity, a sense of balance, and increased energy is usually the wise path.* If you have a hard time imagining a one to ten scale, think of a situation that troubles you and check out the following words:

HIGH ENERGY READING:

light	clear
excited	relieved
bright	alive
challenged	open
happy	growing
connected	

afraid (Because you need to push through something)

confused (You're starting to see both sides of the picture)

ENERGY DRAIN

heavy	stomachache, headache, etc.
should	dull
cautious	worried
tired	bored
obsessed	

afraid (because the situation is abusive, harmful, or chronically draining your energy or because you are afraid to make a break and be on your own)

constantly confused (because you are trying to make something work that doesn't work)

Energy readings connect us to our intuitive self. Once you have an energy reading, the next step is to follow through. Think of who you like to spend time with, when you need to sleep and eat, or what would be fun to do on the weekend, and take a reading. We can use energy readings in our work and creative efforts as well: "That approach 'turns me on,'" "That paragraph has no energy, cut it."

If someone asks to you to be on yet another committee and your gut ties up in a knot, you need to say no. This brings to mind a recent committee meeting that started with one member, Georgina, talking about being burned out, then volunteering to take on several tasks. At the close of the meeting another member, Leah, said to her, "Georgina, I have a mantra for you." And in a low voice she chanted, "Noooooooooo."

"Omm?" Georgina said.

"No! Noooooooooo," she chanted again in a big, round voice. We all chimed in, chanting "Nooooo, NO, NO" in harmony and ended up laughing. It's a chant that many of us need to remember and sing to each other often.

In relationships, we create an energy charge when we are authentic and honest—speaking from both head and heart. When we are being intellectual, hide our feelings or fudge on the truth, we block the flow of energy. Double messages are exhausting to others because our words give one message, but we are unconsciously transmitting another. This confuses people and siphons off their energy. *It's the pretense and dishonesty more than neediness or pain that cause an energy drain.* If someone simply says, "I feel like a big baby today," you can laugh together—which is an energy charge.

You can use energy readings to reflect on yourself. If people tend to withdraw and not choose to be around you, take stock of how you might be draining their energy: Are you negative and pessimistic? Do you frequently complain and not take action? Give unsolicited advice? Keep the focus on yourself, argue, or insist on having things your own way? A deeper concern is to explore your level of fear. People instinctively withdraw from people transmitting high levels of fear.

Sometimes we are in situations that take a lot of energy—caring for children or for someone who is sick or dying. Even then, we can make choices not to get entangled in their pain and problems. We approach them with loving compassion but remember that they are on their journey, learning their lessons.

Following your energy reading helps you preserve your energy, health and peace of mind. One woman commented in response to this concept: "You mean I can just be around nice people, I don't have to stay with people who hurt me? I don't have to take care of all the sick people in the world?" Yes, you can go where the energy is strong and where you feel nurtured and respected.

It is the ultimate act of faith to follow the lead that comes from energy readings because it means acceptance—acceptance of the signals that come from deep within you even when you don't know why. When we start to trust our inner wisdom, the flow of life increases. This brings to mind a line from Chris Williamson's beautiful song, "The Changer and the Changed": "Filling up and spilling over like an endless waterfall . . . Filling up and spilling over, over all."

21

"SOMEWHERE BETWEEN RICH AND NOT TOO POOR": DON'T FALL IN LOVE WITH MONEY OR POSSESSIONS

*O*n the PBS special, "Amazing Grace," Bill Moyers interviewed a ninety-one-year-old African American man from the Ozarks who was a sacred heart song leader. In response to Bill Moyers's question, "How does a man live a life of Joy?" Mr. Williams paused and said, "you've got to be between poor and rich. If you're too poor you can't live happy and if you're too rich you can't live happy. Either way you're worried about money." There's a lot of wisdom in those words. Too much or too little tends to keep us out of balance with ourselves and others.

Rich or poor, if money is a constant source of worry and obsession, it can overshadow the needs of intimate relationships. If we are extremely poor or living at a survival level—constantly worried about having enough food, paying the bills or getting medical help—it's hard to have the time or energy to give to our inner growth or a relationship. If we become obsessed with amassing more money and material goods than we need to be comfortable, we risk creating false gods. Money becomes what we seek, protect, yearn for, and fear losing. Money is a potent form of energy. It reflects a great deal about our deepest levels of security. Like all forms of energy, money can serve us or become a source of stress.

Some people with very little money live simply and rarely worry about it, while others with an abundance of money worry obsessively. Some people with great wealth share generously, and others hoard it, feeling anxious every time the stock market dips. Some people are compulsive overearners while others are compulsive underearners.

At a personal growth training session many years ago, at a place called Cornucopia, we spent an afternoon exploring the concept: *We do with our money as we do with our love.* We used our relationship with money as a window into our lives. We explored the ways we hoard it, throw it away, are stingy, generous, or control people through withholding and rewarding. Some of us were incredibly careful, while others were reckless and impulsive and didn't always have enough left to pay the bills. Some felt they didn't deserve to earn much money, so they didn't try—while some felt entitled to money and exploited others to get it. Nearly everyone had made some bad decisions that had cost them a considerable sum of money, and many had also made good decisions about money. If there was one thing we all had in common, it was that talking about money elicited strong emotions.

Coming into balance with money requires us to examine our motives in how we use it. Taking several friends out to dinner could be a loving act of generosity, or it could come from wanting to impress people; it could be something you could afford, or could leave you without money to buy food for your children. Buying things can be a form of self-love, or a way of hiding your sorrows. Money is an incredible mirror of our inner security. Nowhere do we see this more acutely than after the death of a parent. In some cases, children can generously divide up the property among themselves. In other cases, the childhood jealousies and the lack of feeling loved get translated into fights over money and possessions.

What is your history with money and love? As an example, I'll give you a bit of my own history. As a child I felt lonely because of a lack of connection and understanding. One way I filled the gap was by earning money. If I couldn't have love, I could buy myself things that brought pleasure—a nice skirt, a record, and eventually a little record player. I could snuggle up in my room playing music and leave the painful world behind.

I also controlled my little brother with money. I'd pay him to be a gofer or bribe him by letting him sleep with my favorite teddy bear.

I opened a savings account by the age of twelve and felt a sense of security as the numbers approached a hundred dollars. While there's nothing wrong with a kid having a savings account, the point is that it gave me an illusion of security that covered my intense emotional insecurity and feelings of deprivation. My parents also used money to control. They offered to pay for me to live in a sorority, but not in an international student dorm, where I wanted to live. Later, when my parents did help me out financially, I felt that I was getting what was rightfully mine—as if they were paying me back for hurting me. Over the years that followed, they generously loaned all of us some money as we started our households.

Then an amazing thing happened. My father sent a letter to all four of us adult children, reminiscing about how his parents regretted being unable to help their children with college or getting started in adult life. In honor of his parents and in gratitude for the abundance of his life, he canceled all our debts to him. I had two strong reactions. One was to be deeply touched and feel incredibly thankful. The other reaction—which I hate to admit—was wondering if my siblings had a bigger debt canceled than me . . . and if they did, it wasn't fair. I smile to myself now and feel compassion for the hurt and humanness beneath that jealous thought where I instantly mixed up love with money.

Cut to today. After a tense encounter that left me feeling sad and lonely, I headed home, interrupted by a sudden pull to drop by the Goodwill thrift store. I wanted to buy something pretty to cheer myself up. Thrift stores have an intense appeal because it's like getting something for nothing—free love. The paradox was that as I walked around the store, I felt relieved that nothing fit or was of interest to me. In pondering my relief, I realized that it was because it was the wounded kid who drove to the Goodwill store, but it was the spiritual adult who said: "This won't fill up the longing . . . and besides, we don't need more stuff at home."

As you read my story, notice all the ways in which money was entangled with control, bribery, love, jealousy, generosity, security, and comfort. What is your story with money? Think of how scarcity, abundance, and love fit in. How have you manipulated relationships with it? Think of the amount of time you spend concerned with money, and then ask how money is helping or hindering you on your spiritual journey to love and peace of mind. What would you need to do to have balance? If we exhaust ourselves, work excessive hours to make huge house payments, we are also out of balance. Why not get a smaller house so you live in peace with quiet times to honor your soul? It can be an eye-opener to keep track for a month of everything you spend, and multiply it by twelve to see what your habits cost you over a year's time. See if your values match your spending. As an example, in a treatment program for alcohol and other drugs, people were shocked to realize that their drug habit cost them from $70,000 to over $250,000. It was, pardon the pun, a sobering experience.

Coming into balance with money and love extends beyond the personal level. Kahil Gibran writes in *The Prophet*:

> The master of the spirit of the earth shall not sleep peacefully upon the wind till the needs of the least of you are satisfied.

This suggests that as individuals, families, and part of community, we need to spread the wealth so that the least of us is satisfied. I would go one step farther to include the natural world. If spending our money results in the loss of forests to build huge homes, the extinction of tigers for medicine, or poisons the air and water by cheaply producing lots of material goods or mining gold, we are again out of alignment with money and love. To free our energy for creating intimacy and evolving spiritually, we need to bring money into balance in our lives, earning it honestly, using it in the interest of love for ourselves and all sentient life.

22

THE CIRCLE OF OUR RELATIONSHIPS TO FOOD, MONEY, SEX, TIME, AND LOVE

We've talked about the relationship of love to money. We can also explore the *interconnection* between our relationships to food, money, sex, and time—the basic metaphors for how we give and receive nurturing. Our behavior is usually fueled by our underlying beliefs about being lovable, secure, and sacred. The deeper our insecurities, the more out of balance our relationship to these potent forms of energy may be.

I include time in this list because having control of our time reflects our commitment to the spiritual path. It takes time to drop inside and hear the still, small voice of wisdom that can lovingly guide us in our lives. The white man's Western work ethic has taught many people to feel extreme guilt for taking time for pleasure or meditation. They fail to understand the needs of the spirit for quiet, joy, reflection, or the time it takes to nurture a loving relationship.

Remember the seven deadly sins—avarice, covetousness, greed, sloth, anger, lust and envy? The idea was that a strong attachment to these things interfered with our relationship to God. Unfortunately, in true patriarchal dualistic thinking, instead of seeing food, sex, love, and possessions as something to have in a balanced way, they were labeled bad and sinful— forces so powerful we had to fear and control them lest we be overwhelmed. Celibacy was holier than any form of sex, austerity was better than having creature comforts or taking pleasure in food. Suffering was glorified. As a result, people became obsessed with *not* having sex, *not* having comforts, or *not* taking pleasure in food. Being in righteous abstinence can be as obsessive as being addicted. Denial of need often leads to binge-and-starve behavior or sets up an inner duality creating dialogues such as "No. You shouldn't" versus "I'm going to do what I damn well please!" Unfortunately, our repressed desires usually explode on us. That's why it's not surprising that the righteous preacher who rants about the evils of the flesh, is often found to be having secret affairs. The person who is obsessive about controlling their eating loses all control and goes on a binge.

There are three basic ways in which obsessive relationships to food, money, sex, and time operate. The first is when our underlying insecurities, fears, and desire to control are played out with these elements. We eat instead of getting angry. We spend money instead of crying, or calling a friend. We worry about money instead of letting ourselves know how unhappy we are in our marriage. We deprive ourselves by giving money to our children because we feel guilty about their childhoods. Instead of facing the empty places inside, we get busy.

The second way money, time, sex, and food interrelate is when we switch from one obsession to another. For example, a person who eats compulsively falls in love, and the food obsession vanishes. The obsessive attachment has switched to the new lover. The underlying emptiness has not gone away. When the romance fades, the food hunger returns. People might switch from depression to frenetic activity, addictive relationship to depression, drug addiction to religious addiction, and on and on.

A third type of interrelationship between our relationship to food, money, sex, and time is when one obsessive behavior triggers or intensifies another. It's like the domino theory: If we are upset about a lover, we eat compulsively, drink too much, and flirt with other people. If we are working extra-long hours, we use speed and other stimulants to keep us going. If we don't tell our mate that we find sex uncomfortable, we drink alcohol to hide our anxiety, or take pills to ease our constant headaches. The end of relationships is the Achilles' heel which often triggers one or many forms of obsessive behavior.

One way to explore the interrelationship of these aspects of our lives is to go through the following list.

First, go through the list thinking about food, and write down the word "food" beside any question that triggers a reaction in you, along with any thoughts that come to mind. Then do the same with sex, money, love, time and alcohol or other drugs. If there are other aspects of your life you would like to explore, scan the list with them as well. Let yourself be surprised by your reactions and tune into your body. Notice if there's a sense of happiness, a pang in your gut, a sense of worry or concern, or if you want to deny or rationalize what comes up. Notice your breathing, or lack of breathing. Just notice without judgment. It's all okay, it's information to help you grow.

FOOD, MONEY, SEX, TIME, LOVE, AND OTHER

1. Do you enjoy it?
2. Do you obsess about it?
3. Do you fear being controlled by it?
4. Do you make attempts to control it?
5. Do you have enough of it?
6. Do you want more of it?
7. Are you stingy, hoarding, careless, reckless, or self-depriving with it?
8. Are you generous with it to yourself and others?
9. Do you withhold it from yourself and others?
10. Does it create chaos in your life?
11. Do you binge or starve with it?
12. Do you dole it out in little pieces to yourself or other people?
13. Do you use it to earn approval, impress people, or prevent abandonment?
14. Do you constantly think about having more of it and forget to appreciate what you have in the present?
15. Do you deny your need for it?
16. Is it associated with worry or fear?
17. Is it a problem in your life?

You could also explore the following questions using the words "love," "sex," "time" and "money" or whatever else comes to mind.

If only I had_____then I'd be happy.

I can't seem to get enough of_____.

I wish I had more of_____.

I don't think I'll ever have enough of_____.

I'm afraid of losing_____.

What I really want is_____.

What makes me happiest is_____.

Do you see any parallels, or patterns? What feelings does this bring up?

Extremes are often related. We deny ourselves something when we fear losing control. In general, we feel more comfortable inside when we move from extremes toward the center. A healthy person can set limits, but allows them to slide if there's a good reason. They can budget their money without being totally rigid, take pleasure in food without gorging themselves. They can both give and receive.

Bringing one area into balance can often help with other areas. As I have felt more love in my life, I have been able to let go of possessions and be more generous with others. This, in turn, creates greater peace and simplicity, which helps reduce my cravings for sugar and treats. When I let go of escaping with food, I feel closer to spirit, which allows me to explore more deeply the parts of me that are still wounded. This allows me to be more intimate and loving. When I get off center, the progression goes in the opposite direction. Because it's all energy, one aspect affects another.

Think for a moment about the positive aspects of your relationship to money, things, sex, time, food, and love. Think of times when you felt clear and unworried. What areas have you worked on and how did they have an impact on your life?

There is a circular relationship between intimacy and these elements. The more we create authentic human bonds, connect to community and feel the flow of love within us, the less likely we are to use these counterfeit substitutes to hide our pain. Likewise, the more we bring these things into balance, the more room we have for intimacy.

Changing our relationship to food, money, sex and time is not about deprivation—starving always leads to bingeing. It's about letting ourselves be totally immersed in what we are doing at the moment—be it eating, working, making love, or relaxing—and allowing ourselves to savor the experience. Think of taking a wonderful, juicy piece of fruit, sitting in a comfortable place to eat it, and letting yourself smell it, taste it, suck on it, chew it and totally enjoy it. Likewise with sex, if we allow ourselves to deeply feel the essence of each other, let our passion flow and keep our hearts open, when we are done we will be satisfied and not be left with a craving.

23

REMEMBER THE BEAUTY OF SIMPLICITY

Instead of having more things, we need to have more pleasure with what we have.

—Paul Waschtel

Simplicity is core to intimacy—simplicity of words, thoughts, actions, and lifestyle. Simplicity is not just about possessions, it's about having spaces in our lives—spaces in our closets, on our calendars, and in our hearts. Clutter, whether physical, mental, or emotional, keeps us from connecting to our spirit and from being close to people. Creating simplicity in all these areas allows us to drop into an empty or quiet place, where we give birth to our wisdom and spirit.

I remember going to a funeral and seeing myriad arrangements of flowers. At one level they were beautiful, but at another there were so many, so formally arranged, that I couldn't absorb their beauty. They seemed unreal. Afterward, when someone asked me if I'd like to take some home, I picked out two coral roses and three blue iris and some baby's breath. After I pulled them out of the maze and held them, I felt myself taking a deep breath and relaxing as I was touched by their beauty. Our happiness does not grow with great quantities of personal possessions or lots of money. It grows with a deep level of appreciating the beauty of a few things.

In *The Poverty of Affluence*, Paul Waschtel writes, "Somehow, as we examine the experiential impact of all our acquisitions, we discover that the whole is less than the sum of its parts. Each individual item seems to us to bring an increase in happiness or satisfaction. But the individual increments melt like cotton candy when you try to add them up." He also quotes from a cross-sectional study of happiness by Jonathan Freedman: ". . . Above the poverty level, the relationship between income and happiness is remarkably small."

If we feel whole within—have joy and connection in our lives—our cravings for things dissolve into wanting the basics but no more. We feel burdened by too many things rather than excited by them. Instead we value time, breathing room, and heartfelt connections with others born of genuine, clear communication.

In simplifying our lives it helps to be organized so that whatever you need, you can reach for it and know it will be there. You don't waste time with your adrenaline shooting up as you look through drawers for your insurance policy, or rifle through fifteen dry ballpoint pens to find one that writes. For many, a peaceful, uncluttered living space contributes to a peaceful, uncluttered mind as we learn to breathe deeply and relax.

Simplicity also relates to speaking slowly and simply from

deep inside you in a considered way. Imagine quiet spaces in conversation as people stop to listen, absorb what others are saying, and thoughtfully respond. Imagine comfortable, silent spaces as you allow yourself to *be* with another person.

Creating simplicity in the United States is a tremendous challenge because capitalist society conditions us from an early age to associate value and happiness with objects, status, productivity, and fame. We live in direct contrast to indigenous cultures where artifacts such as pottery and tools are often beautiful, functional, and symbolic all at the same time. They are not a measure of worth, rather, they are integrated with life and have spiritual symbolism.

I had a painful reminder of the depth of my attachment to things when visiting a woman in Nairobi, Kenya, whom I had met as an exchange student in the States. She lived with her father in a tiny home that was at once sparse and welcoming. The old furniture was covered with crocheted covers she had made, and the kitchen consisted of a sink sticking out of the wall, a tiny stove, and a small table. She had made a lovely lunch, which she served with love. She spoke of how lucky she was. When I was about to leave, she asked about a mutual friend in the States, and without hesitation, she picked up the most beautiful small vase in the house, probably one of the three items of value, and said with ease, "Please take this to Pat." A part of me wanted to say, "Are you sure? Is that all right? Won't you miss it?" But I stopped myself because it was clear how unattached she was to that object. It was breathtaking and inspiring. I wished I could do the same so easily. I feel incredibly burdened by my socialization to be attached to objects. It's a prison of the soul because it keeps us from what we're really wanting underneath—love and peacefulness.

It's difficult to remain uncluttered in our culture. People often work full-time while parenting children as well. Junk mail and paperwork grows and abounds. Keeping records for taxes is overwhelming. Some years back, when a tax accountant explained how I needed to keep track of endless receipts, two checkbooks, and a daily driving log, my mind started

swirling around and I was overcome with a sense of despera-
tion. I put my head down on her desk and said with a moan,
"This is so complicated. I don't want to live this way." I wanted
to run from the office and get a job selling socks at Penney's.
How could I feel free when I was mucking around with thousands of receipts and mileage record books?

I remembered when I lived in a little log house with $150
worth of possessions from yard sales and auctions, and all my
clothes fit in a small closet. I taught piano at Ohio University for
nine months, sublet my house in the summer and took off in
my car, following whatever road appealed to me. I also remembered when my tax form was a computer card.

Even if you have a lot to manage in your life, you can pare
down on possessions, cut back on meetings and organizations,
avoid working overtime, take the phone off the hook when
you eat dinner or read to your children, organize a file drawer
to keep track of things, simplify meals, give away old novels
you'll never read again, subscribe to fewer magazines, and
clean out the basement. As you do this, you'll feel your breathing relax. Like everything else, it's all connected—the junk on
the outside and the junk on the inside. Junk love, junk talk,
junk mail, junk food, junk activities, junk sex. Think of casting
them out and freeing yourself to make breathing room for the
spirit and time to have fun with the people you love.

24

SMALL MIND, BIG MIND, SMALL LOVE, BIG LOVE

Zen master Suzuki Roshi taught about the concept of small
mind, big mind. His teachings have had a profound effect on

my life. It is the essence of small mind to focus on oneself as separate from others—*my* hurt, *my* pain, *my* restless mind. Big mind is when we focus on *the* hurt, *the* pain, *the* restlessness. This was very apparent to me recently when I sat in a Quaker meditation hour trying to quiet my mind as it jumped around from one noisy thought to another. As I remembered Suzuki Roshi's teaching I shifted from focusing on *my* restlessness to thinking about *the* restless mind. As soon as I started saying to myself, "I'm feeling *the* restless mind," I felt a kind of energy cord connecting me with the restless part of the minds of others sitting in the room. As I did this, my mind started to feel quieter and I felt more peaceful.

I then thought to myself, I am feeling *the* quiet mind, and again I felt a connection to the quiet mind of everyone in the room. As my mind became quieter, I felt like laughing because I was feeling *the* joy of being connected to something greater than myself, instead of being this little person sitting alone having inner dialogues about my mind. I experienced a sense of cosmic humor as I looked back at myself and thought, How funny to be sitting alone, so worried about a bit of restlessness.

I spoke of my experience in the meeting. Afterward, several people came to me and said, "That was just what I needed to hear, I was feeling so restless in my mind today." This led me to consider that my earlier perception of sitting alone with my noisy mind had been an illusion all along. In all likelihood, I had been coexperiencing the restless mind of those around me. It was only my small mind that forgot this.

When we go beyond small mind to big mind in relationships, we realize that we are in no way unique. We can think of *the* longing to be close, *the* fear of being swallowed up, *the* conflicts, and *the* joys, as inherent to all relationships. From this way of thinking, we become part of the unfolding of the universe itself as we create intimacy and open our hearts to love.

It's comforting to think in big-mind terms. I think of the words from Handel's *Messiah*, "Come unto him all thee that labour and he shall give you rest." To me this means, take the labors of life, open them to big mind, to spirit, to seeing yourself as part of the trembling, suffering, joy, and pain of All That Is, and you will be unburdened. You will no longer feel alone.

Seeking *the* love as opposed to my lover is also part of big mind. It's like seeking to be part of love consciousness in all that we do. Seeking the perfect lover to make us happy and take care of us takes us back to small mind. That doesn't mean it's not all right to want a wonderful lover and partner on the journey. It means that our happiness comes from intertwining our relationship with big mind and big love that open our awareness and consciousness. Big mind helps us on the path toward the inseparable union of seeing God as love, lover, and beloved.

Big mind lightens our frustrations and puts us in contact with cosmic humor, which is the ability to look down on the earth and see millions of people playing out their dramas, getting intense and forgetting to bask in the sunshine, praise the rocks, and sing songs of joy. Cosmic humor is when we see how we trip over our own feet, forget to remember what magical beings we are, and become lost in our own little problems of the moment. It's the part of us that says, *Lighten up! It's just life.*

We can learn to switch to big mind at will. Simply take anything that frustrates you and shift the pronouns to *the* problem, *the* hurt, *the* loss. If someone is late, you can say to yourself, I'm feeling *the* frustration of people being late—just as millions of people do every day. Then imagine thousands of people waiting for someone in China, Russia, South America, and near where you live: Some are agitated, others are reading the paper, while others are using the time to meditate. When we see ourselves from this vantage point, nothing seems so big.

From a big-mind perspective, we realize that life is a flow with inherent challenges that we all face. We're experiencing what people have gone through over the millennia and shall continue to face in the future. When Native American indigenous people do a blessing, they often end with the phrase "All our relations," which is the essence of big mind. It is recognizing all who have come before us, all who live now, and all who will follow, and how they live in us and we in them.

25

UNDERSTAND YOUR
SURVIVAL BRAIN

*U*nderstanding our survival brain helps put us in touch with big mind. Have you ever been bewildered by a sudden outburst of anger from yourself or felt profound hurt in response to a seemingly small event? When pain gets overwhelming, our survival brain says, "Do something! Help me feel better." This leads us to quickly reach for whatever brings comfort. Over time, through a process of trial and error, we find the protective escapes that work best for us. We grab for sweets, escape into a fantasy world, act super-good, or numb our senses watching TV. We get busy, or even harm ourselves physically. From a survival brain perspective, *Whatever you did, no matter how bewildering it seemed, was an attempt to survive.* You were doing the best you could to feel good, assuage pain, or get the approval and love that all people need.

Comprehending our survival responses requires a basic understanding of the brain. The following discussion of the brain includes information from Dr. Paul D. MacLean in *The Brain* by Richard Restak. There are three basic parts to the brain which are interlinked. The brain stem or reptilian brain, the Paleomammalian brain which includes the limbic system, and the neomammalian which is often called the neocortex. I will refer to these as the reptilian, mammalian and neocortex parts of the brain.

The reptilian part of the brain is concerned with vital, survival functions associated with self-preservation—hunting, homing, mating, establishing territory and fighting. It also relates to circulation, breathing, sleeping and hunger. The limbic system is related to emotions that guide behavior. This is where we develop automatic responses to situations starting

with childhood. We learned to automatically withdraw if someone was angry or drunk, we learned to eat when we felt abandoned. The neocortex gives us the ability to reason, reflect,
organize information, use language, have insight, engage in
logic, and anticipate the consequences of our behavior.

In terms of human behavior and relationships, we see the
importance of all of these systems working together. For example, if we feel attacked by someone, the reptilian part of the
brain recognizes our survival is in jeopardy, the mammalian
part has emotions of fear and anger and the neocortex goes into
action to think of a reasonable response to preserve the system
without attacking, killing or doing something that would wreak
serious consequences.

Unfortunately, it doesn't always work this way. In close
relationships it sometimes feels as if we lose the functioning of
our neocortex and react without thinking: We respond as if we
are in danger of survival, even though someone may have simply disagreed with us or been mildly critical. Our knee-jerk
reaction leads us to feel out of control as we start arguing,
defending and counterattacking. A more violent response such
as screaming, hitting and wanting to harm the other person
reflects that we are operating primarily from our reptilian
brain. We are behaving as if our life is at stake.

To further confuse the situation, the mammalian and reptilian parts of the brain store memories in an undifferentiated
way with regard to time and place. The hurts and wounds accu-
mulated in our past are all lumped together in an energy mass
that can feel as alive today as they did in the past. All it takes is
some kind of trigger that echoes past experience to set off a
strong reaction in the limbic system and reptilian brain. We "fly
off the handle," have a "knee-jerk" reaction or get "hot under
the collar," to use some familiar phrases. That's why being able
to keep our neocortex intact is so crucial to relationships. When
we feel a flash of anger or fear, the neocortex can reflect and
help us have a reasoned response.

"Let's take a breath and calm down. What's the reality of
the situation. Is my response reasonable or am I overreacting?"

Without the use of our neocortex, we have the familiar scene that goes something like this: "No, you didn't! Yes I did! You're full of shit! You're the most stubborn person I ever met! I don't know what I ever saw in you. *Slam! Slam!*"

To understand the impact of the stored feelings in your old brain—the reptilian and limbic systems—recall a time when you had an intense flash of anger or hurt that felt out of proportion to the current situation. In reality, your reaction carried the emotional charge from hundreds of past experiences stored in your old brain as well as the current situation. For example, let's say that as a child, Frank was shy and had serious coordination problems. He was often taunted with epithets such as "clumsy," "slow," and "sissy" by his older sister and kids at school. His loneliness and pain covered a deep sense of rage at his tormentors. As he got older, the hurt and anger remained stockpiled in his survival brain, ready to be triggered by any form of teasing or joking about his being clumsy or awkward.

Through tremendous effort on his part, by adulthood he no longer appeared uncoordinated, and he learned to present himself as a friendly guy. Although he thought he had overcome his childhood problems, the emotional wounds remained, often manifesting in sharp bursts of anger that took people by surprise. One day at work, when he felt under pressure, he spilled coffee on some important papers. When his office mate, Mary, playfully teased him, using the word "clumsy," he experienced an intense wave of shame followed by a rip of anger. Even though Mary had always been a loyal friend, at that moment he felt intense hatred for her and wanted to hurt her. With uncharacteristic sharpness he retorted, "You're not so together yourself," followed by a list of past grievances he had never voiced.

Why the sudden outburst? In Frank's old brain, Mary merged with every unkind person and every teasing remark he had suffered as a child and adolescent. Her use of the word "clumsy" tapped into a volatile energy mass of undifferentiated shame and hurt that was ready to explode at a moment's notice. Because he disowned the hurts from the past, he was unable to call on his neocortex. He believed Mary was the *cause* of his reaction—she was insensitive and unkind. As a result, he was quick to justify his behavior rather than apologize—a pattern that had cost him dearly in relationships.

The point of understanding your survival brain is to become more aware of the source of sudden, intense reactions so that you can manage them rather than attack other people or feel badly about yourself. If Frank were willing to reconnect with his past and be conscious of his survival brain at work, he could change. When his emotions were triggered by the word "clumsy," he could call on his neocortex to recognize his response as part of past conditioning and say, "Mary, be nice, I'm really sensitive to teasing—especially the word 'clumsy'—because it happened so much when I was a child." If Mary were sensitive, she could respond, "I'm sorry, I didn't mean to hurt you." That would be the end of it, and the old wounds could start to heal because they were being owned and respected. This is just a glimpse of one of the most important aspects of relationships, which we will return to in later sections.

If you want to increase your awareness of your survival reactions, check the following list for behaviors that trigger strong reactions in you. Rate them on a scale from one to ten and add others that are relevant for you. Most people will have several triggers of varying intensity.

TRIGGER/CATALYST

teased

left out

scolded/criticized

lied to

stood up—someone is late, unreliable

blamed

misunderstood

laughed at (for making mistakes, your body, being naive, and so on) having someone angry at you

making a mistake

having someone tell you what to do/that you're
stupid/clumsy

someone wants something from you emotionally

other, other, other

EMOTIONAL SURVIVAL RESPONSES
(OFTEN TRIGGERED BY SHAME) INCLUDE

sudden anger/rage/feeling stormy/temper tantrums/
break things/get violent

big hurt/sadness

paralyzing fear/being swallowed up/feeling annihilated/
feeling invisible

smooth over the feelings/make nice/fix the situation/
talk in platitudes

sudden feeling of being defective/inadequate

become cold, intellectual, and rational and have
no feelings

other, other, other

If you take some time to pick out the situations that tend to
trigger your emotions, and recognize your emotional responses
from the past, you have some basic information that can lead to
growth. Left unexamined, our survival responses contribute
greatly to the demise of many relationships. When we frequently
fly off the handle, withdraw or lose our temper, we're imprisoned
in the past and are not able to be present for the people around us.
One person criticizes and the other defends or feels very hurt. Or,
one person is upset and the other tries to smooth over the situation. This keeps relationships volatile and superficial because we're
not having authentic connections, we're operating out of the past.

The goal isn't to "get over" having trigger points so much as to recognize them, reflect, and act from a more reasoned stance. In other words, engage your neocortex to guide you. Questions to ask yourself:

What did the person actually say?

Is my response overly intense for the current situation?

Is this an old wound I'm feeling?

What is reasonable for this situation?

What do I really need right now?

Here's an example from my life. Recently, when I was flying home after a long trip feeling tired, I started feeling hurt and angry at my partner. I could hear myself thinking: "She got to stay home and go to the gym while I was working. She probably didn't get the bills paid or take care of the plants or anything." I could hear my feelings heating up. A part of me was ready to walk off the plane and be furious with her. I was totally caught up in small mind and my old brain. When I shifted to big mind and engaged my neocortex, I realized that my feelings were overreactive (not to mention totally irrational) and explored their source—a young child not feeling valued and appreciated. I was able to call when I changed planes and ask for what I truly needed. "Jessie, I'm feeling tired and I need a friend. I'd really appreciate your being at the gate to greet me." How much better it felt to be vulnerable with my needs than walk off the plane with coldness in my heart and anger in my eyes.

Once we understand how our survival brain leads us to have inappropriate reactions stemming from our past, we can realize that other people's intense reactions are not about us. Just like ours, their responses are unwanted intruders from the past. From this vantage point of compassion and big mind, we won't escalate situations by getting defensive and striking back. It doesn't mean that we put up with abuse or that we don't confront a situation; rather, we bring a healing power to relationships by not colluding with old wounded parts that lead us to reinjure each other. We remember that most people aren't out to hurt us, they are responding unconsciously, and perhaps unskillfully, from an old desire to protect themselves and assuage pain.

26

TRUST THE POSITIVE INTENTIONS OF OTHERS

*U*nderstanding the function of our survival brain helps us differentiate childhood conditioning from the present. Using the concept of the positive intention, we learn to listen with a sixth sense, look beneath people's external behavior, and respond to their underlying message. People might see this as contrary to much of the addiction and codependency literature, which says we shouldn't try to figure people out. It's not about analyzing people, it's about listening from a heart place, with love and understanding. The concept of looking for the positive intention comes from various writings and teachings of Ken Keyes.

I remember a talk show I was on. A man gave what sounded like a hostile, judgmental opinion about people having recreational sex. The audience groaned negatively when he spoke, but I had the sense that he was trying to say something of value. "Just a minute," I interjected. "Am I hearing that you think we hurt ourselves when we have sex for recreation, not out of love?" He smiled, showing his relief at being understood. "Yes, yes, that's what I'm saying." I wasn't trying to analyze him, I was simply trying to listen beneath the somewhat unskillful use of words to find his meaning.

It's good to remember that most people are trudging through life the best they can, seeking to be loved, understood, have a purpose, and feel valued. Because of childhood conditioning, we often learned to be indirect when we wanted something—we'd placate, be sneaky, or be super-nice or logical. Skillful parents learn to hear the request beneath the surface behavior. For example, if a child is whining at us, we hear the positive intention, and respond to the possible need. "Do you need some attention now?" We can add, "It's okay if you ask me directly. I want to give you what you want." A man at a training session on relationships I attended said recently, "Everything moves toward love or violence, and violence is a cry for love." Even if someone is yelling and screaming at you, it's because they're trying to fit you into a mold that they can love. It doesn't mean you need to oblige, but if you can start to believe, just a little, that the underlying desire is love, you can see people in a different light. And, of course, when you can hear it in others, you learn to hear it in yourself.

One way to learn this skill is to make a list of all the ways in which you put yourself down, or things you haven't forgiven yourself for. Then explore the possible positive intention underlying each behavior. If you go deep enough, you will usually meet a part of yourself that wanted something positive.

Here are some examples:

BEHAVIOR	POSITIVE INTENTION
I'm super charming and helpful.	People will be nice and never confront me—they'll admire me.
I whined a lot as a kid.	I longed for attention.
I'm distant and unfriendly.	People won't bother me or put me down.
	I won't have to feel my awkwardness.
I chatter and talk a lot.	I want people to notice me. It reduces my fear.
I shoplifted as a teenager.	I wanted to express my anger.
	I wanted to fit in with the other kids.
I get stormy and mean.	I don't want anyone to see how scared and lonely I am.
I taught my daughter to be afraid of men and sex.	I didn't want her to get pregnant as I did when I was young.
I get insistent.	I sometimes feel invisible and want to be noticed so I don't disappear.
Other	Other

Understanding someone's positive intention does not condone abuse even though the abuser may have had a positive intention. The point is to understand that they were acting out of their primitive survival brain, and were inappropriately trying to fulfill some need of theirs for power, control, or love. Their behavior means nothing about your worth. We may have scars, but we don't need to blame ourselves or carry the shame forever. We can go one step deeper and see how we sometimes act like our abuser—we've done to others what was done to us. When we are willing to face our ability to harm others and feel compassion for our lack of skill and unconsciousness, we will be able to forgive both ourselves and our abuser.

Understanding the positive intention with children can be a tremendous aid to parenting. When a young child cries, it can mean that he or she is hungry, thirsty, sick, tired, or needing to be held. Later, when they get defiant, their positive intention might be to be more separate, make their own decisions, and assert their power to gain a sense of confidence. With teenagers, seeing the positive intention is a skill that will prevent a lot of uproar. First and foremost, teenagers are trying to assert their separate identity in order to be strong enough to leave home. They have tremendous ambivalence between "I want out of here so no one tells me what to do" and "Oh, my God, can I make it on my own?" They want the privileges of adults, and they hate being like adults.

The concept of the positive intention gives you a pathway to the center of your heart. When you go deep enough to recognize the positive intention underlying all behavior, you keep coming back to love. At that level of consciousness, hate, cruelty, and greed become a surface illusion covering a deeper level of spirit that exists in all people. In that place, there is no hate or cruelty.

The power of understanding the positive intention of others holds true on a social and political level as well. If we challenge social systems, or protest from a place of compassion rather than anger, we will feel better and be more effective. When we come to the bargaining table with compassion in our hearts, even though we have differences—or think their positive intention is misguided—we are far more likely to be heard and have an impact.

To use the concept of the positive intention to kindle your compassion, the next time you are near a crowd or group of people simply look around you and say to yourself, *All these people have had to live every day of their lives, just like me. They've had to get up and make choices, talk to people and live in their particular body. They went through infancy, had to learn to make friends, had to learn about sex, had to figure out how to earn a living, just like me. They've all made mistakes, been skillful in some ways, unskillful in others, just like me. They all want love, and freedom from suffering, just like me.* As you do this, tune into your heart. You don't have to like everyone's personality, you don't have to want to be friends, but you can turn up your compassion when you think to yourself, "They're all doing the best they can with what they were given."

27

THE SPIRITS THAT HURT OUR SPIRITS: BLOCKING INTIMACY WITH DRUGS AND OTHER ADDICTIONS

*A*ddictions are similar to love affairs. Whether it's food, sex, TV, gambling, or drugs, you can't wait to get it, you put it before other responsibilities, you get mad if you can't have it, you feel afraid of losing it, and you increasingly want more of it. Addictive behavior is when we use any form of escape to cover our feelings. It could be one drink a day, a couple of candy bars

every afternoon—that you look forward to for three hours—
faking your feelings, constant worry about weight, a binge
every Friday night. A full-blown addiction is when we form a
primary relationship to a substance, behavior, or person that
has harmful consequences, affects all areas of life, escalates
over time and leads to withdrawal symptoms upon quitting.

The goal of addictive behavior is usually to escape pain and
feel euphoric, relaxed, or loving, but it's important to realize
that it's a temporary high. If we *depend* on these things for a
high or peace of mind, a hangover is sure to follow because the
emptiness, alienation, or fear we temporarily mask will quake
open again and send us in hot pursuit of another fix. Just as a
love affair is not love, a drug-induced high is not being one
with spirit, it's getting high on spirits. This temporary high can
give us a glimpse of a transcendent feeling, but ultimately we
have to get there by walking the spiritual path, one conscious
step after another. There's no cheap ticket to peace of mind.

Compulsive attachments are like a demon lover, pulling us
in, controlling us, seducing us into thinking that they are crucial to our existence. It's a double bind—our old survivor brain
thinks they are necessary to our existence, but, in reality, they
cause internal conflict: We engage in a life-and-death battle
between the part of us seeking true spirit and the part of us that
wants a fix. Part of the cunning nature of addiction is our
propensity to deny that we have a problem. "I can stop any
time" or "My life is fine." If you quit for a time to prove you
don't have a problem without examining your underlying
emotions, you are still in an addictive state because your addict
part is trying to con you into believing that there's no problem.
It's a classic ploy. You haven't truly let go, you have remained
in a state of denial that is likely to keep any true insight and
growth from occurring. After a few months you can say, "See, I
have no problem," and resume the addictive behavior. This
well-honed denial system is born of the terror of living without
our escape hatch, which keeps us from dealing with our feelings.

When we're in an addictive or compulsive state, we are in a

trance that excludes connection to others or to spirit. We know love exists but it doesn't penetrate the walls of our hearts. There is a sense of unreality or a feeling of passing through life without quite being there.

To move toward intimacy means releasing the grip of addictive and compulsive behavior and crashing into reality. Life is messy, uncertain, and confusing, but in being genuine and real we are able to connect with others. Letting go of addictive behavior is a leap of faith because you often don't know the trouble it caused until you let go of it. If we go deep enough beneath addictive or compulsive behavior, we will find that our true desire is to be one with spirit.

Spirit can be defined as the immortal part of each us—an energy that is beyond time and definition. It has no labels, it is simply a wondrous "ah," the breath inside the breath that is inexplicable. Spirit removes the artificial boundaries of small mind that says we are separate and alone. It's like a memory that we are creation itself, magic, a tingling vital energy force that is part of the cosmic energy field. We can only grope for words to explain it with phrases like "I had a feeling beyond words when I gave birth" or "The solution magically came to mind."

The longing for spirit and peace of mind is powerful motivation to let go of addictive behavior. Instead of approaching the release of addictive behavior as depriving yourself of something, keep your focus on what you have to gain—growth, self-respect and something so peaceful and vast that it's worth any discomfort to get there.

It's like saying "I like the hot fudge sundae, it would taste good, but I love the feeling of being healthy and alert even more," or "I like watching TV five hours a day, but I want to feel true connection with people even more," or "I want the security of this dead relationship, but I want to know myself even more."

Even if it's not an entrenched addiction, every compulsion or moment in which we hide from our authentic self takes its toll. One man commented, "I can't quite put my finger on it, but when I quit alcohol, although I didn't drink very much, my relationships changed, my state of mind changed, everything—it was like seeing the world through a different pair of eyes. My meditation practice went deeper and life seemed more real."

Usually beneath addiction is a cry for help—I'm lonely, I'm scared, I'm hurt, I need love. If you have compulsions or addictive attachments, you can ask yourself: What does it give me? What does it protect me from feeling? How might life be different without it? Could you let yourself drop into those feelings and sit in the middle of your restlessness, hurt, or pain? Your ability to tolerate this discomfort is your ticket out of isolation and addiction to love and spiritual connection with others.

When people let go of addictive attachments with the intention of exploring their inner world, feelings and memories often rise to the surface. The pain we were burying is felt. We become anxious, depressed, and wonder if it's worth it. Yet, somewhere inside we feel a birthing of spirit, a sense of safety born of living life on its own terms. We are not led around by our compulsive cravings. We start to feel free.

If you feel stuck in any way, or your relationships aren't all you want them to be, take a careful look at your favorite escapes/comforts and consider letting them go so you can make room for love. List them, and think about the positive intention of using them as well as the harmful consequences. I particularly suggest abstaining from alcohol, other drugs and the daily use of TV. Even if it is just one glass of wine after work, a couple of hours of TV a night or an hour at the computer, explore what happens when you break the routine. Sit in your discomfort and meet your inner world. Do it as an experiment to get to know yourself. Very often that one little drink when you walk in the door is like taking a step away from intimacy with your partner. It's like wearing a protective shield so you don't have to feel.

Imagine the voice of spirit whispering in your ear that you have the ability to meet the world as you are—trembling, afraid, beautiful, strong.

28

TRUST IN THE HEALING POWER OF THE TRUTH

There are very few human beings who receive the truth . . . by
instant illumination. Most of them acquire it fragment by fragment.
                                                        —Anaïs Nin

*I*n *Mutant Message Down Under,* Marlo Morgan tells of her four-month walkabout in a desert with an aboriginal tribe who call themselves the Real People. She witnessed how adept they were at sending messages via telepathy. When she marveled at this, she was told that they never tell a lie—"not a small fabrication, not a partial truth, nor any gross unreal statement. No lies at all, so they have nothing to hide." As a result, no one was afraid to have their mind open to send and receive messages via telepathy.

The closeness of our relationships is measured in large part by the level of our honesty—our ability to know it, speak it and hear it. The truth keeps relationships alive because there are no secrets or deceptions to stop our energy from flowing back and forth. Every time we hold back inside, we make distance from ourself and others. Yet truth-telling takes a level of discernment. It doesn't mean that we pour out our past history of lovers and escapades. It doesn't mean we blurt out everything that pops into our mind without reflection. It means that we do all that we can to stay clear in the present by not deceiving people or hiding our feelings. With some people, deception comes from what they don't say. They maintain a stoic front and withhold the truth, which might be: "I'm afraid," "I don't know the answer," "I need your help."

Opening up to the truth isn't easy. It demands an emotional honesty that starts with a covenant to know oneSelf—the heart of our feelings and thoughts. It requires moment-to-moment awareness as we move through our days, tuning into signals from inside, pushing through fear to reveal our inner experience. It's far more subtle than owning up to the cookies we've swiped. Truth-telling involves being aware of our motivation.

Marlo Morgan writes, "I learned as long as I had anything in my heart or my head I still felt necessary to hide, it would not work. I had to come to peace with EVERYTHING—to lay my mind out on a table like the Real People do, and stand by as my motives were exposed and examined." We can ask ourselves: Is my motivation to be caring, or is there an edge of maliciousness or an attempt to change the other person?

Telling a neighbor you saw her husband flirting with a woman in a bar is not in the spirit of truth-telling if you do it to hurt her or to feel important because you have big news. On the other hand, if your neighbor is a close friend and has told you she wants to know if her husband is fooling around, the same message could be in the spirit of truth-telling.

The truth might stir up conflict, but this can be positive if the motivation is to heal, not harm. If we silence our voice, deny conflict, withdraw or fake politeness, part of us withers away and our relationships become shallow. For most people, fear is the barrier to telling the truth. We're afraid it's not the right time, we might hurt someone's feelings, someone might get mad or might leave. It's better to make an occasional mistake or have a painful outcome than to live in chronic fear. You can always build a bridge back, but the tension in your gut goes on forever. When the concept of telling the truth was new to me, I often felt a sense of nameless terror when I brought up concerns and feelings. My most common lies were not asking for what I wanted, not owning up to a mistake, or not saying directly that I was hurt or angry. I also realized how often I told partial truths, hedged, denied conflict, or simply tried to put problems out of my mind.

At one point in my life, I waited three years to bring up a painful situation with a neighbor. Every time I thought of her, I felt fear rip through me. When I finally phoned her, a white-hot energy pulsed inside and my arms were tingling because I was so scared. When we talked, she said what I feared—that she didn't want to be friends anymore. Even so, it was a great relief to talk, and, paradoxically, afterward she was much friendlier. After the conversation, when I felt a great release of energy inside, I thought of the fear and pain I had caused myself by waiting for so long.

Telling the truth is not only about bringing up conflicts and problems, it's about revealing our love and caring. When we are uncluttered by past resentments and hurts, our love is free to flow to each other. Gratitude and appreciation become central to our exchanges with others.

The truth also comes through silence with soft eyes, smiles, gestures, and touches that transmit feelings from the heart: A smile that says, "I'm happy to see you"; a nod of the head to say, "I hear you"; a firm grasp of the hand to say, "I'm here. I'm with you." The last time I saw my father alive, he was sitting in a wheelchair in a nursing home. While he couldn't talk coherently, he still had a wonderful, strong grasp that expressed the love and care he could no longer voice with words. As we sat there in the stillness, I could feel his spirit through his firm grasp. Memories of watching him chop wood or sand a desk he was making, or the talk he gave us on the value of solid handshakes washed through me.

The challenge of telling the truth is to let go of the outcome. The truth isn't the truth if we expect people to reciprocate in a given way, but becomes dependency or enmeshment. Likewise, as a listener it's important to hear someone's truths as part of their journey, spoken in the spirit of staying clear and honest. If we accept the outcome of living by our truths, we will come to know love and freedom. Ultimately, telling the truth is at the heart of our ability to love and feel the breath of spirit, or as Hazrat Inayat Khan writes, "God is truth, and truth is God."

29

TRUST WISELY

Nothing dispels mistrust like the revealed heart.
                    —Stephen and Ondrea Levine

A friend told me of a woman who canceled a trip with her at the last minute. When she asked her the reason, the woman replied, "I don't trust you."

My friend asked her, "What do you mean by that, what don't you trust?" and the other woman simply repeated, "I just don't trust you." The concept of trust often gets bantered about in relationships in general, unspecified terms. What people are often implying is, "I don't trust you to give me what I want" or "I don't trust you to be the person I want you to be." We need to define what we mean by trust.

Do we trust someone to be on time, to listen, to not steal our things, to be sexually faithful? *Trusting wisely* means that we build trust slowly, over time, as people demonstrate their trust-worthiness in different situations. For example, if Carl says he wants a relationship with Sherie, yet breaks appointments and pulls away, Sherie needs to trust in what she sees. In my empowerment model for groups, I include the step, *We daily affirm that we know what we know, we see what we see, and we feel what we feel*. This suggests that trust begins with ourselves. We can't control others' feelings, but we can learn to trust our instincts and observations and make wise choices for ourselves. We can learn to trust that we have the strength to persevere when life is tough or things don't go our way; we can say no or not sacrifice our values to please someone. The ability to trust wisely grounds us and protects us from harm. When we can see a con, we can protect ourselves; when we see love, we can open our heart.

A most helpful teaching on trust I have had was from Ken

Keyes, author of *Handbook to Higher Consciousness*. He taught that we could trust all people to be exactly as they are—to run off their programming. *In other words, we can usually trust that the best predictor of future behavior is past behavior.* If someone drinks too much, you can trust that they will probably continue drinking too much. If someone is chronically late, you can trust that they will continue to be chronically late. Of course, people can make changes, but it's up to them; our job is to *see people as they really are and decide if we want to be with them, as they are right now.* A change would be a nice surprise, but don't bank on it.

There's an apt expression, "One time shame on you, two times, shame on me." This means that if I trust you once and you break the trust, then shame on you; if I trust you again in the same situation—unless I have evidence that you will be different—shame on me for playing the fool. We often continue to "trust" someone because we hope they'll be different. For many years, I kept telling personal secrets to a family member who routinely repeated them to others. A part of me *wanted* her to be a close confidante even though there was repeated evidence that she never kept a secret. It was like a childhood part of me denying reality in the hope that she would change. I needed to act as an adult and trust that she would always tell my secrets—especially to family members who would probably use them against me. When I stopped confiding in her, I felt a lot of sadness because I was giving up the illusion of having her as an intimate family member.

It's important not to hide behind the word "trust" in order to stay naive or as an excuse for remaining in a harmful relationship. Because a woman fears losing her husband, she might say, "I need to trust him not to have any more affairs" instead of trusting that there is a history of affairs and no evidence of any change. We have to give up our wishful thinking in order to develop the ability to trust wisely.

Often, people will visit their families, saying, "It's going to be different this time, we're going to get along." I suggest that people avoid resolutions of this sort and trust that people will be the way they are. Grandpa will give monologues, you will probably pick a fight with your sister, and Mom will probably drink too much—and that's the way it is. Paradoxically, when we enter a situation with the stance of trusting people to be as they are—including ourselves—we will bring a different energy because we are seeing from a big-mind perspective. We will feel much lighter as we observe ourselves amid the great human comedy acting out our own personal soap opera. Our lighter energy will usually have a positive effect on the whole situation, and for sure we will feel better.

30

THE BITTERSWEET TASTE OF TRUST

When we build trusting relationships that allow us to feel safe and loved, we become increasingly free from fear, drama, and chaos. In the resulting quiet, we often drop to a deeper level of feelings and consciousness. Sometimes the feelings are peaceful and happy; other times, buried pain and grief rise to the surface.

This happened to me quite by surprise when my partner left for a six-month trek in Antarctica. Because it was a new relationship, we didn't have a long-term foundation of trust. She was scheduled to call me once a week—I couldn't call her—and I found myself being both anxious and excited before her calls. Would she remember? Would she be sure and let me know if she was called away and couldn't be there? I looked forward to those calls like a kid waiting for Santa Claus. After a few weeks, when she had called on time, I stopped worrying and started trusting that she would call. One might think I would feel relieved, which I did. Yet, in the resulting quiet, I started missing her with an ache that was more profound and painful than anything I had ever experienced. I wanted to get busy, to run, to eat—to do anything but simply sit in the loneliness that existed because of how much we loved each other. I could truly understand why people stay in chaotic relationships, emotionally detach, keep busy, worry, and stay preoccupied to avoid feeling.

As I allowed myself to surrender to my feelings of loss, I started thinking of all the people who were separated from loved ones, not knowing if they were safe or would make it home. I kept thinking of how terrible it would be to have a child or a friend away fighting a war and not knowing if they would return. I kept thinking of all the pain so many people in the world are feeling. The big ache inside became a source of compassion. After a while, the feeling turned to one of sweetness and peace. It's hard to describe, except to say that I felt connected through time and space to many people. I wasn't this person alone missing my lover, I was one of many people going through a common human experience that bonded us together. I also noticed that I wasn't overeating as I had been when I didn't allow myself to feel my sadness.

One of the reasons to create relationships with people who are loyal and caring is to free ourselves from endless drama so that we can reach deeper into our hearts. It is scary at first, but it takes us to spirit. When we create dramatic, traumatic relationships, we stay so busy surviving we don't have time for the breath of spirit to enter us. Every step of the way to intimacy has the potential for a bittersweet experience. We open up, we feel more deeply both the roses and the thorns, and then, for a little while, the sweetness of peace comes over us.

31

LISTEN TO THE SOUNDS
OF SILENCE

Stop the words now, open the window in the center of your heart . . .
—Rumi

*T*he breath of spirit is all around us, but we need to take time to breathe it into our hearts. Imagine sitting quietly, listening to your breathing, taking time to feel your heart space. Feel the area around your heart soften, relax, let go. It is your soft heart that allows you to be stirred by a tender glance, a sensuous breeze, a sunset, a flower, or a loving touch.

In our upside-down world we've come to value possessions and work more than the most precious commodities of all—time and stillness: time to relax, be conscious of our breathing or feel the presence of a loved one near by; stillness to hear and feel the subtle nuances of life, the beating of our heart, to know God.

The quality of our relationships reflects the quality of our spiritual life. Questions to ponder today, tomorrow, and always, are: What is life for? Why are we here? What will we have learned when it's time to pass on?

Even with full-time jobs and busy lives, we can make choices about how we spend our time. We can pause to breathe consciously several times a day. We can clear out our appointment book for a weekend, eat from the same pot of soup for three days, and wear the same clothes several days in a row. At a workshop on simplicity, one of the suggestions was to spend a day following your heart, doing whatever brought joy, the rationale being that when you live in the moment in connection with your heart, you will feel fulfilled and happy.

I remember, as a faculty member at Ohio University, being interviewed for an article on ways in which faculty members spent their leisure time. I said I liked tennis, old movies, but most of all I enjoyed hanging out in the country with a bunch of friends, with no particular plans. When I read the article, I felt a bit sheepish. Other faculty members studied hieroglyphics, learned foreign languages, read up on god knows what. My discomfort was eased when a student said I had given him hope that being an adult didn't mean you had to be completely serious. It can be difficult for people to allow themselves a few hours for following their hearts, not to mention a whole day or weekend, particularly where they were brought up with a strong work ethic and a heavy dose of guilt.

When I moved from the Midwest to a small college town in the Rocky Mountains, I felt a dramatic shift in the way people spent time. In Minnesota it was, "I'll meet you for a walk next Tuesday at Lake Harriet at four o'clock. I've got to go by six o'clock." I remember asking a friend to take Sunday afternoon off and have fun, and hearing her blurt out, "I can't do that, I had fun yesterday." Shortly after I moved out west, a friend suggested an afternoon bike ride. When we were done I expected to hear the familiar "Gotta go now, get some work done"—the work ethic pulling her away to some nameless task. Much to my delight she said, "I have some food at home, do you want to come over for dinner?" When dinner was nearly over, I was surprised again when she asked, "Would you like to rent a video and watch it with me?" A long, leisurely day had become almost a foreign experience. I felt a gentle wave of euphoria sweep over me.

It takes time to open the love window—time alone in quiet, and time with our partner, family, or friends. We come to know the details of another's life not just by words but by time together. It can't be forced or rushed. I dislike the term "quality time" because it suggests doing things intensely. The concept doesn't include the importance of simply being near a loved one, relaxed, talking a little, eating a little, and just enjoying each other's presence. Children need "time on the fly"—a caregiver who is available over a long period of time so the child can alternate between exploration and a quick visit for reassurance—a hug, or help. Time together in silence provides an anchor for relationships. We go from *doing* things together to simply *being* together. We slow down.

I remember with great fondness our family's summer camping trips back in the late 1940s and 50s. We had an old army surplus tent, a tiny rowboat, and minimal equipment—just enough to be comfortable. Few people camped at that time, so we were often alone or with a few other families or relatives who had joined us. One part of the family ritual was to be quiet for an hour after lunch. You could read, sit, write, embroider, draw, or sleep, but you had to find one place and stay there and be quiet. This was not a punitive or controlling rule, rather, it was presented to us as a nice thing to do. I would put a cot under a tree in a special place with just the right amount of sun and shade. I'd usually have a pillow and a book. Sometimes I'd gaze up at the trees and look at the bark, the pine needles and the sky. Other times I would read for a while and fall asleep. I remember looking around at my mother and father, quietly reading. As I write this I am visited by the sense of peace and profound safety that came from these quiet times together.

When I talk with couples about their relationships in general and their sex lives in particular, it is clear that both work better when the couple spends relaxed time together experiencing pleasure, often without words. Sexual union flows out of a heightened awareness and sense of connection.

Silence is the great healer and the great truth. It's where we came from and where we are going. Quiet and meditation have incredible power to calm us down, heal our physical bodies and bring us in touch with the spirit of another person. It takes time to dissolve into silence and let the lists, worries and plans recede to the back of our minds—like a bit of static on the radio rather than a loudspeaker blaring in our faces. After a while we might even feel moments of true quiet. So, turn off the radio, the TV, the computer. Set down the book you are reading and simply take a few moments of silence as you breathe deep and relax your belly. Think of silence as a form of prayer that will bring you to your heart and help you connect with the heart of another.

PART IV

◆◆◆

MANY SMALL STEPS

32

"MAKE AND KEEP AGREEMENTS WITH GREAT CARE"

—the Goodenough Community

Most of us have felt the dull clunk of disappointment or despair as a happy state of anticipation is suddenly deflated by a last-minute phone call: "Sorry, something just came up, I can't make it," or worse, someone acts as if they weren't sure you made a date: "Were we supposed to get together today?" Still worse, a person never shows up and you sit watching the clock tick away, fighting off feelings of anger and hurt or wondering if anything will ever work out.

The Goodenough Community's covenant, to "make and keep agreements with great care," is considered central to healthy relationships and healthy community. To develop intimate relationships, we need a steadiness and reliability we can count on. In *The Little Prince*, by Antoine de Saint-Exupéry, the Fox explains the importance of dependability.

> If, for example, you come at four o'clock in the afternoon, then at three o'clock I shall begin to be happy. I shall feel happier and happier as the hour advances. At four o'clock, I shall already be worrying and jumping about. I shall show you how happy I am! But if you come at just any time, I shall never know at what hour *my heart is to be ready to greet you.*

How sweet it is to feel free to open our heart in anticipation of someone coming to be with us or share an adventure. As we learn to keep agreements with great care and choose others who do likewise, we lower the level of drama and chaos in our lives. We free ourselves to love.

Being able to make and keep agreements with great care is

intricately intertwined with the spiritual journey because it means that we know ourselves deeply. We can know in advance we'll enjoy going to a movie on Saturday night, being on a camping trip in August, or taking a walk later in the day. We know we have the power within us to create happiness doing these things.

There are different types of agreements. There are specific agreements of time and place—to meet someone for a movie or for dinner. There are the ongoing agreements of friendships, which might include returning phone calls, keeping confidences, initiating contact, and bringing up problems. It helps to be explicit about our agreements in order to have clarity and accountability.

Like litter on the side of a highway, most unhappy relationships are strewn with broken agreements in all shapes and forms—breaking dates at the last minute, staying at work when you promised to spend time with the family, refusing to go for counseling, "forgetting" to pick up food for dinner or pay the bills, spending big chunks of money without consulting your partner, having affairs, or getting pregnant. Keeping agreements is a measure of our commitment and should not be undertaken lightly because agreements imply *a commitment to do what it takes to maintain them.* When we say we will love and honor someone, we are committing to a deep level of inner work. Whenever we make an agreement, we need to ask ourselves, Is this an agreement I really want to make? Is it realistic for me at this time? Will I do what it takes to keep this agreement?

A couple I admire talked about the process of making agreements and commitments with each other. "When we got together we were careful not to promise each other the moon because we couldn't deliver it. In fact, we didn't promise a lot. We'd make agreements step-by-step and see how they felt. Then we'd make deeper agreements. We wanted to be true to our word."

The value of being careful with agreements has lost its meaning for many people in our throwaway, fast-paced society.

People become dissociated and self-absorbed due to exhaustion, overstimulation, and a frenetic pace of life that includes the continuous assault of junk mail, junk music, and junk food. We detach from our feelings, move into survival mode and become glib with our words, thoughts, plans, and agreements. When we're out of touch with ourselves, it's easy to forget that we matter to others and that they are affected by a broken agreement.

The Goodenough Community uses the expression "great care." This reminds us that people are sacred, tender, and vulnerable. Every time we don't keep an agreement, it's like a little scratch on the other person's heart and a little scratch on our own heart because we have tarnished a human connection and haven't been true to ourselves. Eventually the heart becomes covered with scar tissue and it is a momentous job to get underneath the tough covering and become vulnerable again. If we are in touch with the tenderness and fragility of our own hearts, then we will remember to treat others' hearts with *great* care.

It is incredibly important to keep agreements with children. Young children look forward with pure delight to spending time with a parent, being read a story, going to the store or a movie. In anticipation of the event they will have pleasurable fantasies and a heightened sense of excitement, sometimes for days. When the event is casually canceled, it's like dropping a huge dose of gloom on a child's spirit. Over time, broken agreements lead to a broken heart. To survive, the child pretends not to care, not to be angry, and not to need anyone. This often leads to emotional problems and compulsive or addictive behavior.

Some people resist making plans and agreements, saying that they want to be spontaneous. While being spontaneous can be fun, a person who won't make plans in advance is often experiencing a fear of feeling trapped. This reflects a tremendous ambivalence about intimacy that is often connected to childhood abuse or neglect. A person who repeatedly refuses to commit or make agreements in advance is an unlikely candidate for an intimate relationship.

Making plans doesn't mean we need to be rigid—we can agree to keep a plan open-ended. For example, you might agree to spend time with a friend Friday night, and call that afternoon to see what the two of you feel like doing. Making and keeping agreements with great care is a learning process. We learn to be realistic and not overbook our schedules so that we are always "running late." If someone makes a request and you feel confusion, you can always say, "I'll need a couple of days to think it over."

No matter how careful we are, sometimes we make an agreement and then get a stomachache or think, "Why the hell did I say yes to that!?" If this happens, call back immediately and tell the truth. "I've reconsidered and realize I'm overcommitted and need to back out. I'm sorry." You don't have to grovel or make up fake excuses. Sometimes our heart wants to do something, but our inner gauge gives us a signal that we are overdoing it. Sometimes we can do part of the plan. In any case, it's better to change plans immediately than to get a migraine headache and cancel out at the last minute, or not show up at all. You don't have to be perfect, but you need to be honest as fast as possible.

One other aspect of making agreements with great care is not throwing out glib invitations when we don't seriously intend to follow through. Saying "Oh, we'll have to get together sometime" or suggesting "future things we can do together" can stimulate people's hope and excitement, which is deflated when there is no follow-through. When you have the impulse to make an invitation, stop, take a breath, go inside and ask yourself, Do I really mean what I say? One rule of thumb is, *when in doubt, don't*. Go home, think it over, and when you're ready, call back with a date book in your hand and set a time.

Being steadfast with agreements is a contribution to goodness on the planet. It shows our love and respect for others. It's a way we ground our energy and that of the people around us. I think of making and keeping agreements with great care as an art—the art of balanced living, the art of knowing yourself, the art of being good to others.

33

AT THE HEART OF A
NO LIES A YES

*P*art of learning to define our world and have honest relation-ships is developing the ability to say no. We need to distinguish between chronically saying a fearful no to life and saying a respectful, clear no that defines our limits and protects our energy. Without the ability to say no, we let ourselves be con-trolled by listless, gray "shoulds" and the needs of others. We forget to care for ourSelves, and often become depleted, depressed or feel swallowed up. We are energy fields—what goes out needs to be replaced.

Developmentally, we must learn to say no before we can say yes. Some time around two years of age, you will hear chil-dren say no with delight because it gives them an exciting sense of definition and power. As part of maintaining our integrity, we need to know that we have the right to say no to commit-tees, sex, food, caring for others, talking or listening. Saying no to things you don't want to do is like being given permission to say who you are, set limits, and create a protective shield around you. It affirms our right to exist, have our voice, and define ourselves.

Unfortunately, in our culture, so obsessed with obedience, children are often punished for saying no—they are seen as being obstinate, difficult, rude, or noncompliant. While chil-dren need to be respectful and have appropriate limits, squelching their no's lowers their self-esteem because it takes away their ability to define and protect themselves. This condi-tioning spills over into adulthood, where saying no or setting limits carries a threat of abandonment, punishment or guilt. Yet every time we say yes when we mean no, we build up resentments that will manifest in our bodies or come out in sideways remarks, in withholding, and resentment. We will also add a debt to our secret scorecard that one day bursts out: "I gave you everything, and now see what you've done to me." The wise person doesn't "give everything," he or she gives wisely.

To cut through old guilt programming, you can tell yourself you have the right to take care of yourself. It's better for everyone because it has integrity. You can ground this belief in your body by making big no gestures, getting in a power position and pushing outward with your palms, picturing the person or situation you want to say no to. Martial arts can be helpful. It's even more powerful when you combine big belly sounds with the movements—Ho! No! Many people, especially women, start giggling when they do this or quickly drop their arms. To help center yourself in your power, think of the ways in which you've felt ripped off and hurt, think of yourself as a mother bear or a lion protecting her cubs—find some way to feel fiercely protective of yourself. You might say, "I'm not going to give myself away again! I'm going to take care of myself." Eventually, you will feel a nice, warm energy in the center of your belly that says, "I exist, I'm worthy of self-protection."

As you change, you might go through some withdrawal, namely gripping, gooey guilt—the basic withdrawal symptom from caretaking. But remember, *relief will follow.* When you won't play the role of the one who gives all, or the nice guy, other people might feel hurt or be angry with you. Remember, *whenever we carry anyone on our backs, we both become cripples.* By taking people off your back, you free them to learn to walk and you will feel lighter, happier, and more able to feel the breath of spirit. Most of all, as you get more comfortable in saying no, you can relax, laugh, and start saying a true YES.

34

THE GLORY OF YES

"*Yes*" is a beautiful word when it comes from the heart, unfettered by guilt and shoulds. Think of saying a big yes to love, joy, openness, generosity, creativity, truth, and adventure. Feeling full of yes, or Yes, I Can! energy helps us take on new endeavors, quit bad jobs, get training, stay in school, or stay sober. When we say a big yes to life, we feel more secure in the world and less concerned about money and possessions. Yes is the knock on the door that opens us to the realm of pure potential, to the belief that all things are possible. Yes is our connection to God/great spirit. Yes says, "I'm willing to feel it all, know it all, live it all, to be one with All That Is."

Think of a big yes gesture you could make with your body. What would it be? How would it feel? A big yes opens the will to *I can*. Many people feel afraid to say yes because they fear the strong flow of energy that emerges as a result. Imbibing in yes energy may open up buried pains and hurts you carry in your body. But remember, the pains and hurts you carry are affecting you right now. They are alive, though out of sight. If you bring consciousness to them, you can experience them, heal them, and let them go. If you leave them buried and out of consciousness, they create more and more pressure, requiring you to spend more of your life energy keeping them at bay—and keeping other people at bay as well.

We need to discern the difference between a reckless, impulsive yes and a spontaneous yes that comes from one's center. A true yes from the spirit involves consideration for your well-being and that of others and won't have predictable harmful consequences. Impulsiveness is when we forget all caution or safety and risk great harm to ourselves and others. Even so, it is probably better on occasioon to err on the side of being impulsive than to live in fear and shut yourself off from life.

Yes opens the pathway to generosity. As we walk a path of love and integrity—the big yes to life—we will eventually experience a sense of abundance and generosity with others that is authentic and genuine. In turn, our generosity reinforces the flow of our energy because it is based on faith: All love given returns, often twofold. There's a paradox in the relationship of giving to opening our energy. We don't want to give from an empty place, yet sometimes we have to nudge ourselves. Our ego wants to create distance and keep its well-defined boundaries, and an act of generosity, of helping others, of sharing deeply about ourselves is scary. Yet when we break through and give, we often feel a rush of energy come through us.

If you experience fear at the thought of saying yes, or if you say to yourself, "I need to wait until I feel safer," remember this: The fear doesn't go away when we stay at home, stand on the edge of the diving board, or wait until we feel comfortable revealing our inner world. The fear goes away when we walk out the door, jump in the pool and speak of our fear. You can do it shaking, nervous, uneasy, or breathless. The important thing is that you do it. When you step right into the middle of your fear and take action, no matter how scared you are, you open the door to your heart and your joy. You move into the land of yes.

Yes takes us through the door of fear and frees us to dance in the center of our own lives. When we dance to the beating of our hearts, we will attract others who are dancing to the same drummer. As we join together in a circle of yes, the spirit of love and intimacy come alive and we bond together to free our spirits and live together in peace.

35

IF IT ISN'T WORKING, STOP DOING IT, OR, THE BAKING-POWDER BISCUIT THEORY

*S*tatements we've all heard include: "I've tried for fifteen years to get him to . . . "; "If I've told her once, I've told her a hundred times to . . . "; "We've been arguing about this for twenty years. . . . "

A person can have a clear, scientific mind for research or be a fabulous auto mechanic yet leave their logical mind at the door when they come home.

When clients talk about the ways in which they've tried and tried to get others to change or do something, I start talking about baking-powder biscuits. "If you made baking-powder biscuits a hundred times without the baking powder and they always went flat, what would you expect the hundred and first time?"

"They'll go flat." (Everyone always gets the answer.)

"So why would you keep doing it, unless, of course, you want little dough pellets to throw at someone?" I then ask.

This usually stops people short. For the most part, people repeat the same old pattern because it has become an entrenched habit, they've stopped thinking, or they don't take the time to be creative.

Maxim: If something isn't working, stop doing it; do something else, do anything else, but don't keep repeating the same old pattern. You are wasting precious energy and your partner, friends, or children are getting stuck in the same rut with you.

If you're constantly pleading with people, *take action instead.* If a friend is constantly late, tell them that you are setting a limit and leave without them. If you're getting a lot of criticism and ingratitude about dinner, don't cook one night—or for a week. If you've been pleading with your mate to take you out on the town, go have fun with friends—and come home smiling and pleasant. If you've been pleading with a friend to call you more often, stop calling them and call someone else.

If we keep getting in the same old dead-end conversations, we need to stop the pattern. Have you ever had something to say on the tip of your tongue but knew it would lead to a predictable, heavy conversation that would feel like falling into a cesspool? What if you resisted the urge to bring it up? Imagine what it would be like to control yourself and not say it. Part of you will feel a wrenching pull, the other part will probably feel relief, as if you had freed yourself from the clutches of an entrenched habit.

When considering what to say or do, use the imaginary energy meter that goes from yes to no, or lightness to density. If you have serious doubts, or even minor doubts, don't do it. Instead, breathe, take a walk, and pray to the Universe for a more creative solution. If you can predict exactly what the other person will say—like an old script or a road you've traveled a hundred times (or more)—why travel it again? If it hasn't worked the first hundred times, what makes you think it will work on the 101st?! Better to go make biscuits . . . and put baking powder in them.

36

RESEARCH SOLUTIONS AND PASS YOUR KNOWLEDGE AROUND

We are all part of a vast field of information and knowledge. We don't own knowledge, it comes through us, it exists in the universe. One way we connect to universal intelligence is to give and receive knowledge with others, keeping our minds open to new ideas and concepts. As we "play" with ideas and solutions together, we enter into a force field of wisdom. Our generosity in sharing what we know with others opens the energy flow within us, particularly in our hearts.

Many people have a hard time saying, "Help, I'm confused," particularly when it's about something private, such as relationships, sex, or bringing up children. We sit alone, trying to reinvent the wheel, gnashing our teeth as the same thoughts circle around in our mind and we feel stuck. By asking someone for help, suggestions or input, you open up the energy field for both of you. You can think of it as collecting data. People usually feel flattered to be asked how they've solved a problem, and often, in the process of talking together, a totally new idea will pop into your mind. This kind of conversation creates intimacy because it is personal, creative, and serves an important purpose.

When I first planned to write a book proposal and didn't have a clue as to how to do it, a woman friend who had written several books gave me a copy of one of her proposals. I looked it over, got the gist of it, made a list of her subtitles and started. Since then I have sent copies of my proposals to others wanting to write books. I like doing it. It feels like keeping the energy flow in motion.

While people may feel comfortable talking with others about how to fix a car, or bake bread, when it comes to relationship problems and sex, couples often draw the line. "You don't talk about *that*!" Single people are more likely to talk about their love life, dates, and dreams with others—at least the women do—but when people get married or are in committed relationships, the door often closes.

My dear one, Jessie, and I researched how couples solved the problem of hiking at different paces. Now I know that sounds like a small deal in the course of life, but it was creating a lot of stress between us, and we'd already spent two therapy sessions talking about it. So we asked numerous couples what they did when they hiked together. Jessie and I gathered all the information. The next time we went hiking, I said, "Now let's stop and agree on a plan so we don't spoil the day and spend another eighty-five dollars on a therapy session." We discussed all the alternatives and came up with our own plan. It worked quite well.

The benefits of talking with other couples went far beyond getting ideas for our hiking conflict. It normalized our conflict, gave us a window into other couples' lives, and gave us an intimate experience with them. The goal is not only to brainstorm a solution, it's to find out *how* people arrive at solutions. I have been repeatedly amazed at the willingness of couples to talk about the intricacies of their relationships—from sex to money—when asked. The most common stumbling block is that no one takes the first step: "Say, we're having a problem with _____, we'd like to know how you deal with this." Of course, it's best to ask a couple who appears to handle their life well.

We gather information from others in myriad ways. In my mother's generation, exchanging recipes was common. After my mother died, I was touched when looking through her old cookbooks and seeing all the recipes she had gotten from others—Mira's Lemon Chiffon Cake, Edna's Mexican Chicken—written on cards or pieces of paper attached with glue, paper clips, or in little pockets of the cookbooks. It was like a little community of her friends all represented by recipes. I smile to myself as I remember seeing her write out recipes for others, including many I have in my cookbooks. Sharing our knowledge is like sharing food—the basic sustenance of life. It spices up our lives, saves us time, and brings us closer to each other.

37

AT THE HEART OF YOUR THOUGHTS YOU ARE WISE: FOLLOWING YOUR THOUGHTS TO THE CORE

*W*e often have immediate responses that seem to pop out of our mouths: "I don't want to!" "No, you can't!" "It's too much!" Sometimes these are the voices of wisdom, other times they are abrupt knee-jerk reactions that come from old conditioning in the limbic system of the brain. They often shut people out, create distance, and keep us at a superficial level of awareness. If we take a thought and follow it deeper and deeper, we often find the heart of our feelings and get down to the real issues. When we can speak from these vulnerable core places, we are more likely to work through conflict and feel intimate.

Here's a situation that came up between Linda and Nancy in a therapy session. They were about to leave on a much anticipated vacation together to New Zealand. Linda casually mentioned that she would probably have to call her mother while they were there because it would be her mother's birthday. Nancy had a hot reaction: "I don't want you to do that."

Linda got defensive. "Why shouldn't I? She's my mother. You don't get to tell me what to do."

I asked Nancy to take a deep breath and follow her thought deeper—what was the next thought under her sudden reaction. She paused for a moment.

"It would cost a lot of money and we don't have much money." I could still hear a hesitation in her voice.

"Follow that to a deeper thought."

"When you talk to your mother, you can never get off the

phone, and then you complain about how much it cost. It was two hundred and fifty dollars the last time you called from a foreign country." Nancy continued thinking.

"Just breathe and take your time. What else do you hear?" I said. Then she came closer to the real answer.

Her voice softened. "I feel as if I'd be losing you somehow." She paused.

"Say more," I said.

"I feel kind of stupid about this, but when you talk to your mother you get all upset, sometimes for days, and then I feel left alone. I want so much to be with you and enjoy our trip together."

As Nancy sank into deeper and deeper levels of truth, the shift of energy was palpable. Her breathing deepened, her voice calmed down and her body relaxed. She also gained the attention of Linda, who became pensive thinking about what Nancy was saying.

"I do get upset when I call my mother," Linda said finally. "And I don't really want to spend the money either. But I'd feel so guilty if I didn't call her."

Linda took some time to follow her thoughts to the core.

"I don't really want to call her either but thought I had to— you know, because I'm her daughter."

The next thought was, "I keep hoping if I call her she will start calling me more often," and finally, "I feel really hurt by her and kind of angry too because she doesn't remember my birthday."

Nancy and Linda were able to come to a resolution quite easily at this point because they were sharing from the heart. If they had stayed on their initial course, it could have been a sore point for the whole trip.

When we follow our thoughts to the core we keep asking, What's below that? What's the feeling under that? You might feel yourself dropping deeper and deeper out of your head and into your body as you listen for answers to come. When we follow our thoughts to the core, we invariably end up at a feeling level: "I'm scared that you don't care about me," "I felt left out," "I'm worried that our plans won't work out," "I love you." At the core we will usually find our personal agenda, which may include a request. Nancy had wanted to feel close on the trip and to be careful with money. Nothing wrong with that, but when it came out in a bossy way, Linda was not able to hear the care. She felt pushed around and her rebellious side reacted.

When trying to solve a problem or work through a situation, let yourself hear *all* your thoughts and feelings. Don't censor anything. Often people have important thoughts they dismiss because they don't seem relevant or because they seem contradictory. Say or write down everything until you feel a sense of being cleared out. Sometimes if you sit for a minute longer, deeper thoughts will come to mind. This is your inner world speaking to you.

One way to gain access to our deeper thoughts is to put our focus in the area of our heart, and breathe into it. You can imagine the area softening and becoming spacious and soft. You might want to touch the area over your heart and keep your focus there as you listen. Imagine that you are putting your problem or concern in your heart with kindness and compassion. Then follow your thoughts deeper and deeper. In this way you will find your truths.

38

FOLLOW A COMPLAINT
WITH A REQUEST

*T*here is a certain satisfaction to righteously complaining, whining, or pointing out the faults of others: "She always phones me after I'm asleep," "He never remembers my birthday," "These kids just don't care about helping around the house," and on and on. It's usually easy to get sympathizers to join the chorus with us, chanting about how incompetent or insensitive other people are.

The problem with complaining and not taking action is that we stay stuck in our little cocoon of righteousness. We are also acting as if we are powerless victims of all those mean and insensitive people out there. To take our place as full-fledged adults, we have to ask for what we want. In other words, we need to *follow all complaints with a request.*

This sounds quite simple, but it gets a lot of resistance from people. Here's why: When we are infants, we don't have the words to tell people we are hungry, wet, tired, or need to be held. We just wail away and hope they figure it out. If our parent or caregiver is responsive, we feel loved. If our needs are not met for long periods of time, our ability to comfort ourselves expires and we're left with an aching hunger inside. This makes it difficult to move to the next stage of development, where we learn to use words to ask for what we want and become more adept at comforting ourselves when we don't get what we want. Instead, we have the unconscious belief that if people really loved us, they would know what we need. This often carries into adulthood, where people expect others to read their minds, figure out what they want, and give it to them. If others don't comply, we interpret it as meaning that they don't care, they don't love us, or they want to hurt us. As adults, it's not reasonable to ask someone to read our minds; it's our job to stop being mad at Mommy and ask for what we want.

Cher and Harry are a case in point. When they were about to move away from Cleveland, Cher complained bitterly that Harry had never taken her to a Cleveland Indians baseball game. "He never seems to care about what I want. He knows I love baseball. I don't know why he never took me." Note the powerlessness in her statement—there is no sense of being proactive to meet her own needs. The child part of her is waiting for someone to take care of her.

I felt a sense of trepidation as I asked her the obvious question, "Did you ever *ask* him to take you to a game?" She got upset. "If he cared about me, he'd know!" Then she turned on me. "You just don't understand." I withheld making the next obvious remark, which was, "Did it ever occur to you to invite him to a baseball game and order the tickets yourself?"

So long as we wait for people to figure us out and give us what we want, we are asking our friends or loved ones to play Mommy or Daddy to us. This brings a disturbing inequality to relationships that is deadly to intimacy and friendship. It's like being a little person in a big body making the plaintive cry, *Please come take care of me, I can't do it myself.*

If you hear this cry in yourself or another, have compassion for the cry, but don't become trapped by it. When we treat someone like a wounded bird, they are likely to remain a wounded bird, and that includes ourselves. We all have the capacity to grow up and ask for what we need in life. We will never get it from a childlike position of waiting for others to give it to us, although, paradoxically, deeply bonded couples often have a sense of telepathy and ability to sense what the other needs.

Whenever you find yourself complaining, stop and find the request at the heart of the complaint: Instead of saying, "She sure has nerve calling so late," tell her, "I'd like you to stop calling me after ten at night." Instead of hollering, "You kids are always leaving such a mess," say in a clear way, "I expect you to pick up your toys in the living room . . . and if you don't, they will disappear." Ask your beloved to make dinner for you, or take you to a baseball game. If you're afraid no one will remember your birthday, tell friends you would like to be remembered on your birthday and give them the date. Better yet, give yourself a birthday party.

39

LAUGH THROUGH YOUR TEARS: IT'S ALL A PASSING SHOW

*T*he purpose of our journey is joy and love. Today. We aren't out to win the personal growth game, to be pure or perfect. We're here to revel in our humanness, love each other in our imperfections, feel compassion, and have a good belly laugh when we trip on the path.

Just this week I was in a committee meeting where five intelligent adults, including myself, got totally trapped in our thinking and essentially shot ourselves in the foot. We made assumptions, and neglected to see the obvious pitfalls of our logic. Our mistaken decision cost us about $120. Later, when I realized the mistake and called people back, we'd start by trying to figure a way to bail out but always ended up laughing and saying, "We blew it, didn't we!"

You can't cover all of the bases all of the time. Everyone makes mistakes on occasion. You, me, all of us. Just today I got a check in the mail for $70 with a note saying "Thanks for sending the book order, you also sent us back our check." The more you can be accepting of your mistakes and goofs, the more you transcend feeling like an unloved child being constantly scolded. It's not serious. It's just a little bleep in the cosmic scheme of things. It helps to be gentle with yourself and become a loving witness of your journey.

I've been to ashrams, personal growth training sessions, and support groups and have repeatedly seen people get deadly serious about their growth. They're trying so hard to be pure that their energy dies. There's no humor. The purpose of personal "work" is to be clear enough inside to bask in the sun, speak your truth, and see the cosmic humor when you make a mistake. We're not going anywhere, we're here right now. This is it. Today. So we might as well breathe deeply and accept it the best we can.

I'm currently trying to accept that I'm fifteen pounds heavier than I'd like to be. I'm going to a high school class reunion next month and I wanted to lose at least eight pounds. I increased my exercise, cut the fat in my diet even more and no luck. Until today, every time I looked in the mirror I pictured myself being thinner at the reunion. Today I thought, To hell with it. This is how I'm going to be. It's in my genes. I'd like to be lighter, but, that's enough daydreaming and putting myself down.

The shift in my feelings came from a simple process of putting myself in my heart. I imagined my heart center becoming soft and spacious and then had an image of me in my heart—fifteen pounds overweight. I heard the words, "You've exercised regularly, you're thinner than your mother was at this age. It's okay. I love you." We can want to make changes, but the true mark of the spiritual journey is to accept ourselves on our path today.

Another way to lighten up is to enjoy paradox and seeing all sides of a situation. I was amused at the flock of reporters and people from the FBI who swarmed our area when the alleged Unabomber was arrested about eighty miles from my home. I had the image of a bunch of kids getting to play cops and robbers. I mean, how many people does it take to search a ten-by-twelve-foot cabin and scope out the area? Everyone was so unbelievably serious. On the one hand, the arrival of the press and the FBI was good for local business. People flocked to the Mom and Pop stores in the area, and all the motels and hotels were packed for miles around. And, hey, maybe it will mean that fewer people move to Montana because they think we're all a bunch of kooks. On the other hand, we might attract more reactionaries. Oh well. Hey, the sunshine just came out after a week of gray days. Time to breathe and relax.

Remember, you are on the journey of this moment. We'll all die one day and hopefully we won't be full of regrets. If you can have a sense of humor in the midst of sorrow, you are dancing with the spirits. While my sister was dying, her dear friend Arnelle and I often cracked jokes, hugged, and cried, all at the same time. Then we'd take a break, go to a thrift store and find clothes for each other. On the day before Lenore died, she sat on the front-porch swing, a skeleton of her former self, and posed for a picture with a faint look of amusement on her face while her husband, Bill, held a big, red, juicy tomato in his hand, as if offering it to her.

In compiling one-page biographies for my fortieth high school reunion, I've had great pleasure in reading over their answers to the question, "What have you learned since high school?" No one said lose weight, earn more money, work harder, or be serious. What people often said was, Do it. Don't wait. Have fun. Give thanks, and enjoy the people you love.

So embrace the whole big predicament of living, and remember to laugh. It's all the unfolding of the universe within us and around us. It's all a passing show.

PART V

•••

JUST BETWEEN YOU AND ME: SENDING AND RECEIVING MESSAGES

40

NO RECIPE BOOK, JUST FOOD FOR THOUGHT

Mohammed's son pores over words,
and points out this and that,
but if his chest is not soaked dark with love,
then what?

The Yogi comes along in his famous orange.
But if inside he is colorless,
then what?

—Kabir

*T*here is no recipe book for communication. While we can learn the basics of clear speaking and good listening—and this can be useful—we also need a heart soaked dark with love and a colorful inner world. We need to be centered in ourselves and able to translate impressions and feelings into words. We need to bring our presence to listening so we hear not only the words, but the spirit and intention beneath the words.

Language enables us to share our feelings, ideas, and consciousness with others. The tone, rhythm, and pulse of our voice, and patterns of speaking and listening, all play an integral part in communication and reflect much of who we are. Our words transmit meaning and our voice communicates aspects of our emotional state—afraid, relaxed, tight, shallow, integrated.

Communication is also a form of alchemy between two people—an energy vibration that matches and flows together creating a sense of being in sync. It's not based so much on whether people talk quickly or slowly, interrupt or give advice, rather, it's the rhythm, flow, timing and fit between any two given people.

Other skills for communication are about tuning into the experience as it happens, noticing if the messages are being received and understood. It requires an ability to sense if another person is "with you" and if you are feeling emotionally connected to the process. It also involves being able to comment on the process of the interaction—are we hearing each other, what's not working, are we out of sync?

Words can help us connect and they can throw up a wall. Words can carry love and kindness and they can also inflict pain. Words can be spoken with conviction and a sense of truth or they can ring false. Words can generate emotional states. Often, after we've spent a memorable time with someone, we remember the warm feelings far more than the words, yet the words helped create the warm feeling.

The intention of this section is to give you food for thought and some reference points for observing communication patterns in yourself and others. The more you bring self-awareness to your communication, the more you will be able to make conscious choices about your patterns of speaking and listening. Because I grew up in a family without a blueprint for expressing feelings or resolving conflict, I have had to learn about communication through observation, practice and my training as a psychotherapist. It is an ongoing process, one that is both fascinating and challenging.

Our spiritual journey is deeply reflected by the evolution of the voice and by the ways in which we communicate with others. Our fears, softness, sharp edges, peacefulness, and joy are all carried to others by our tone, words or lack of words. As people become more whole and in tune with themselves, they usually speak with greater simplicity, resonating from both head and heart.

41

LEARN THE MAGIC OF GOOD COMMUNICATION

When I was five years old, my mother and I visited her best friend, Helen Haig. I had a special and warm feeling in my chest when I was around her—something I longed for but seldom felt at home. Helen Haig would look me in the eyes, talk in a natural voice, and ask me questions. As a result, I felt like something more than just a little girl. I was Charlotte, a real person.

When someone talks to us from a loving heart, we find our own heart. Through the act of listening, understanding, and responding we help each other find our voices. Recently, when I was interviewed about intimacy and community, the interviewer, Mary, responded with such interest and enthusiasm that I found myself having a flow of new ideas pour through me as we spoke. I heard my voice speaking clearly, putting ideas together better than I ever had before. The separation between the interviewer and myself dissolved as we created an energy field that allowed the best of both of us to emerge.

The connective power of communication happens when a message is sent, received and responded to honestly. Like creating a weaving, one starts by reaching inside, listening, and speaking from the heart. The other person takes the thread of thought, listens, absorbs the meaning of the words, mulls them over, and responds back from his or her heart—two people unfolding in the moment. The outcome of the conversation is unpredictable because it is a form of mutual creation.

Even when we are afraid or awkward, heartfelt words will break through our isolation and unify us at the heart. It's the loving intention that creates the alchemy of connection, not an eloquent ability to use words. When we interconnect at this deep level, we enter sacred ground because I, you, and us/spirit/God merge together. We invoke spirit to fill us and surround us because our connection is based on love, kindness and truth.

The healing power of connecting at a heart level operates whether we are resolving conflict, working to find a creative solution to a problem, sharing stories of our lives or planning a weekend together. If we think of an exchange of words as an exchange of energy, then we can understand why every cell in our body is affected by our interchange of words and thoughts. We don't only receive or send words, we receive and send energy. We learn to enter into another's experience. The magic of heartfelt communication comes to life when we speak from a sense of stillness within. I think of the phrase "Be still and know I am God." In speaking from the center of our stillness, we speak from the God place within—the home of our heart and spirit.

MAINTAINING THE I, YOU, AND US IN COMMUNICATION

A great deal has been written in psychology literature and self-help books about empathy, understanding, and self-disclosure in communication. The question is, *How do we engage with each other in a way that supports our separate autonomy while creating a sense of intimacy? How do we maintain the I, you, and us?*

We can again consider the Buddhist notion of attachment. Namely, anything we do that places a demand or expectation on another person creates attachment, hence suffering. For example, if I tell you about my fears with the expectation that you will do likewise, I have created an attachment. To maintain my separate sense of self, I need to speak from my heart, honestly and clearly, because the spirit leads me to do so. Your response remains entirely up to you. When and if you respond, it will reflect your inner world. As we stay separate in this way, we will truly get to know each other and create the sense of *us*, of intimacy.

For many people this feels brutal and uncaring. Aren't we supposed to nod our heads, smile, repeat back what the other has said and draw them out? Yes and no. We can ask questions of others if we feel led to do so, but we don't do it because it's the right thing to do. If we say "Wow" or "No kidding" or give a big smile spontaneously, that's fine. But if we do it to "help" the other person, it can be patronizing or overinvolved. The point is to stay grounded inside our center so we go beyond *using* good listening techniques to *becoming* a receptive, spontaneous listener. We communicate care and empathy through our heartfelt presence and attentiveness more than with words. Empathy is about being able to resonate with another's experience, it doesn't mean we agree with the other person.

A way to play with this notion is to observe your emotional state as you listen. Do you feel revved up and breathless, feeling you have to help the other person out, assure them that they are okay, and validate their opinion? Or can you relax, be quiet inside, and simply be a loving witness to what they are saying, showing your care and concern through your eyes and a few words to show you've heard them? In a therapy group, where most people felt responsible for filling in the empty spaces and helping others talk, a woman brought a cartoon from *The New Yorker* that said "Dare to Be Boring." It became a theme in the group—to be proud of "being boring," of allowing quiet spaces in conversation and not immediately helping others out.

In observing myself, I notice that I am different in different circumstances. When I'm interviewing people or in a therapist role, it's as if I vacate myself and drop down inside. I would call it deep listening. If I ask a question or paraphrase what another person has said, it's to understand them—what it's like to live in their world. At the other extreme, if I am uneasy in a social situation, I might feel agitated and anxious inside, causing me to either interrupt or chatter.

In a community retreat, we did an exercise in which we took turns listening without giving any facial or verbal feedback. We had exchanges with numerous people. Some took the assignment so literally that they turned into stone and it felt like talking to a brick. Others listened with soft eyes, a sense of care and an occasional slight nod of the head that communicated warmth and kindness. This exercise helped me be aware of how much we take our cues from others in conversation. Without any form of feedback, I felt acutely aware of my words and became more conscious of what I was saying and thinking rather than being led by the other person's response.

One aspect of self-disclosure is telling your story. This is best done as it feels relevant to the present. Too often people gush out the horrors of their past, overwhelming another person who may not want to know so much so soon. If we reveal our history as it becomes relevant in the moment, it feels alive. For example, if you are visiting a place from childhood, telling the memories that come to mind is likely to be alive and immediate. They'll have energy because you are reexperiencing them as you speak. It is not crucial to intimacy that we know everything about a person's history. It's more important that we are connected to what we're talking about.

Another level of self-disclosure is having a meta conversation in which you reveal your experience in the moment—you comment on the process. For example, if you are in the middle of a conversation and you start feeling tense you could say, "I feel tight in my chest." If the conversation feels flat, you could comment on that or ask the other person if it feels flat to them. This keeps you connected to your experience in the moment.

Overall, we create intimacy in conversation when we speak our truths as they come to us, not looking for validation from others but feeling grounded and going where the energy is strong. We talk about what is alive for us, so our words and feelings resonate together.

42

LEARN TO GROUND YOUR WORDS

*B*y speaking genuinely and listening from the heart, we both ground ourselves and the person with whom we are conversing. When people talk *at* each other, interrupt, look away, dominate, speak in platitudes, chatter, argue, talk about irrelevant details, talk too loudly or too softly, the conversation can feel ungrounded. It's like loose wires shooting out energy in all directions but not connecting to anything. Whether we are listening or responding, we can help keep a conversation grounded so that it can flow.

Grounded communication is supported by the breath and a soft, relaxed belly. You can create a sense of allowing your words to ride on your breath, like waves coming in and out. If you release your breath as you talk, exhaling completely, you allow yourself to drop down deep inside. When a person raises their voice and talks fast, with great intensity, they are usually holding their breath, which causes their chest and shoulders to be raised or tight. The effect is often like a child desperately wanting to be heard but not believing anyone will listen. If someone is talking loud and fast *at* you, you can use the same technique. Relax and exhale softly, blowing the tension out through your mouth that you are picking up from them. You might gently ask them to talk a bit more slowly or more quietly. It often helps to reassure them that you want to hear what they are saying.

Another way to ground a conversation is through eye contact. You might look away for a moment as you gather your thoughts or ponder what someone is saying, and then circle back by making eye contact. We can also become aware of whether we are giving people soft eyes, distant eyes or cold eyes. It's often said that the connection to the soul is through the eyes. Even so, at times it can be such a struggle to pull out the words that the best we can do is mumble and avert our eyes. There's a dance to eye contact, because if we look too long it can feel intrusive, but without it we lose our connection and the listener might start feeling like an object.

When telling about an experience, we ground our words when we include feelings and relate what the experience meant to us. *The more you are connected to your feelings and relate the essence of an experience, the more the listener can engage with you.*

As the listener, it helps to enter into the other's experience as much as you can. You might create mental images of what they are saying. Sometimes we have an urge to break in and say, "I've done that too," or "I knew someone who did that," or our mind wanders (What's for lunch?). If this happens, you can take a relaxing breath, let the thoughts pass through your mind and bring your attention back to the other person. You might involve yourself by asking a question that keeps you connected. What was that like for you? What did you learn from that? If you don't feel able to listen attentively, then politely say so.

Another way to stay grounded in a conversation is to notice if the listener is looking at you and responding with interest or is restlessly looking away, tapping their fingers and mumbling a vacant "uh-huh." If they show signs of restlessness, don't talk faster and louder, but stop talking and check in with your listener. "Am I going on too long? Do you need to go?"

You can also provide a sense of grounding by nodding or saying a few words that let the other person know you hear them. (This is different from "helping" them out because it lets them know you are present.) The power of supportive listening was wonderfully demonstrated in the movie *Being There*, where Peter Sellers portrayed a man of marginal intelligence who would listen very attentively to people (because he had a hard time following them and didn't have much to say) and say things like, "Um hmmm. Yes, I see . . ." People mistook him for a brilliant man and he ended up as a consultant to top government officials.

Grounding your words is deeply related to your ability to relax and feel grounded in yourself. As people start observing themselves, they often realize that they are quite anxious when they talk with others. Meditation, clearing out trauma, and practicing deep breathing are all ways to help you come back to your center more rapidly in conversation. We let go of our anxiety when we realize that conversation is not a performance, but, rather, a flow of energy that helps us connect with another soul.

43

FEEL THE RHYTHM OF CONVERSATION

*T*here are different rhythms to conversation, just as there are different rhythms to dance music. The important thing is that conversation feels like a dance together rather than two people standing alone or constantly stepping on each other's toes.

One rhythm of conversation is when we take turns in talking about ourselves in response to questions such as, "How was your day?" "What's new in your life?" "Tell me about your dreams." For a while one person is the primary speaker and the other the listener. Then we switch. Over time, it's important that both people get equal airtime or else the relationship becomes unbalanced.

Another rhythm of conversation is exploring ideas or seeking solutions to a problem with two or more people. In popcorn style, everyone tosses their ideas on the table no matter how unusual. It's called brainstorming. Someone's idea might build on what another person has said, or they might be on a completely different track. There is no attempt to control the energy. I think of brainstorming as opening to the wonder of the universe as we collectively let our minds be receptive to any and all solutions.

A slightly different rhythm is when we're exploring ideas together with a particular goal in mind. When I was writing my first book, I hired a woman, Kate, to help me get my ideas organized. In preparation for each chapter, we would sit down and talk over the notes and outline. I'd describe an idea, which would trigger Kate's thoughts. We would build on the ideas and become animated and excited as our exchange refined and expanded the original ideas. Our conversation was in the interest of finding the best ideas—not in winning or being right— just the pure joy of creating together. It felt like being in the service of something bigger—of finding truth. What we came up with together was more than either of us could have come up with alone. This kind of creative exploration requires that both people set aside their egos—thoughts such as I'm the smartest one, I know the most—and work toward a higher ideal.

Another rhythm of communication is two people discussing the intimate concerns of their relationship. In this case, it is important to sit close and give each other undivided attention. People often try to have an important conversation with someone who is reading the paper, fixing the plumbing, attending to a child, or in another room. A rule of thumb is to have your faces within four or five feet of each other and to sit on an equal plane facing each other so that there's an open channel between your hearts.

Before engaging in any conversation, take a moment to sense the other's presence. You don't need to look deeply into their eyes, simply tune into their energy: Is it light, bright, heavy, or gray? Do you sense fear or worry? Just note it. To honor the spirit of your coming together, you might think or say *Namaste* (meaning, I honor the light/divinity in you). Before starting to speak, tune into your breathing and center yourself. This sounds like a lot to do, but, in reality, it takes fifteen to twenty seconds. This pause before talking is important, just as the moments of silence in music give emphasis to the sounds.

The rhythm of intimate conversation is to engage back and forth, where one speaks and the other responds to exactly what was said before contributing their own idea or thought. It's like a continuous circle. Because the words are so full of feelings and meaning, it's best to say only a few sentences at a time so that they can be absorbed.

Another rhythm of communication is between teacher and student. We often think of teacher-student communication as going in one direction, but a skillful teacher keeps the energy flowing in a circle. This brings to mind a workshop I attended recently on hypnotherapy and ego states with John and Helen

Watkins. Throughout the two-day workshop I felt bright and awake. They were down to earth, humorous, emotionally available, and obviously cared for the people they had worked with. They gave thoughtful consideration to questions and comments as if they were learning from us. By contrast, the following morning, when I heard a different speaker, I could hardly stay awake. I wasn't tired and the man was saying intelligent things, but he was very intellectual and spoke of his therapy clients in a disconnected way. As a result, I felt like an object being talked *at,* in contrast to the earlier workshop where I felt we were all part of a creative process.

Every conversation is a dance with another person. There are different steps and rhythms. Being skillful at the dance requires the ability to feel the beat, to lead and to follow, and to enjoy the sounds of the music.

44

LISTENING 101:
REPEAT AFTER ME

*L*istening with care takes us to deeper levels of connection and intimacy. We not only hear the words, we learn to hear another's heart and tune into the spirit of their message. Becoming a receptive listener also takes practice. In graduate school I attended a class on listening in which we heard short tapes from emergency 911 calls. We had a little quiz on what we had heard, and although most of us thought we were pretty good listeners, we were amazed at how much we missed. It felt as if we were straining our brains to retain four or five sentences—and that was only trying to get the facts straight.

Because listening is an art we are not routinely taught in

our families or in school, we literally have to exercise our brain to become finely tuned to hearing others. In many ways, compassionate listening is a form of meditation because we detach from the chatter and emotional clutter of our own being and give our attention fully to another person.

Reflective listening is when you listen to a person and then repeat back what they said. The process is also called mirroring, reflecting or active listening. I prefer the term "receptive listening" to active listening because "active" triggers the concept of doing something. Receptive means that I relax and receive. My partner dubbed the process "Repeat After Me." It's not hard to understand in theory, but it's difficult for many people to do, especially when they are upset, angry or afraid.

The purpose of repeating back what another has said is to quiet your ego and completely hear the other person. Much of the time, people stop listening halfway through a sentence in order to prepare their rebuttal. When you plan to repeat back what someone says, you get so busy listening that you don't have time to prepare a counterattack.

One of the most challenging times to do reflective listening is when the other person is upset or hurting. Many people have an instant impulse to rush in to "fix it" by giving advice or calming the person down. This reflects our discomfort with strong feelings and communicates judgment—"You shouldn't feel the way you do." A more reflective response could be, "Oh, you're upset." We stay right there with the other person in their upset state.

There are several ways to practice receptive or reflective listening:

1. Verbatim listening.
Sit facing another person and agree on who will go first. The least threatening way to begin is to describe what's going on in your life, or tell about your day. One person says one or two sentences and the other person repeats them back verbatim, changing only the pronouns. At the end you can ask, "Did I understand all you said?" If the other person says,

"No," then ask, "What didn't I hear?" When the person repeats it, reflect it back. After about five to ten minutes, switch the roles of listener and speaker. It's very important to practice at this level without changing the words because people tend to jump into interpretations or shift the focus. Let's say our couple's names are Alex and Emily. Alex starts by saying, "The day started out good, but I felt upset at work when I heard there are going to be layoffs." Emily responds, "Your day started out good, but you felt upset at work because you heard there were going to be layoffs."

2. *Paraphrasing plus feelings.*
After practicing the first level until you feel proficient, you can go to a second stage in which you repeat back directly or paraphrase without changing the meaning. You might also add something that implies you are connected to their feelings. When Alex says he had a good start to his day but he got upset when he heard there would be layoffs at work, Emily responds, "Your day started out okay, but you heard there might be layoffs at work. Sounds scary."

3. *Paraphrasing with feelings and questions.*
At the next level, you continue reflecting back the message, but you ask questions that take the person deeper into their feelings or give a broader perspective to the event. Along with saying, "Your day started out okay, but you heard there might be layoffs at work. Sounds scary." Emily might later add, "Did they give you any more information?"

Alex says, "No, they are going to to let us know more in a week." Emily responds, "A whole week to wait. How is that for you?"

When Emily responds, "How is that for you?" she leaves the response field wide open. She doesn't introject her frantic thought that it would be a living nightmare to wait a whole week. This is fortunate because Alex says, "Well, I don't like it, but I'm good at keeping busy and not thinking about things. Besides, I've done some thinking . . . If they do lay me off, I might go ahead with my idea of starting my own business."

Another way to practice Repeat After Me is to bring the conversation to the me-you level—how we feel about each other—instead of talking about what we did apart from each other. The least threatening place to begin is with appreciations (although some people have a hard time hearing anything positive about themselves).

Start with the first stage again. Each one mentions one or two things that they appreciate in the other, and the friend or partner repeats it back. It's good to start in a positive vein for several reasons. First of all, it's good for anyone to hear positive feedback. Second, you want to pair good feelings with the concept of talking with each other. For many couples, talking has disintegrated to irritation, anger, and criticism, so why bother? If your brain gets the message that talking can be fun, affirming, and productive, then you're more likely to want to talk.

Once you have practiced showing appreciation, another step is to bring up conflict or dissatisfaction. It's often tough for a couple to stay on track because people get scared and start defending. Because most people need the assurance that they are loved, and easily fall into shame when someone voices disappointment, you could say something like "Because I value our relationship, I'd like to clear the air about something . . . Okay?" It's like sending compassion to the scared part of the other person and letting them know you are not trying to hurt them. Some people might call this caretaking. I call it compassion. It brings a sense of spirit into the conversation, puts the other person at ease, and gives you a contract to talk. Whenever we enter into areas of conflict, we become more vulnerable because we risk resurrecting dreaded feelings from childhood of being scolded, shamed, or called into the principal's office. We also feel the risk of losing or harming the relationship.

There will be times when the last thing on earth you want to do is repeat back how your partner or friend is feeling about what you have done or said. You'll want to argue and say, "You're wrong." I urge you to swallow your pride, defenses, and fears and do it anyway. It is the bridge that brings us back together when we start to feel separate. I also encourage you to be sure and get your turn. It needs to go both ways. It's best to agree in advance that either person in the friendship or couple can ask for Repeat After Me time.

As we learn to be a receptive, reflective listener, a sense of calm and peace sets in in our relationships because we are bonding through understanding and kindness—we're flowing together rather than trying to fix the other person, change their feelings, defend ourselves, or give advice. We're simply be-ing with them as an equal and a friend.

45

LET YOUR SECRET VOICE BE HEARD

*R*ecently, my friend Toni described a difficult encounter she had with a friend named Yolanda. After planning a trip, Toni had a change of heart and wanted to change the plans but was afraid to tell her friend for fear she would be mad or disappointed. She didn't want to lose the friendship. She had talked about her predicament with a friend who encouraged her to speak up and be assertive—she had the right to change her plans!

Toni practiced what she was going to say and called Yolanda. She started the conversation attempting to be brave and forthright when she really felt scared and guilty.

"Yolanda, I need to change the plans for our trip." She attempted to sound resolute, but her shaky voice belied her fear.

Her friend Yolanda responded, "What! You said you were sure. Now you're backing out on me."

"You don't need to get so mad. I have the right to change my mind."

"Sure, you've got the right, but what about our friendship?" You can imagine the rest.

What was missing from the conversation? Compassion—an acknowledgment of her concern for Yolanda's feelings. Instead of trying to be brave—going in with a rehearsed statement that sounded off center—she could have said the whole truth: "Yolanda, I'm really nervous about bringing this up, I care about you and don't want to disappoint you, but something has come up and I'd like to change our plans." This would be a much more accurate reflection of the truth because that was exactly what was going on in Toni's mind.

Many times people have an inner dialogue going on when they start to talk with someone. It can help immeasurably if you let the conversation flow from your internal experience in the moment—your inside voice. "I feel awkward bringing this up," "I don't want to hurt your feelings," or, simply, "I'm afraid."

In the middle of a conversation if you go blank, simply say, "I'm drawing a blank. I don't know what else to say." You can even report your body sensations. "I'm starting to get a headache. I need to slow down for a minute." You can relay your positive responses as well. "It really feels good to clear the air" or "I'm feeling so relieved."

We create intimacy and move beyond fear when we report our internal experience. For many people this concept brings a kind of astonishment and delight—a new path that helps lead them out of a quagmire of dead-end, unhappy, clunky conversations. Revealing our inner voices seems so simple, yet it's illusive because we come from a culture that teaches us to get it right, perform, and have our act together before we speak. But intimacy is not about performance. It's about telling the truth, staying present and revealing our inner world as it unfolds before us.

Revealing our secret voices can also be applied to giving

presentations, talks or when teaching. The fear most people have when they do a presentation is that they will go blank, get lost, or forget what they are saying. When I've had that happen to me, I've said, "I'm sorry, I just blanked out. Could someone tell me what I was talking about?" Usually, people feel a sense of relief. It's more comfortable to have someone ask for help without shame, than to nervously sink into embarrassment. Paradoxically, after I got comfortable about saying I was nervous or went blank, I stopped being nervous or going blank.

The concept of letting one's inner voices be heard is especially helpful when you need to change plans or bring up sensitive topics. My partner, Jessie, and I were scheduled to go backpacking with our friend Tom and his son. I had acquiesced to a trip that felt a bit too challenging for me and found myself having constant inner arguments about going. The morning of the trip I awoke feeling as heavy as a rock, and said to Jessie, "I'm dreading being exhausted and worn out instead of having a relaxing time. I hate to cop out on people, but . . . " She said she also felt doubtful about the trip and agreed that she didn't want to go. As I reached for the phone to call Tom, Jessie said, with a sense of fear, "What are you going to tell them?! They're good friends of ours."

"I'm going to say the truth.

"Hi, Tom. I've really looked forward to being with you and don't want to cop out or have you think I don't care, but . . . I'm really overwhelmed at the prospect of such a long trip on a short weekend . . . I woke up as heavy as a rock." He responded kindly by saying, "I understand. If you don't feel right coming, don't feel you have to come. We'll be fine." We had a brief chat, wished each other well, and I noticed that the rock was gone from my chest and I felt full of energy.

Jessie and I went on a much easier trip and I got the relaxation I had wanted. On our way home we dropped by Tom's house to see how his trip had gone. After the usual greeting, Tom said, "As it turned out, we were relieved you weren't there. The trail map was twenty years old, the trail was totally overgrown, it was steeper than we thought, and it took nearly ten hours before we got there. We would have felt terrible dragging you along."

We all laughed with a sense of camaraderie and relief.

For those of us brought up to be super-responsible and discount our feelings, it can be terrifying to change plans with someone. Before I learned to let my inner voices be heard, I could make myself sick over the prospect of breaking an agreement with someone. Some of the most common fears people have are: "If I change the plans they'll never ask me out again," "I don't want to hurt their feelings," "I shouldn't have gotten myself into this in the first place," and "Maybe they'll be mad." When you're feeling tied up in knots, listen to all your inner voices and lay them on the table one by one. Most people will be understanding. If they are not, then it might require further discussion or you might want to reflect on the relationship: "Is this a person who can never see beyond his or her own needs?"

It's also important to let all your voices be heard with children. I remember my daughter asking to have friends come and spend the night when I was exhausted and wanted some peace and relaxation in the morning. I also was happy that she wanted to have friends over.

So I said to her, "There are two parts of me having an argument about this. One part says that you have a perfect right to have friends over and I know that's fun for you; the other part says that I'm tired, I want to sleep in, and I don't want to make popcorn at night or get up and make breakfast." Just saying this gave us a way to work it out. They would make their own popcorn and breakfast and not interrupt me repeatedly during the evening.

Often after that, when she saw me mulling over a decision, she would say to me, "Tell me the two parts." It's good to let children know that we have inner conflicts—it helps validate their inner conflicts as well. If I had said, "No, you can't have anyone over, why don't you just relax?" (which would have been a projection because it was me who wanted to relax), I would have been seen as the mean parent, she would have been mad, and we would have ended up in an argument. If I had said yes, but not talked about my needs, I would have felt resentful and irritated.

46

AVOID ARGUMENTS

*F*or some people, arguing is a way of life. Some couples connect by bickering and arguing together; it feels natural. Very often, however, the circular energy flow of an intimate connection is broken when we argue. If you want closeness in relationships, avoid arguments that stem from the rigid part of the ego wanting to defend its turf. If your motivation is to win, control, or overpower another, then take a moment to reflect. What will you really win? It won't be a connection with another person. There will only be two losers feeling separate from each other. Arguing leads people to raise their voices, become impatient, interrupt and feel tight inside. When neither person feels heard, they often state their case over and over again with increasing intensity. As a result, both people become more polarized in their beliefs.

Arguing often reflects fear, insecurity, and an inability to appreciate differences. In reality, arguments have little to do with the subject matter. It's usually the unconscious survival voice saying, "If I'm lovable, you'll agree with me. If you disagree with me, there must be something wrong with my way of thinking—therefore I must make you agree with me."

I remember the pain I felt as a child when I'd come home excited about what I'd learned at school and my father would automatically take an opposite stance, tear down what I was saying and insist that I present proof. My initial joy in wanting to share what I was learning disintegrated into feeling swallowed up and battered with logic. I would struggle to extricate myself from the pressure to argue with him, and run to my room holding back an urge to cry. Much later, I came to understand that my father's way of feeling secure was having people agree with him—especially me. I felt swallowed up because his self-esteem was equated with swallowing me into his reality. The message was, "I need you to take care of me by being the same as me." Again, this reflects that he was operating from a survival mode.

Arguing is different from discussing differences of opinion. Voicing our stance in order to define ourselves or clarify our beliefs is the way we maintain our selves as separate people. It's like saying, Here we are, two different people with two different sets of ideas or two perspectives on the same situation. I like purple and you like red. I want to live in the country, you want to live in town. I believe in social programs for young mothers and you don't. There is room for both of us—we're learning about each other and our self-esteem doesn't rest on the other person agreeing with us.

We go from argument to discussion when we bring in a third entity—spirit or love. Instead of wanting to be right, we want everyone to be respected and heard. Instead of wanting our way, we want what's best for the whole. We remember that we will be happier living in unity with another rather than feeling split in two. We can continue to believe that we are right, we can present one case for our beliefs, but we need to give up winning and realize that someone else may feel as right about their stance as we do about ours. Discussions may be spirited and heartfelt, but the goal is not to exclude anyone or prove them wrong. If we give up trying to convert people to our way of thinking and become aware of our differences, we are then faced with deciding if there is enough glue in the relationship to hold it together. Sometimes we try to change people because we don't want to see that we're very different or incompatible.

If someone is picking an argument with you, you can say, "I don't want to argue with you—it doesn't feel good," or "I think this is a subject I'd prefer to avoid," or "I would like to agree to disagree." Some people will back off right away, but others will persist. Just repeat to yourself, "I don't want to argue with you." One time this happened on an airplane with the man sitting next to me. He saw what I was reading and started to argue with me in a hostile way. I told him that I didn't want to argue and he responded: "You're sure touchy. I bet you're one of those feminists." I sidestepped the feminist bait and said, "I don't like the way it feels to argue." He persisted and I called for the stewardess to change my seat. At a certain point, if someone insists on arguing when you say no, it's time to get away. Your boundaries are being invaded against your will, which is a form of violence.

If you tend to argue or always take an opposite stance on any subject, you might try doing something different and see how it feels. Try listening and understanding the other person. The part of us that wants to be right or win is usually a little three-year-old who desperately wants to be noticed or told they're important. Instead of giving into the impulse to win or be right, you can say to yourself, *I understand your need, but having your way won't help you feel better—getting along with others will work much better*. It's a paradox that what you think will make you happy—winning or being right—is what will actually make you lonelier.

A simple phrase that can be useful is simply this, "You can be right, or you can be close."

47

WHEN TO CONFRONT SOMEONE, WHEN TO SAVE YOUR BREATH

When are we being a good friend and when are we interfering where we have no business?! There are no easy rules, particularly when it comes to these questions. Can you think of a time when someone confronted you or made a suggestion and it was of great benefit to you? I am thankful for the people who said to me, "You shouldn't marry. . . . " They were right, I married him anyway and it was a disaster, but I always felt grateful that they cared enough to tell me what they saw. I am grateful to the woman who said to me after my divorce, "Why are you looking for a piano teaching job when you could live in Europe and study on the money you have!" It had never occurred to me—and it changed my life.

While we don't have the right to interfere with another's journey, we are here to help each other wake up—to be a friend indeed. People have tremendously different reactions to someone giving them a suggestion or advice. Some people feel cared about when others offer suggestions or give feedback. Other people have a rebellious kid response—Don't tell me what to do! We decipher individual differences as we get to know people. But we also need to respond to the pangs in our gut.

My rule of thumb when I think a friend is going down a dangerous path is to say it once and then let it go—at least for six months—well, maybe four. It's a dance between trying to prevent a friend from self-destruction and interfering where you have no business. I am most grateful to Linda, my office manager, for bringing me up short when I was headed down what could have been a deadly path.

Five years ago when I got word that I had a suspicious mammogram, I put it out of my mind and didn't schedule a visit with a surgeon for nearly six weeks. I was busy, and I couldn't believe I had cancer. The day before the appointment, the surgeon's secretary called to change my appointment to later the same day or else three weeks later. Changing the appointment to later that day meant moving a lot of my own appointments and made me mad—"Don't doctors think anyone else has important things to do?" So I said, "I'll come in three weeks." Linda, who overheard the conversation, was obviously agitated. She told me with great clarity and strength, "I think that's a mistake. I think you should go right away. My husband's sister put off going to the doctor and she died two years after the diagnosis." She also spoke with obvious sadness about another friend who put off going to check out a lump and died several years later.

Linda did not usually interfere. I could hear the tremor in her voice. The intensity of her worry and concern was like an icicle coming into my brain, waking me up to the potential danger of putting off the visit. I realized I was probably cutting off my nose to spite my face, and I immediately called back and took the next appointment. I am deeply grateful to Linda for her sharp, strong intervention, which woke me up. Yes, it was cancer, but it hadn't spread to my lymph nodes. And who's to ever know if that might have happened during the three weeks I would have waited to visit the surgeon.

If you are going to speak up to someone, say it clearly and honestly, including your own agenda. ("I feel extremely nervous when I see you . . . ") Be sure you have the other person's attention when you talk. If the other person resists your words, don't push. It's time to save your breath. If the person is listening, say all you need to say as succinctly as possible, then stop. Sometimes your input will be pushed away, and other times the message will be heard. Sometimes the person will be resistant but thank you later.

The same thing applies when giving personal feedback. If you find yourself talking about someone behind their back, it's probably better to talk with them directly. This can be scary, but it's the source of intimate relationships. I had a dear friend who seldom made eye contact. Repeatedly, people mentioned it to me but no one said anything to her. I finally told her that I felt uncomfortable trying to talk when she didn't look at me. She said that no one had ever mentioned it before. When she learned that other people had felt uncomfortable with her lack of eye contact, she felt hurt and said, "Why didn't anyone ever tell me?"

You might want to explore your typical reactions when people make suggestions or give you advice. Do you immediately feel defensive or are you willing to listen for a moment and consider that it is coming from care? I'm not talking about people who constantly give advice and try to tell everyone what to do. I'm talking about people who are expressing deep concern for you. If several people give you a consistent message about your behavior, you might want to remember that it's hard for most people to offer suggestions or feedback and that they are probably doing it because they care. It is often a gift if we can stop and listen. If people see you on a destructive path, or find you closed to feedback, they may distance themselves to preserve their energy.

I am thankful for all the people who have had the courage to tell me when they thought I was making a mistake or when they didn't like my behavior. Their attempts to intervene were good, clear energy given to me from the heart. When I remember back on some of these times, I know they gave it careful consideration and that it was not easy for them.

There is a delicate balance between being our brother's and sister's keepers and butting in where we have no business. We can't always know when to confront, give feedback or pray silently for someone's well-being. We can't know if they are going to hear us or resent us . . . or maybe resent us in the moment but think over what we said. The best you can do is be guided by your intuition, speak from your heart, and let go of the outcome. As part of the community of all people, it can be important to speak up when someone is on a destructive path because we all need to care for each other.

48

AVOID TALKING IN PAGES AND PARAGRAPHS

One time when a cocounselor and I were having a tough time working together, we went to a supervisor. She commented, "You both talk to each other in pages and paragraphs. I'm not sure either of you has heard the other." That was wise counsel that helped me tune into my own patterns of conversation. Talking in pages and paragraphs is a common habit that separates people because most of us cannot absorb or hear that much information at once, particularly when we are talking about emotional issues. We need time to both hear the words and process them at an emotional level so that we can respond.

Talking on and on without the other's attention is a tremendous waste of energy and tends to end up in scenes like this:

Ella asks Jack, "Say, did you pick up the cleaning?"

"No. What cleaning!?" Jack says, surprised and nervous, thinking he's going to be attacked again for messing up.

"Did you forget again?!" Ella says, exasperated, reinforcing Jack's anxiety.

"You never told me to."

"Yes I did," Ella says as her temperature climbs.

"When?" Jack says, attempting to stand up for himself.

"Last night when I was doing dishes."

It's true she had said, "Please go to the dry cleaner's tomorrow," but it was said in the midst of pages of words while Jack was putting silverware in the drawer, looking the other way, and humming to himself. He had tuned her out about four pages earlier.

People who talk at length often feel puzzled or angry when others don't remember what they said. That's because the meaning gets lost in a confetti of words. When I do listening exercises with couples, it frequently comes as a shock that, at most, 50 percent of what they are saying gets heard. And on some occasions, the excess verbiage hits an overwhelm button and the listener forgets everything and goes blank. Unfortunately, this gets misinterpreted as not caring as opposed to having the circuits overloaded.

A basic rule of communication: *Get to the heart of your message, speak only a few sentences at a time, breathe, and check to see if your listener is with you.* If you want to tell a story, ask your listener, "Do you want to hear what happened to me yesterday?"

If they say yes, tell your story. It's still good to be aware if they are tuned into you, which you can tell by the level of their attention.

If you are the recipient of pages and paragraphs of words, you don't need to sit and space out. You can say politely, "I don't mean to be rude, but I'm getting overwhelmed" or "I'm still mulling over the first thing you said, could we go back to that for a minute?" Cutting in on someone is not easy, but what's to be gained by feeling invaded by words, building up resentments or holding the phone from our ear and not really listening. If you don't say something, in all probability you will withdraw and the other person will wonder why or feel hurt. You might also be tempted to talk about them behind their back. Part of creating intimacy in our lives is breaking through our old patterns by kindly talking with our friends about what keeps us apart instead of faking politeness and staying superficial. Of course, this is a matter of timing and judgment.

If you muster your courage and say something, some people will politely acknowledge that they talk a lot. Others will experience your request for limits as a withdrawal of love, particularly if they talk compulsively as a protective shield for their fear. One signal that someone talks compulsively is if you feel drained when they talk; this is because their underlying neediness is pulling at you through the words. Another signal is feeling unusually afraid to break in and bring up the subject of their talking at length. You probably sense that you are treading on tender ground—exposing their protective shield—and you are merging with their fear. If you decide to say something, assuage your friend's underlying fear by reassuring them that you care about them.

A friend of mine, Annie, told this story. She had a dear friend, Jean, who talked in paragraphs and chapters that went on as long as half an hour without a break. She gave up visiting her even though she loved her. One time when she phoned to say hello, Jean commented that Annie rarely stayed with her when she was in town. She sounded hurt. Annie finally harnessed her courage to talk with her. "Jean," she said, "this is hard to say. I care about you and I don't want to hurt your feelings, but I stay away because I get overwhelmed when you talk for long periods of time, often about people I've never met. I get exhausted. That's why I stay away—it's not that I don't love you."

Even so, Jean was hurt and didn't understand what Annie was saying. When Annie explained that hearing detailed stories about other people had nothing to do with their friendship, she said, "I feel as if you're not interested in my life."

"I am interested in *your* life," Annie protested. "I'm interested in how *you* feel and what *you* are doing. But I'm not interested in details about people I've never met." Jean looked bewildered and responded, "I don't really understand, but because I love you I'll try not to tell stories about other people." Annie felt great relief and wished, even though it was very hard, that she hadn't taken so long to bring up the subject.

If you think you talk compulsively, take some time to reflect on yourself. Do you go from one subject to another without a break? Do you stop to ask others about their lives? Observe yourself with compassion and understanding. It can be painful to acknowledge compulsive talking and realize the impact it has on others. It's also painful to connect to the underlying insecurity and fear.

If you are trying to break a compulsive talking habit, ask friends if they are willing to use some kind of signal to remind you to slow down. You can tell them what would feel best for you—touching your arm or saying, "I'm feeling overwhelmed." Like any compulsion, talking excessively doesn't go away without effort, but with effort, one can change. You will make room for deeper connections in your relationships. Eventually, you will enter into the realm of being with others in silence.

This brings to mind a Christmas morning when I sat around a cozy fire with Jessie and Maggie, an eighty-one-year-old friend of ours. We had brunch, shared some simple gifts and ran out of words as we sat around the fire. As we quietly began leafing through some coffee table picture books, a warm sense of peace filled me. We were communicating in a very real way that we were comfortable enough not to talk, but simply to be. It's what I remember most vividly about Christmas.

49

OBSERVE YOUR COMMUNICATION STYLES

We change as we become willing to observe ourselves and feel the discomfort of recognizing patterns that do not improve intimacy. The following examples are to be taken as food for thought—not as right/wrong prescriptions. The learning comes as you apply them to your experience through observation and self-appraisal and try them out for yourself.

SOME COMMUNICATION STYLES TO EXPLORE

EXCESS DETAIL.

We connect with others when we relate the essence of our experience, not the external details. If someone asks you, "How was the wedding you went to?" it doesn't require a twenty-five-minute, nonstop response including a detailed account of the beading on the wedding dress, the types of all the flowers, the names and jobs of "important" people who attended, and a blow-by-blow description of every bit of food. It's better to say how you felt about the wedding and one or two things that interested you.

GETTING DERAILED.

This is when a person starts to tell about an event, then gets derailed by a side issue and loses sight of the initial subject. It's as if something keeps pulling them farther and farther from their center. Andy asks his friend Jim about his weekend trip. Jim responds, "I saw my friend Joan. You know, she grew up in Illinois and went to college at Oberlin; you know, she was very good in flute. When she was growing up, she would get up and practice before school. The whole family is musical—two of her brother's kids are both studying music in college. One of them is at the Cincinnati conservatory, which is having a fund-raising concert next week. . . ." The report on the weekend with Joan is totally lost. As a listener you also feel lost—which is probably how the speaker feels. Inner thoughts you might have are "Please get to the point" or "Why are you telling me all this?"

GIVING DETAILED STORIES ABOUT OTHER PEOPLE.

For the most part, telling someone detailed stories about people they've never met is boring because it puts the energy outside the circle of your connection. If you have friends in your life who mean a lot to you, it can be very tempting to want to tell people about them, which is fine as long as it relates to your experience. For example, I could tell you (which is true): "I had a dear friend, Torrie, who was about the only person I could talk to during my depressing marriage. She did two important things: She confronted me on complaining about my marriage and not doing anything, and she introduced me to feminism, which gave me the courage to get divorced." While I'm talking about Torrie, it's in relationship to my life. I could also say, "I had this wonderful friend Torrie who helped organize women for peace trains, had her phone tapped, was a wonderful mother, wrote articles, etc., etc.," all of which is of value, but it is not connected to my experience. It's "out there." If someone asked me what I admired in her, this would be relevant; otherwise, it has nothing to do with the essence of my story and my life.

GIVING SOAPBOX ORATIONS ON "HOW BAD IT IS."

Some people's way of relating to others is to speak in rhetoric about the sad state of the world. When you've prepared a nice dinner for six with candlelight and roses and someone launches into a righteous, heavy, political harangue about how bad it is, the flow of conversation stops, the energy in the room goes flat, and people suddenly have to get home early. There is definitely a place for social action and taking stock of the world, but conversation is about exchange at a feeling or experiential level, not one person talking *at* another.

SHIFTING THE FOCUS

Another approach to observing communication is to look at the ways you or others shift the focus of the conversation to other people or away from the emotional experience of the one who is talking. Shifting the focus blocks connection or emotional intimacy.

Here is a summary of ways in which people shift the focus in conversation:

1. "I had a friend who did it too." Shift to talking about other people.
2. "I did it too." Take the conversation back to ourselves.
3. Change the subject.
4. Minimize or negate what the person is saying.
5. Ask for facts and figures.

Here are ways in which we connect:

1. Ask a leading question that takes a person further into their story or experience.
2. Make a supportive comment that shows we are listening.

EXAMPLES OF SHIFTING THE FOCUS IN CONVERSATION

1. "I had a friend who did it too." Shifting to talking about other people.

ROSA: I've been having difficulties with my daughter lately. She's been acting strangely at home and I'm getting worried.

PHYLLIS: Oh, I have a friend who is going through a terrible time with her daughter . . . She started getting into drugs, etc.

2. "I've done it too." Taking the focus back to yourself.

> ROSA: I've been having difficulties with my daughter lately.
>   She's been acting strangely at home and I'm getting
>   worried.
>
> PHYLLIS: Oh, I used to have problems with my daughter. We
>   went through a terrible time when . . .

3. Changing the subject.

> ROSA: I've been having difficulties with my daughter lately.
>   She's been acting strangely at home and I'm getting
>   worried.
>
> PHYLLIS: Yeah, there sure is a lot to worry about these days.
>   My husband, Ted, is terribly worried about possi-
>   ble layoffs at work.

4. Negating the other person's concerns.

> ROSA: I've been having difficulties with my daughter lately.
>   She's been acting strangely at home and I'm getting
>   worried.
>
> PHYLLIS: Well, don't worry about it too much, these things
>   pass. She'll probably get over it soon.

5. Ask for facts and figures.

> ROSA: I've been having difficulties with my daughter lately.
>   She's been acting strangely at home and I'm getting
>   worried.
>
> PHYLLIS: How old is your daughter? When did she start giv-
>   ing you trouble?

How did you feel reading the above dialogues? Now we'll
try them again in ways that connect.

1. Ask a leading question that takes a person further into their
   story or experience.
2. Make an empathic comment that shows you are listening.

ASK A LEADING QUESTION THAT TAKES THE PERSON FURTHER INTO THEIR STORY OR EXPERIENCE

> ROSA: I've been having difficulties with my daughter lately.
>   She's been acting strangely at home and I'm getting
>   worried.
>
> PHYLLIS: She's been acting strange lately, what do you think is
>   going on? or So you're worried about your daughter.

In both of these ways, Rosa is invited to continue talking about her worries with her daughter.

> ROSA: (she's been waiting to talk a long time) I'm worried that she is pregnant and not telling me.
> PHYLLIS: You think she might be pregnant. Oh, my gosh.
> ROSA: Yes, I heard her throwing up the other morning.

And so on. We now have a conversation with a circular energy flow.

After Rosa has been heard, validated, and given a chance to talk about her concerns, Phyllis might say, "I can really relate. You know, I've had a terrible time with my daughter as well. Do you want to hear about it?"

The inner experience of listening in this way includes the ability to relax inside, put one's agenda aside and be present. You will be amazed at the differences in your life when you get centered enough to listen well and speak from your heart. Most of all, as you listen with greater resonance to others, you become a better listener to yourself.

50

TAP INTO THE WONDER OF STORYTELLING

I want to differentiate between compulsive or excessive monologues and storytelling. Storytelling is an age-old practice that links one generation to the next. Through stories about their lives and their forebears, people have passed on the history of their people and culture. I remember sitting up until two in the morning with my mother's cousin Margaret as she told the story of her three-year internment at a Japanese prison camp during World War II. I was enraptured as she spoke, totally in awe of her tenacity, undauntable spirit, and compassion for all people. I'll never forget her referring to the Japanese as "the people we called the enemy then." The magic of that evening will be with me for the rest of my life.

Storytelling brings us home to our hearts. It requires no props, no money, nothing but revealing history, our experience, and our inner world. It doesn't matter if you're gifted at weaving a yarn or simply speak from your heart. What matters is that you tap into the wonder of your own life and share it with others. Telling the stories of our lives to each other brings a richness of spirit and validates our specialness. Storytelling ignites our imagination as we create pictures and scenes from words. It is also a wonderful way to build community.

When people come together to form a group, they often start by telling what brought them there and then describe their vision and hopes. The more we know about each other's journey, the more compassion we have for each other. As a psychotherapist I have found that when I know someone's story—what they have survived and all they ways in which they have coped—it is impossible not to care for them or feel compassion. This level of compassion helps us work together effectively.

We build community as we get to know people in their ordinary humanness—not as job descriptions or degrees. When we talk about the times when we have felt happy, sad, scared, or proud, we are on equal ground, as people on a journey. I recently attended a retreat where we had an evening for hero stories—what were we proud of having done in our lives? At another retreat with psychotherapists and counselors, we spent several hours going around the circle speaking of the things that brought us pleasure, starting with early childhood. I was astounded by all that I learned about the people in both gatherings. The hero stories were absolutely amazing and reminded me again that all great things are done by ordinary people with extraordinary courage. In the therapists' gathering I learned that one person sang gospel songs, another had a huge garden, another wrote poetry, another liked to hike, one spent a lot of time training dogs. I remember the sense of peace and awe that settled in as we touched the spiritual dwelling place of each other—our lifelong sources of joy and pleasure. Through these rituals, I often learned more about a person's life and heart in one single evening than I had in years of knowing them.

I started this section talking about storytelling as a way of passing down our history to the next generation. If your children are not interested in hearing your stories right now, tape them or write them down. (And remember, the best stories involve conflict, feelings, fears, adventures or mistakes.) There will be a time when they will savor them. If your parents are alive, ask them to talk about their lives. Try to get beyond facts about where they lived; ask them what worried them, what made them happy, what school was like, how they met each other. This is often a good way to bridge troubled waters between adult children and their parents. You might tape their stories for future reference. I am thankful for the stories my father wrote about his early years riding the rails to bail hay as a high school student, and the account my mother wrote of her first two years of marriage working beside my father, a forest ranger in Montana. I would love to have more. I think of all the words we exchanged in our lifetime together—I wish more of them had included stories of their lives.

51
AVOID MAKING FIX-IT STATEMENTS

*F*ix-it statements are a common form of communication that creates distance between people. A fix-it statement is when one person tells about a problem or experience and another person jumps in to help, make it go away, rationalize, or analyze, rather than simply listen and meet the person heart to heart as a loving witness and friend. A lack of secure identity mixed with fear underlies fix-it statements—fear of feelings, of connecting, or of conflict. Fix-it statements often start with phrases such as "It's probably because . . ." or "They didn't mean to do it. . . . " They almost always take the conversation from a feeling level to a "head" level.

Here's an example:

I was having lunch with a group of women at a conference we were all attending. We got to talking about the speakers. Arlene said, "I had a hard time with that first speaker, he didn't feel very well prepared."

Instantly, another woman, Joanna, rose to his defense, "Well, *it's probably because* he hasn't had much experience."

Someone else said, "I wish they would have more panel discussions. I'm getting overwhelmed with so much information."

Again Joanna rose to defend. "Well, they probably had a limited budget and that would have cost too much." In response to every comment, Joanna offered reasons or excuses. My inner experience was frustration and disappointment because I wanted to hear the women's opinions. I sat there wondering what to say, when, much to my relief, another woman said, "Joanna, could I say something to you?"

"Yes," she replied, sounding surprised.

"I feel as if you are telling me it's not okay to have an opinion. I'm just telling my reactions to the conference. It doesn't mean I don't like it or that I'm not learning something, but I'd like to feel free to say how I feel. I've spent a long time learning that I get to have opinions."

Joanna quickly replied, "I'm not saying that."

"But every time I have an opinion, you make up rationalizations or reasons instead of just listening. I don't feel as if you ever hear me."

Fix-it statements essentially send the message don't question, don't be upset, don't be mad, and don't have feelings— all projections of the person's inner fears. The internal survivor

voice screams, "Danger, smooth things over as fast as possible."
People who make fix-it statements usually feel a lot of shame
or mistake observations for negative judgments. Their shame
results in translating statements like "I didn't like that talk" to
meaning "I think the speaker is a bad person and this is a lousy
conference and it's all bad—and I'm bad too." Even observations such as "She certainly wore an odd dress" are translated
to "She's bad and I don't like her."

In reality, we are only afraid of hearing "judgments" to the
extent that we judge ourselves in the same way. For example, if
someone criticizes you for being quiet, it won't bother you
unless you feel ashamed of being quiet.

Lively conversation can result from people sharing perceptions and observations in the spirit of getting to know what
others think. It requires an ability to tolerate and enjoy differences and not make negative translations of opinions. It's a way
in which we open ourselves to others. It can be dull when
people don't have opinions and voice their perceptions and,
instead, all sit around agreeing with each other.

To take our place at the table of adulthood, we need to recognize the difference between our childlike trigger points and
current reality. If opinions, questioning, observations, and judgments scare you, check out the source of the fear. It might help
to remember that at the level of big mind, there are no judgments, only lives unfolding and lessons to be learned. If you
feel compelled to make fix-it statements, here is something you
can say to yourself: *An observation is an observation. An opinion is
an opinion. It doesn't say anyone is bad, it doesn't mean I'm bad, it
doesn't mean the conversation will escalate into a battle or our relationship will fall apart. We can have different opinions and different observations. People can disagree. There is nothing here to fear. I am not a
child and these are not my parents.*

As we soften our fears, we learn to participate and listen
without fear of strong feelings or "being judged." Like a story
unfolding before our eyes, we bring ourselves as witnesses and
observers, attached to big mind, which says, "Ah, now isn't this
interesting."

52

THAT'S NOT WHAT I MEANT: THE PROBLEM WITH INTERPRETATIONS

One of the greatest causes of unnecessary fights and hurt is misinterpreting what others say. Instead of hearing what someone actually said, we interject voices from the past and then react based on these misinterpretations. In general, the more important the relationship, the more we are likely to mistake our partner's words for voices from the past. That's because the more intimate we become, the more our unconscious blurs the lines between our current family and our past family.

I sometimes call it the 80–20 ratio. Eighty percent of a hot or strong reaction is about events from the past and the other 20 percent is about the current situation and needs to be dealt with. Sometimes it's a 100–0 ratio and we completely mishear the other person.

The formula that gets people in trouble is this:

Message from speaker	→	Listener makes interpretation based on childhood or past experience—feels shame—	→	Listener reacts on the misin- terpetation

As an example, my partner, Jessie, and I were tying down a canoe on top of the car. Her knots looked like something out of a knot-tying guide and mine looked like the first day at Girl Scout camp. I was at the back of the car mumbling to myself as my knot came loose. I glanced around the side of the car to watch her and mumbled to myself, "How does she do that?" As we proceeded, I could tell that she was getting irritated.

"Are you mad about something?" I asked her.

"Yes. I don't like it when you tell me to drop everything and come help you. You don't think what I'm doing is important."

"What!?" I responded in amazement. "I was mumbling to myself. I didn't tell you to drop everything and come help me."

"Well, it seemed like you did."

"That's your interpretation . . . it's not what I said."

I could stick up for myself because I finally have learned not to always back down. A few years back I would have had a totally different reaction. "Oh, dear, she's mad at me. What did I do wrong? Now we'll have a bad day together." I might have started to apologize so she wouldn't be mad at me. Our relationship would have become stuck because she would have continued to project her interpretations on me (You're telling me to drop everything and help you) and I would have continued to cave in and not stand up for my reality.

Because Jessie was willing to look at her misinterpretation and I was able to stick up for myself, the conflict was over in a short time.

Later, after reflecting on the incident, Jessie said, "I think I was hearing my dad. He always said, 'Drop whatever you are doing and come help me.' He never asked me, he never thanked me. He just bossed me around and punished me if I didn't do what he said."

"Jessie," I said, "I honestly didn't want to boss you around. I was admiring your knots and wanting to learn for myself."

Jessie became quiet. "I guess you're right, but it sure felt like you said those things . . . But, it's true, you didn't. I guess it all happened in my head." A great relief set in for both of us.

It takes two people playing their parts to work through misinterpretations. The one who was misinterpreted needs to stand up for him or herself. The one who misinterpreted the message needs to be willing to sort out what was actually said and what happened in their head.

HOW TO RECOGNIZE AND AVOID MISINTERPRETATIONS

1. Note the intensity of your reactions to others. If it's a highly charged flash of anger, hurt, or fear, stop and ask yourself, What did the other person actually say?—verbatim. If you can't remember it verbatim, ask the other person kindly to repeat what they said.

2. Identify and own your interpretation. What were the words *you said to yourself that were an interpretation*? Some examples: "You always tell me I'm doing it wrong," "You're always criticizing me," "You hate me," "You're bossing me around," "You're going to leave me," "You don't trust me," "You don't care about me." Check back in your mind. Does this reaction (interpretation) relate to old experiences stemming back to childhood?

3. Do not react out of your interpretation. Tell yourself, *This is an interpretation; it is not what my friend/partner said.* Acting out of an interpretation will keep me stuck and is not fair to the relationship.

4. If you like, check out your emotional reaction with your friend or partner: "Were you feeling critical of me?" "Are you mad at me?" "What was going on with you?"

5. Listen to the answer with your heart and mind. Even if the person did have an abrupt tone, or was upset, they may have had no intention of putting you down or criticizing you. They may have been asking a question, stating a feeling or making a request. (On the other hand, if you repeatedly feel stung by someone's remarks and they constantly smile and say, "No, I was just being friendly," it might be that you are picking up an undercurrent of anger. I talk about that in the next section.)

RESPONSES TO SOMEONE WHO MISINTERPRETS YOUR REMARKS

1. Don't collapse when someone has a strong reaction. If you know truly in your heart that you are being misinterpreted, defend yourself calmly. If you get off center, start shouting or start feeling like a bad kid, then you've both lost it and you'll waste a lot of time on a bogus argument that has little to do with the two of you.

2. Kindly but firmly say, "I didn't say that. I only said . . ." You might also add, "Truly, I wasn't feeling critical, I just . . ."

Most violence in relationships is triggered by misinterpretations that send people reeling back into a childlike state. We perceive people as attacking or abandoning us and we react from a survival mode as if our life was in danger. From an adult stance, people can't abandon us—they may leave, but we are able to take care of ourselves. Some people spend much of their lives in a two- to five-year-old state, chronically misinterpreting what others say, exploding into rage and violence: "You're going back to school so you can get a job and leave me." "If you won't have sex, it means you don't love me . . . or you're having an affair."

The more we misinterpret others, the lower the level of intimacy. Our vision is clouded by past events and we are constantly reacting to others out of a childlike state. We are still being defined by past events and allowing our self-esteem to fluctuate based on what others do or say. To move toward intimacy, we need to listen to our misinterpretations and resolve the underlying causes. As we become able to differentiate what others *actually* say and what we are saying in our head, we set the process of growth in motion.

53

TRUST YOUR INTUITION

While it is important to look at your misinterpretations, it's also useful to discern when someone *is* giving you a double message. If someone says they love you but their behavior is repeatedly uncaring or mean, you need to listen to your gut feelings. Discerning the difference between misinterpreting others and recognizing abuse can be very confusing. On the one hand, you say to yourself, "Maybe I'm overreacting. I really shouldn't be so mad/sad/hurt." On the other hand, you are upset, angry, scared, and something feels wrong. At this point, trust yourself and listen to the cues from your body.

For example, if someone is conning you, you may have an

uneasy feeling in your stomach or a flicker of a thought—This doesn't feel right. Other symptoms of being abused or receiving double messages are confusion, feeling hazy in your mind, having a knot of fear in your chest or gut, feeling paralyzed about taking action, or getting obsessed with thinking about the person. You might tend to make excuses, blame yourself, or minimize the situation: "Oh, I'm too critical," "They really didn't mean it," "It just happened once," "They're often so nice," "I know they didn't mean it." If you're analyzing or making excuses, drop down into your gut and say, How am *I* feeling about this situation *today*? Don't futurize, today is what counts. Most of the time you will find that you are feeling afraid, angry or hurt.

It's important to be conscious of these feelings and not dismiss them. If it seems safe and appropriate, make an attempt to share your perspective and feelings with the person you're concerned about. By doing this you take a proactive stance and test the relationship—can the other person handle conflict, reflect on themselves, and own their part? If you don't check out your misgivings, you might be conning yourself out of knowing you are being abused or exploited.

If you voice your concerns and the other person explodes, gets abusive, becomes extremely defensive, or starts shaming and blaming you, you can know your hunches were right and that it's time to get help for the relationship or leave. Living in chronic fear, worry, or with chronic preoccupation of another usually leads to a numbing of the spirit and depression, which does nothing to change the relationship.

There was a movie called *Gaslight* with Ingrid Bergman and Charles Boyer. The essence of gaslighting is when you hurt, lie and sabotage someone, but pretend to be caring—the definition of sadistic. When confronted, the alleged gaslighter flatly denies doing it and the other person feels crazy and confused. In the movie, the heroine suspected that she was being lied to, but didn't trust herself and stayed until her husband nearly killed her.

Gaslighting is intended to break your will, lower your self-esteem and cripple you emotionally so that you will never have the strength to leave. If you feel you are becoming crazy and afraid in a relationship, stop making excuses, stop trying to figure him/her out and go talk with someone who knows about abuse. Spend time away from the situation and see if you feel less confused and foggy. At a certain point, you don't need to understand why you feel confused and scared, you simply need to know that you can't handle being with the person. It's draining your life energy. Your journey literally stops when you stay in an abusive situation where your mind feels scrambled.

I am reminded of the Zen master who said, "The best thing is to take action and be right. The second best thing is to take action and be wrong. The worst thing is to take no action at all."

54

SPEAKING FROM THE HEART IS THE KEY

A few nights ago in a support group I attend, a new woman came. She spoke in a trembling voice, with her eyes averted, looking at the floor. Her inner struggle to speak was palpable. Yet as she spoke of her life and her fears, I could feel my heart soften. I felt permeated by the love that was awakened in all of us by her courage. She spoke few words, but she gave greatly of herself.

Our willingness to give generously of our feelings and thoughts, to struggle openly to find the words, to reveal our inner fears and joys are the most profound gifts we can ever give. Likewise, to be a loving witness to someone else's journey, to listen with an open heart and put ourself in someone else's shoes, helps us feel union with another. The starting place is to breathe deeply, relax into your belly, and tune in to your inner world. The daily practice is silence—silence that allows us to hear the voice of our spirit.

PART VI

◆ ◆ ◆

"STAYING CONSTANT THROUGH CONFLICT"

—the Goodenough Community

55

CONFLICT: THE SEEDS OF GROWTH AND INTIMACY

Conflict signals that our differences have met. We are separate people with different ideas, wants, and beliefs. Conflict is not bad. It's how we deal with it that profoundly affects all our relationships, be it with an intimate partner, our work associates, neighbors, or friends. A relationship without conflict can mean that both people are in tune with each other, but it is more likely to mean that both people are not being honest and real with each other, or that one person is routinely acquiesing to the other. Unresolved conflict blocks the energy flow between two people or within a group of people. The healthy resolution of conflict restores a sense of flow and deepens the bonds between us. Dealing with conflict often means that we name what is going on and bring our differences to the surface, where they can be exposed and explored.

Impending conflict raises fear in many people—fear that's deeply embedded in our unconscious mind, often dating back to childhood. The fear of conflict reflects difficulty in being autonomous or able to maintain our center. We fear feeling wounded or absorbed by another. We may also fear that there will be no resolution. The other fear of resolving conflict is that we will actually get through it and be more intimate with each other. While most people say this is what they want, very often unresolved conflict keeps us at a "safe" distance. It creates a lot of noise and static that keeps us from the quiet of intimacy.

There can be great satisfaction in resolving conflict, a "good for us" feeling, like giving each other high fives. Yes, we did it! It can help immensely to think of conflict as something not yet finished, a work in progress. Think of conflict and resolution as part of a whole, not two separate entities. It's a form of contraction and expansion, like the tension and release that our muscles do throughout the day, the dark of winter that makes the returning light so exciting. Conflict and resolution are a natural part of music, as expressed by dissonance to consonance. Consonance brings satisfaction only because it follows dissonance.

Conflict exists whether we recognize it or not. If we don't deal with it openly, it lives in every muscle and fiber of our being. Like tension without release, it converts to stress that causes headaches, disease, low energy, stomachaches, frightening dreams, and a general sense of dullness and disconnection from others. It builds up a knot of emotional tension that can lead us to make the well-placed dig, withdraw, explode, drink, or engage in other addictions. In my family, where conflict was nearly always swept under the rug, my preoccupied father took stomach acid pills daily, along with aspirin for his frequent headaches and my mother ate compulsively. I had a "nervous stomach" and started experiencing depression by age five, my older brother went fishing every day and became silent, and my sister was mean to me. It was sad, because underneath our unhappiness we were all good, caring people who longed for closeness but didn't know how to create it. Many years later when my mother observed me teaching an assertiveness class, she said with a sense of sadness, "I sure could have used that class bringing up you kids."

Unresolved conflict stalks us through life—always there somewhere, hiding in the back of our minds, ready to jump out when we least expect it. We wake up from a dream feeling angry about a quarrel that happened five years ago. We resurrect our partner's affair and sling it at him or her when we're feeling insecure.

The final stage of dealing with conflict is letting go of the hurt and anger, and forgiving oneself. We can say *Namaste* to the other person or persons. In many books on death and dying, people are encouraged to clear out anger and conflict with others—to forgive and be forgiven—so that they can make their transition with peace and love in their hearts. But why wait until you are dying to clear your heart? If you keep the channels clear between yourself and other people during your life, you will know love and be far less frightened of dying . . . not to mention living. And it's never too late to apologize or clear the air with others.

When a relationship goes dead, there is usually a history of unspoken hurts, disappointments, resentments, and apologies that need to be made. Many people think the love is gone from their marriage when it's not, it's simply buried under a garbage can of unresolved anger and hurt. In their avoidance of conflict, they have enmeshed themselves in a mass of fear. No one says what they truly feel or want. It's like burying their soul—a living death. I have often seen the love return to people's eyes after they clear out the anger and hurt. It's a joyful feeling, like removing dead leaves from the garden in spring and finding flowers sprouting up.

There is a difference between raging and dealing appropriately with conflict. When we fight and blame instead of dealing with conflict respectfully, the negative energy ricochets around, affecting everyone. This brings to mind an example from my own life. Many years ago, my young daughter, our cat, and I shared a household with Ellen, her young son, and their cat. We were all in the kitchen getting breakfast when Ellen and I started having sharp words with each other in a blaming way. As our voices got hotter, her son suddenly jabbed my daughter, who in turn smacked his cat, who instantly ran across the room and clawed our cat. Ellen and I, seeing the chain reaction of our fight, burst out laughing. "Well, there's the family system in action," she said. I agreed. Our hot words solved nothing and our unskillful approach to conflict spilled over onto our children and cats with amazing speed.

If you tend to focus on your fear of conflict, stop and think about what you have to gain by resolving conflict—bringing up the fears, hurts, and pains that litter the landscape of your relationships. It will start to release the knot of fear from your gut, the toxic energy throughout your body, the anger and grief that block your heart, and the tension that clouds your mind. It will

often give you insight into yourself. No matter what the outcome, you will move closer toward truth and clarity—basic
sources of intimacy and the ability to love.

To take the sting out of the thought of engaging in conflict
resolution, you might think about some of the following:

1. It's natural to have conflict because people are different.
2. It's more important to find unity or clarity than to be right
   or win.
   I'll write that again in **bold** print because it's so important.
2. **It's more important to find unity or clarity than to be**
   right or win.
3. No one is right, wrong, good, or bad, we're just different.
4. Conflict is about having a problem to solve.
5. Conflict is about staying open and clear with each other.
6. If we don't come to an agreement, then at least we can
   agree to be different and we'll know the truth.
7. There's usually a win-win solution somewhere.
8. It's respectful to others to clear our conflict—it frees us all to
   move on.
9. Resolving conflict keeps us from living in fear.
10. Resolving conflict usually helps us feel closer or find clarity
    in a situation.
11. Resolving conflict with our primary partner helps us keep
    our passion and sexual feelings alive.

The first step to resolving conflict is to value clarity and
openness with others and realize that unresolved conflict creates distance and physical problems. The second aspect to
working through conflict is for both people to agree "to stay
constant through conflict." That means approaching a conflict
situation with the agreement that no one will run away, no one
will shame or blame, no one will use force, manipulation, or
violence. Instead, we will listen respectfully, try with all our
heart to understand each other, speak our truths, and work
together in the name of harmony and unity until we reach clarity or find a solution everyone can live with.

56

DANCING WITH FEAR

Fain would I climb, yet fear I to fall.
—Sir Walter Raleigh

We need to be kind to our fears and at the same time move through them if we want to love and be loved. Franklin Roosevelt said, "The only thing we have to fear is fear itself." My sense is that he referred to living in chronic, paralyzing fear, which disheartens people. In many day-to-day situations *the only thing we have to fear is denying our fear.* We don't need to be afraid of fear. The first step for many in coming to grips with fear is simply owning it: "I'm afraid." Fear can be an important signal that we are feeling off center, losing control, or have lost faith. It's also common to feel fear when we venture into the unknown. Acknowledging fear is counter to much of our cultural conditioning, particularly for men, who are supposed to be fearless no matter what.

When we deny our fear it tends to paralyze us or results in shame and anger. I remember going to a counselor with some housemates when we were having difficulty. When the therapist said to me, "I think you feel a lot of fear," something inside me relaxed and I was curious to explore what it was about. It was like getting a diagnosis for what was going on inside me.

In our journey to intimacy, we repeatedly face fear as we break through old barriers and risk new behavior. We feel vulnerable as we allow our hearts to open and our voices to be heard. If we constantly back off from situations that create anxiety or fear, we back off from life. The greater our tolerance for discomfort and fear, the greater our ability to break old patterns and experience life more fully. Once we learn to name our fear, the next step is to expand our perception of fear so that we see it within the context of our whole journey. "Here I am experiencing fear. That's normal, it happens to everyone. It's part of life. It's just another form of energy." When we go from small thinking to big thinking, we will gradually learn to dance with our fear.

There's a fear vs. excitement ratio in entering into the unknown. If we are inexperienced, cautious, or security conscious, the higher our level of fear. Our mind jumps to what could go wrong. As we practice pushing through our limits, the excitement goes up and the fear goes down. Over time, we condition ourselves to enjoy the energy release and freedom that comes from breaking through old patterns and expanding our world. Pushing through limits in any area where you experience anxiety can affect other areas.

When we chronically say, "I'm afraid what others will think" or "I might make a mistake," we can ask: What am I actually afraid of? What harm can come to me? What will happen if someone says no or goes away? People often say, "I'm afraid I'll be rejected." It's important not to get stuck with that thought. People don't reject us—they agree with us, like us, understand us, don't understand us, or don't like us. There's a fit or there isn't. As adults, we can't be rejected unless we reject ourselves. We need to keep reminding ourselves not to tie our self-worth to the words of others.

Fear can be contagious. Have you ever thought of bringing up a concern with someone and suddenly felt a rip of fear inside? It could be that you were picking up their fear. In giving lectures and workshops, I can feel when fear ripples through the audience. The energy drops and feels tense or flat. If that happens, it's important to ask people what's going on for them.

To discern whether you are caught in your own fear or have taken on the other person's fear, ask yourself: Could I bring up the same concern more easily with other people in my life? If the answer is yes, it is likely that you are tapping into the other person's fear and you instinctively know that you are treading on tender ground. The tendency in these kinds of situations is to back down and not speak up. You need to assess the real level of danger before you decide what to do.

Sometimes our fear signals real danger. If we are living in chronic fear, we may be picking up the covert, violent energy of people around us—their deceit, their rage, or the possibility that they may do us physical harm. In this case, fear is a natural, self-protective response that is screaming at you to watch out, speak out, or get out.

Looking back in my life, an important lesson I've learned is that no matter what the outcome, *it is usually better to bring up a conflict and get it out in the open than paralyze my life and my spirit with fear.* In my desire to overcome fear paralysis, I made a covenant with myself: "I will not live in fear. If speaking my truths results in loss or pain, so be it. If it means a relationship falls apart, so be it. I will not live in fear." It's like committing to sobriety at a spiritual level. This doesn't mean we barge in with our opinions and thoughts without being sensitive to others. It means we promise ourselves to be true. Usually when we are consumed by fear, we are trying to control a situation—often to prevent separation, anger, hurt, or pain. Letting go of being controlled by fear frees us to breathe again, to come back to our center.

When we are sinking into fears that serve no purpose, one way to lift ourselves to a higher dimension is to stop, breathe consciously, and consciously intensify the feelings of fear. Then focus on the feeling of fear and detach the thoughts connected to the fear and breathe into it. Usually the fear will become a feeling of energy that slowly dissipates. If we can let it just be there, it doesn't need to overwhelm us.

Another way to transform fear is to recite a line or two from a sacred text or a reading that lifts our spirits. We don't get rid of the fear, we simply move to a higher plane of consciousness. Just thinking, God is love, or Ram, or "The lord is my shepherd, I shall not want," or reciting "The Lord's Prayer" can take us from small mind to big mind, from fear to release. When we say words that have been spoken millions of times by millions of people, we tap into an enormous energy mass. Singing or chanting can also have a tremendous effect. It's hard to stay afraid when you are singing because the breathing relaxes the body. My all-time greatest ally for lifting myself out of fear or anxiety is to sing:

> Ask and it shall be given unto you;
> Seek and ye shall find;
> Knock and the door shall be opened unto you [Luke 11:9].
>
> Sing allelu alleluia.
>
>
> We do not live by bread alone
> But by every word
> That proceedeth from the mouth of God [Matthew 4:4].
>
> Sing allelu alleluia.

As we deepen our faith in spirit, we become able to put our fear in the hands of the universe, or God. As we accept pain, sickness, loss, accidents, love, and death as part of life, not as something to be medicated or feared, fear subsides. When we are able to trust our calling and accept the journey we've been handed, we trust in a wisdom beyond our comprehension, remembering that no matter what happens, we are part of sacred creation.

57

A TIME TO LET IT GO—THE OVERPROCESSED RELATIONSHIP

*T*here is a time to talk things over, a time to back off, and a time to drop the subject. While it is important to stay clear in relationships, it's good to remember that endless processing of a relationship can be a defense against intimacy. Sometimes talking at length is the only way people believe they can be close, but it's a counterfeit form of intimacy if the underlying need is to fill up empty spaces, and it doesn't leave room for the spirit to emerge. The purpose of processing difficulties in a relationship is to free yourself to enjoy life, not to make discussion the center of existence.

One of the harmful side effects of therapy, addiction recovery groups, and personal growth books is that people often think they have to analyze and discuss absolutely everything. We get caught in the web of overinvolvement with self. It becomes a form of recovery narcissism. Any little feeling, hurt, mood change, or problem becomes the subject of endless discussion and analysis. Why did you say that to me? Can we talk about your tone of voice? People analyze an incident or misunderstanding for three or four hours, speculating on causes stemming from childhood upbringing, one's astrology chart, the weather, their menstrual cycle, and so on. We get caught in narrow, small-mind thinking. Sometimes this can be fascinating or productive, but more often it's because we're not clear with ourselves and we're avoiding the conflict or feelings that would arise if both people said what was really on their minds. Speaking the truth doesn't take much time: "I'm hurt. I need some time alone. I need to know you care. I'm angry."

When the energy in a discussion gets heavy and dull, it's often better to stop talking and take time apart to seek clarity. You might meditate, pray for guidance, or put your concern on the back burner to season. Often it helps to engage in activities that lighten your spirit—see a friend, take a walk, read something inspiring, go to bed early. In this way we are more likely to find our center, which allows our truths to rise to the surface instead of forcing ourselves to "figure it out."

Processing relationships is a common topic in therapy groups. One day a client, Ginger, came to group and said, "I need to confront my friend because she hasn't phoned me all week." Ginger had a history of getting caught up in heavy, analytical discussions and having people go away from her.

"Let's explore that for a minute," I said. "Why are you confronting her?"

"Well, I've called her three times in the last week, and she hasn't called me at all. I think she should know how I feel."

"Who defines how often she is supposed to call?"

Ginger looked stunned. "Well, shouldn't she call me back?!"

"I think it is good when people return calls, but what will probably happen if you 'confront' her?"

"Oh . . . " (sigh) "She'll probably make a lot of excuses or get mad."

"So you don't think it will resolve anything?" I responded.

"I suppose not. But I thought you were supposed to bring up your feelings with people."

"Well, yes. Sometimes. *But you are creating your feelings with your demands. You've written a script for her.* You think she's supposed to call you as often as *you* want her to. What if you let go of the demand instead?"

"But how do I do that?" she asked.

"You change your demand to a preference. You can say, 'I'd *like* her to call, I'd *prefer* that she call,' but the reality is, she gets to decide how often she calls. Your job is to accept her as she is."

Ginger was obviously taking it all in. "But don't I ever get to talk about it?"

"Sure you can, but when you are in a demanding, hurt place, the conversation is not likely to go well. You're coming from a childlike place. Wait until you accept that she has the right to call as often as she likes and are interested in her reasons. Then it's likely to be a more productive conversation."

The essential element of getting out of a quagmire is to shift from a small mind, small heart to a big mind, big heart perspective. If a conversation starts sinking into the muck, stop. You can take time for silence or breathe into the feelings, notice them in your body, and let go of the thoughts. You might recall a time when you felt close. From a big mind, big heart perspective you can say to yourself, "We're having *the* relationship problems, it's just a moment in time, this too shall pass." This helps us enter into the big awareness of cosmic humor and compassion.

58
BUT YOU DIDN'T ASK *ME!* THE PROBLEM WITH UNILATERAL DECISIONS

A unilateral decision is when one person in a partnership of any kind makes a decision and acts on it without consulting the partner or others involved. People tend to make unilateral decisions when a sense of unity—of us—is lacking in the relationship. They also make unilateral decisions when they are afraid of "giving in," want their own way, or have no sense that win-win solutions exist. It is often a path to unnecessary hurt and conflict.

Unilateral decisions place people in a double bind, which essentially means that you feel damned if you do and damned if you don't, no matter how you respond. For example, if your boss *tells* you to work late when you have other plans, you are in a double bind. If you acquiesce to his or her demands, you are likely to get a stomachache, be angry, and have to break another appointment. If you stand up for yourself, you risk getting put down, losing your job, or being called difficult.

Unilateral decisions can be little things like turning on the car radio without asking the others in the car if they want the radio on, inviting someone over for dinner without consulting your partner, or moving a frying pan to a different cupboard without telling anyone. It can be big things like announcing that you are going to move or that you just bought a new car or you are leaving a relationship.

It's important that we avoid unnecessary unilateral decisions with children as well as with partners and friends. While
there are times when we must assert parental authority—"Yes,
you have to go to school"—much of the time we can elicit
cooperation by giving a child a voice in decisions. "Would you
like orange juice or apple juice?" Unilateral decisions can raise
havoc with teenagers. "I forbid you to see Charlie" is practically
an invitation to see Charlie. "No TV until you bring your grades
up" will result in kids sneaking out to watch TV or acquiescing
and taking the anger out in other ways.

Unilateral decision making often comes into play with gift
giving. The basic principle of gift giving is that a gift is a gift
when we give the person what they want—not the "gift" we
want or think they "should" have. In my family, if I asked for a
blue nightgown I was likely to get the "surprise" of pink paja-
mas. I remember many a Christmas morning feeling let down
and abandoned. I couldn't understand why they didn't give me
what I wanted. I faked being polite so they wouldn't call me
ungrateful, but my sadness and hurt led to feelings of depression and often resulted in my overeating. I remember vowing
that I would never do the same with my children.

Unilateral decisions are different from spontaneous surprises. If we know someone well and are tuned into their life,
it's lovely to surprise them with flowers, a book, clothing, a
card, or something we know they would enjoy. When two people are deeply bonded, they start being telepathic and can intuit
or know the other's tastes and preferences.

Unilateral decisions come out of fear, insensitivity, or a lack
of feeling bonded in a relationship. Making unilateral decisions
can be a conscious or an unconscious act. It can be done as a
way of asserting one's importance, expressing anger or to keep
chaos and drama exploding in a relationship so we don't have
to look at underlying issues or get close.

Making a unilateral decision is often a way of avoiding face-
to-face conflict with someone. Because we don't feel entitled to
pleasure or doing what we enjoy, we sneak off to do what we
want. We play the role of the naughty kid and set our partner

up as the mean or restrictive parent. This lack of integrity is harmful to relationships. If unilateral decisions are frequent, it's time to look underneath these feelings and explore the relationship bond. How much of it is grounded in two adults being together and how much of it is about people replaying scenes from childhood? Making decisions together can be a form of intimacy if we operate from the belief that we both care about each other's happiness and that in most situations there is a win-win solution. It doesn't mean we give up something that is important to us, it means our differences are overt and everyone knows what's going on.

Part of a true marriage is to think in terms of "us" when making decisions. It's doesn't mean we'll agree or that it will be easy, but when we show concern for our loved ones and are willing, we deepen our connection to self, spirit, and our beloved.

59

WHAT ARE WE TALKING ABOUT? SORTING OUT CONTENT FROM PROCESS

Sorting out content from process is like being able to see the forest *and* the trees instead of just the trees. Being able to observe the process of your conversation takes you beyond concrete facts to the essence of what is happening. The distinction is this: *Content is the subject you're discussing. Process is about the nature of an interaction.* For example, the content of a conversation might be arguing over *whether* you agreed to go out Friday night—"No, you're wrong, we didn't agree to go out Friday night." A process comment might be, "We're starting to argue and defend ourselves, let's back off and try to hear each other." It can be crucial to shift from content to process when we get stuck or start arguing.

Content and process are both important. If you only talk about content, you're likely to make narrow decisions or start bickering over details. If you only talk about process or essence, you might never get a decision made or take action. Generally, we need to start making plans by first naming the essence of what we want—to feel closer, to make a decision about something while being respectful of each other. We need to agree on our process of decision making. We each take turns presenting our ideas and make a consensus decision. Then we need to move to content—how many, when, what, where?

Over and over I see people getting caught in conversations in which one person is trying to talk at a process level and the other keeps going off into content/examples. One way to distinguish between content and process is to separate the subject of a conversation from the examples used to illustrate the subject. Here's an example:

Cathy is troubled about her relationship with Jeffrey. She feels a wall of distance between them and notices that they are not hugging anymore. She brings this up at a process level: "Jeffrey, I notice we're keeping a lot of distance. We don't hug each other anymore. I have the feeling something's not being said here." The subject is: distance in the relationship. The example is: We're not hugging anymore.

Instead of responding to the *subject* of distance in the relationship, Jeffrey responds at the *content* level by using her example. "I think you're right, I think we should hug more."

Cathy sighs. "I don't think you understand what I'm really talking about."

"Yeah, I do," Jeffrey responds anxiously. "We're talking about hugging more."

"No," Cathy says, "that's just an example. I'm concerned that we don't feel close."

"We were close the other night at the movie," Jeffrey responds, his anxiety level rising as he interprets any words of dissatisfaction as meaning he's done something wrong. What he doesn't realize is that his inability to hear the essence of what she is saying is likely to cause the demise of the relationship.

When people constantly get caught up in content, side issues, or examples, it's often because they fear conflict, feelings, or facing the reality of the situation. In the above example, Jeffrey had always been afraid that Cathy would leave him; when she brought up a problem, his fear turned into profound anxiety and he couldn't follow the conversation. In his mind, any kind of difference or displeasure meant the collapse of the friendship. As a result, instead of responding to her concern, he tried to convince her that everything was okay. This only made her feel more distant and hopeless about having an intimate conversation.

If you recognize yourself as acting like Jeffrey, keep reminding yourself that when someone brings up a concern, it's because they want to make things better. It doesn't mean you're bad or did anything wrong. Try to hear them and listen to their concern. Even though every part of you wants to defend, know that the relationship has the best chance of surviving if you can talk about problems and concerns. Believe me, I know. I was like Jeffrey. I remember forcing myself, over and over, to stay and listen to people's concerns. And much to my repeated amazement, instead of people going away, relationships got better.

In another example, Anya is temporarily staying with her friend Sandie. Anya is depressed and focuses on everything that is wrong in the world. The constant negativity is affecting Sandie, who decides to bring up the subject. "Anya, I'm having a hard time living with your negativity. It's starting to rub off on me. When you keep talking about all the teenage drug problems, I just want to run and hide."

The subject is: Sandie's discomfort with Anya's negative energy. The example is: extensive talking about teenage drug problems.

Anya responds to the example instead of the subject: "Well, the drug problem is very serious with teenagers, and I think you should be concerned."

Sandie responds, "I know the drug problem with teenagers is serious, but I need to talk about your being so negative in general."

Anya, feeling scared, says, "I don't know why we can't just get along and not get heavy. You just want someone who is happy and superficial all the time."

Sandie, realizing they are on a merry-go-round, doesn't take the bait but wisely brings the conversation back to the process level: "Anya, I'm frustrated in trying to talk with you because when I bring up a subject, you go off in a different direction or defend yourself. Are you feeling afraid?"

At this point, Anya takes a breath and instead of defending, she says, "Yes. I'm afraid you are going to ask me to leave."

Now they are connected and talking about the real issues at hand. In general, if a conversation is getting tangled up and not getting anywhere, come back to the process, as Sandie did: "We're stuck. We're getting irritable. Where did we lose each other?" Then take a moment and ask the following question: What is the subject of this conversation? You need to agree on what you're talking about.

Another process remark to bring a conversation back to center is to say, "I'm feeling confused, could we summarize what each of us has said so far?" Then it's up to everyone involved to reach inside and say what they are thinking or what is bothering them. Another type of a process remark is to notice the energy level. If it's gone flat, you might ask, "The energy just dropped. Is there something that's not being said?"

Another way to sort out process from content is to remember that process is often related to how we are feeling, while content is usually more about people, places, and things. In a very personal example, I remember telling two different people when I found out I had cancer. When I told Jim, an old friend from high school, I could hear a tender sigh over the phone as he paused and said, "I'm so sorry." His sigh and warm words conveyed great care and love. When I told my friend Ellie, I was barraged with questions: "Did you get a second opinion? When is your surgery? Are you sure it's cancer?" I felt myself getting distant and irritated. So instead of responding to these content questions, I moved the conversation to a process level. "Ellie, that's too many questions, I need to know how you feel." Her voice cracked and she started crying. "I feel terrible. I feel as if it's happening to me," she said. My body relaxed, and my heart connected with hers.

Having an easy flow from content to process is about listening to the essence of someone's words and not responding to their examples or getting sidetracked.

It's about tuning in on different levels, observing yourself and others, and being able to break in and say, "I think we're getting lost."

The same is true for organizations. If they would pay attention to process—to having a respectful flow of ideas and concerns to and from all sections of the organization—they would save time, money, improve the health of everyone, and lower stress. Reflecting on process is a way of saying that we're all equal here, we all have ideas and we need to work together in a respectful way. It takes us from a hierarchical, authoritarian stance to that of being in a circle, working together with concern for the well-being of everyone.

60

WARM ANGER, BURNING RAGE: HOW TO KNOW THE DIFFERENCE

*A*nger often gets a bad rap in New Age literature, the addiction field and spiritual teachings. People are encouraged not to get angry because it is said to be harmful. I believe that anger has an important place in relationships, but needs to be distinguished from rage and be expressed appropriately.

A rip of anger through the body can be a natural survival response to being invaded, threatened, or attacked. It says, "Look out! Danger!" Anger gives us boundaries. It says, "Someone's trying to con me or rip me off." You may even feel the back of your neck get tense or a flash of heat go through you as your adrenaline shoots up, preparing you to take action. Anger often signals that we need to set limits and take care of ourselves. It doesn't mean we attack or blame, it means we're aware of our feelings so we can act appropriately.

We need our anger response system to feel safe in the world. People who stay in abusive relationships often have had their natural response to danger programmed out of them in childhood. Sanctions against anger can come from the family and the culture including sex-role stereotypes—an angry woman is called a "bitch." As a result, people develop an intimidating internal censor that responds to any hint of anger with *Danger, Do Not Get Angry*. Instead of getting angry, we cry, get sick, or make excuses for the other person.

If we don't recognize our anger, it is likely to manifest in other ways: We may get confused, feel trapped, be super nice, have a headache, get rattled, make sarcastic remarks, get a tight stomach, become preoccupied, or get very ill. Some people start to feel dizzy, feel a nameless sense of terror, or want to hurt themselves when they start feeling angry. The first step when you have these symptoms is to ask yourself, "Am I angry?" If that feels too strong for your internal censor, ask yourself, "Am I irritated, put out, or upset?" You could also ask if you think you are being invaded, used, betrayed, or ripped off. If the answer is yes, you are probably angry beneath the surface even if you don't feel it directly. If you tend to deny your anger, notice if the anger is being reflected in violent dreams. It can be helpful to have a conversation with the internal anger censor. "Now look. I understand you squelched our anger as children to protect us, but it's all right now to get angry. It's a natural part of life."

My guidelines for expressing anger or discontent are to sort out your thoughts and be specific about what's bothering you.

The goal is to clear the air, not blast or hurt someone. A caring way to start is by acknowledging the value of the relationship: "I'm concerned about something and want to get clear so that we can feel close."

The basic formula for expressing anger or other feelings is this:

I felt angry_____ when you did/said_____.

Don't say, *You made me angry*. In reality, we make ourselves angry in reaction to what someone did or say. It is crucial to be specific. "I felt angry last Tuesday afternoon when you didn't call." "I feel angry that you are having an affair with George." "I feel angry that you are not contributing financially to this relationship."

Expressing anger appropriately is a learning process that requires timing and judgment. When you first start recognizing anger and expressing it, you might do it awkwardly, unskillfully, or lose your impetus and end up whispering or whining. But like all things, with practice it gets better. It takes a while for a mouse to roar. Even if you do it halfway, that's better than not doing it at all. To use a personal example, when I was going through intensive treatment for childhood neglect, strong feelings about being date-raped a decade earlier came back in full force. I decided to call the person and say how I felt. Much to my amazement, I found a phone number and reached him on the first call. When I got on the phone, he successfully side-tracked me about eight times, asking questions about my divorce or talking about his career as a social worker. I was able to say that he had hurt me and that I was angry even though my tone of voice sounded more like I was about to invite him to dinner. When I hung up the phone, I felt like I was part wonderful and part wimp. Even so, I felt tremendous relief.

NOW, TO DISTINGUISH ANGER FROM RAGE

Rage is usually triggered by shame. Shame is a deep, engulfing feeling of being defective, worthless, bad, or evil. If we are not willing to look at our shame, it often turns to rage. Here is the process: Something hits an emotional nerve—we feel exposed and tell ourselves we are bad, stupid, or wrong. We tell ourselves it's not okay to feel this way. This causes us to feel shame. To escape the dreaded feeling, we resort to rage—yelling, screaming, shaming, blaming, or being physically abusive to others. We might shoot daggers with our eyes or verbally hit below the belt.

Rage is not appropriate. It stings, wounds, and harms. It's a toxic invasion of the energy field of another person and doesn't deal with the real issues. It's like going on a binge. If someone is having a rage attack, the best thing is to get out of the line of fire. Don't try to reason with the person because they are too young to reason with. They are basically having a two-year-old's tantrum or feeling like a wounded animal protecting him or herself.

Rage attacks may reflect a lack of early bonding, neglect, or abuse. It can be a learned habit from a parent. If you are trying to give up a pattern of raging, take stock of how well you are able to connect with your own feelings and how often you blame external circumstances for your behavior. Blame or external referencing reflects your sense of powerlessness to get your needs met, express feelings, or take care of yourself. It's basically a victim stance of saying that the world is doing it to you, that you have no power.

If you have rage attacks and can't get them under control, get help. Unpredictable rage in a household leaves everyone walking on eggshells. It blocks intimacy and creates an atmosphere of fear. It often results in children having learning problems or becoming depressed, eating compulsively, having stomachaches, and on and on.

Rage explosions can operate like an addiction—some people use the term "rageaholics." People don't say what they need or feel, so the tension build ups and they explode. Rage is often associated with alcoholism and the abuse of other drugs that cause a shift in brain chemistry that removes inhibitions. Other times, one person is feeling immense frustration from being lonely due to a withdrawn or uncommunicative partner. I have worked with numerous female rageaholics. They often go unnoticed by professionals who do not think to bring up the subject with women who appear kind and friendly. If you have rage outbursts, be kind to yourself—they signal that part of you is hurting and feeling out of control. Which brings me to the next point.

As we come to balance in our lives, our anger will diminish. If we develop a sense of spirituality, choose loving friends, learn skills for intimacy, speak our truths, and develop compassion, there will be fewer occasions that trigger anger. This doesn't mean that we won't feel a flash of anger now and then, but we'll be able to stand back and observe it, not letting it take over and lead us to impulsive, hurtful behavior toward ourself or others. While we may feel angry, it won't separate us from wisdom or the ability to be thoughtful.

Paradoxically, it helps prevent anger when we know we have the strength within to defend and protect ourselves in the face of danger so that we feel safe in the world. When we have a self-respecting warrior within, we transmit a sense of power and self-respect that doesn't invite victimization. We need to develop a self-image that includes being both strong and gentle, angry and tender, powerful and kind.

61

EVERYONE CAN WIN: CONSENSUS PROBLEM SOLVING

Surely you would not honor one guest above the other; for he who is more mindful of one loses the love and the faith of both.
—Kahlil Gibran, *The Prophet*

*C*onsensus implies a commitment to a process in which everyone is heard and valued in the interest of unity. It is an exquisite process that integrates the needs of individuals with the needs for group cohesiveness. Indeed, the two are seen as inseparable. It's a structural way to take care of everyone so that no one has to fight to be heard. While our surface differences may take center stage in the beginning, as we go deeper we find common ground.

Consensus is a spiritual process because it puts human values before material goods or winning. Instead of making a decision, we collectively allow ourselves to be led to a solution by listening to others and listening deeply within. I feel deep gratitude to the Society of Friends, or Quakers, for all I have learned about consensus problem solving.

I spoke with Jeanine Walker, a longtime Quaker friend who is deeply grounded in the consensus process. She said, "Consensus asks us to go to a deep level, where unity is possible. Sometimes that means going really, really deep. It may take time, but when everyone is included in making a decision, they are likely to support each other in carrying it out. Consensus also helps deepen our individual inner unity—our head and heart connection. In Chinese writing there's a figure called 'shen,' which means heart and mind as one. That's what we seek with consensus. There's no separation the way there is in win-lose situations. That's why it feels so good. Whenever we have important things to do together, we need to get beyond win-lose."

Consensus problem solving is at the core of building a strong and vital community. As individuals we become more clearly defined within as we put all our thoughts and feelings on the table. We maintain the group integrity because it truly reflects all the members. It doesn't mean that everyone gets their way completely, nor does it mean that we go against our values, or give up our beliefs and values to please others. It means that by gathering together with love and respect for each other, we will be led by spirit to find a wise solution.

True leaders in a democratic system understand aspects of consensus. For example, right after an election it is customary for the one who lost to send congratulations to the winner. This gesture invites unity. Likewise, the winner asks whoever lost for their blessing and support in the hope of reuniting for a greater good.

Voting creates winners and losers: The resulting split often harms the sense of unity and connection in the group (or in the relationship) and leaves the "losers" feeling as if they have a score to settle. It's like breaking the circle. Consensus is hard for many people brought up valuing rugged individualism and the belief that people get what they deserve. Consensus implies that we are all important links in the circle and that our individual happiness and peace of mind depends on knowing that all people are cared for and respected.

On a simple level, consensus decision making might mean that you and I want to be together on a Friday night, but want to see different movies. Consensus requires that neither of us pressures the other to go to our movie. Likewise, we don't agree to a movie we don't want to see because that would violate our self. With consensus, we look for a movie we could both enjoy or we find something else to do. The task is to maintain unity and keep both of us happy.

It is a powerful experience to be part of a large group reaching consensus; it's like a force you can feel building. To give an example of consensus problem solving and a model that can be used in any organization, I will tell you about our Missoula Quaker meeting's decision to buy a meeting house instead of renting space from others. The group had been unable to reach consensus for two years or more. Some people wanted to buy a meeting house, others thought we weren't ready. Someone would bring up an issue and another person would disagree. Then someone commented that we had forgotten to use our Quaker process of consensus. A small committee of us got together and planned a special meeting. The outline was essentially to:

1. inform and include everyone
2. give everyone a chance to be heard completely
3. listen with our hearts

4. consider what was best for the unity of the meeting
5. pray together
6. say where we stood
7. see if we reached consensus

Everyone was informed of the meeting and was invited to send input if they couldn't attend. We started the gathering with a few minutes of silence to get centered and bring our presence into the circle. We were asked to listen to each other with our hearts and think in terms of everyone having a piece of the truth. We used a talking stick—a practice that comes from Native American tradition. The person who holds the stick is the only one to talk. All the others are to listen. We also asked for silent spaces between speaking. As people talked and others listened, you could see shifts occurring. One person spoke of worries about paying for a meeting house, but when someone presented a financial plan that seemed workable, their fears appeared to be allayed. Some people talked about the burdens of ownership, and others talked about contributing to the community by having a space organizations could use. We went around and around the circle as long as anyone had anything to say. There were no arguments or even discussion, rather, a circle of us reaching deep within to say our views, absorb what others were saying, and tune into the will of the group. There was a sense of birthing—a combination of struggle and a miraculous sense of moving together.

After the talking stick had gone around the circle several times and we felt a natural resting place, we each wrote our name on a piece of paper and put it face down in a pile in the middle of the room. This was to symbolize bringing ourselves together as a whole. Following this was a period of silence for each of us to listen for spiritual guidance to do what was best for the meeting. After the silence, people were invited to speak again. As they did, we could feel consensus building as more and more people felt clear about buying a meeting house. People who did not feel comfortable with the idea said things like, "I still don't feel right about it, but consensus is building and I will step aside in the interest of unity." There was a breathtaking moment when we passed the stick around the whole circle and no one had anything left to say. Several of us started smiling. Then one woman threw something in the air, jumped up, and said, "Hooray. We did it!" There was a jubilant feeling in the room. We won. We all won. We had pulled together as a community and agreed on a major step for the Meeting.

When one is accustomed to consensus problem solving, it feels painful when a group of people vote on a decision and the "losers" are left either hurting or mad. It seems so obvious that we need to make decisions in a unified way to prevent group divisions or later hostilities from taking place. In some cases groups use consensus minus one or two.

As you participate in a consensus process, you can ask yourself:

> Am I in agreement?

> Am I in partial disagreement, but is it better for the group to take this action than to take none?

> Am I in such disagreement that I must record my opinion and then stand aside in the interest of unity?

> Am I in such complete disagreement that I must block consensus?

If people have participated along the way, it would not be a surprise to the group for a person to block consensus because they would have been active in the process. Obviously, this process would not work if people have power needs to control or are not invested in unity. The process I have outlined draws from Quaker consensus process with a few adaptations of my own. You can modify the form to fit your situation.

Consensus becomes a way of life. It keeps us tuned into ourselves and the good of the whole. It leads to love because it helps us let go of ego demands, and see, over and over, that when we take everyone into consideration, we all feel better.

62

GOD IS IN THE DETAILS: CAREFUL PLANNING, FEWER CONFLICTS

Careful planning helps us prevent conflict. This could include planning how to spend a weekend, build a shed, have a potluck dinner, or make a major change in our lives. It also works in organizations and community groups.

Careful planning can be simple or complicated; ideally it helps people have a good time or accomplish the job at hand as smoothly as possible. I remember facilitating a therapy group that planned a marathon retreat. We took great care in planning the food, arranging rides, getting accurate maps, and so on. At the end of the retreat, a woman said, "You know, I was mad when we took so much time to plan this—I mean, that was therapy time—but I've learned something wonderful. Everything went so smoothly and everyone had what they needed. It freed us to focus on the work we came here to do."

When Harry and Sally attempted to plan their weekend, it would go like this: Sally would say, "I'd like to see the movie *Forrest Gump*." Harry would respond, "It didn't get a very good review." Harry would then say, "We should go to a basketball game," and Sally would say, "Basketball is boring." Every suggestion was met by a negative response, and most weekends disintegrated into putzing around the house, doing a bit of laundry, and watching TV. Sometimes Harry would go off to a basketball game while Sally stayed home feeling left out. It left them both feeling unfulfilled and frustrated. We worked on a process for making plans that stated the essence of what they wanted to experience together—a foundation that is often left out.

Here is a step-by-step plan for making plans. If you observe people who are adept at planning, you may notice that many of them naturally follow this procedure. It may seem a bit complicated or drawn out at first, but with practice it can become second nature.

1. Agree together on the essence of the experience you want.
2. Brainstorm ways to actualize the essence of what you want.
3. Each person presents their ideal plan/solution.
4. Note points of agreement.
5. Explore differences and gray areas.
6. Say the things you are not willing to do.
7. Ask if there are other considerations to be taken into account.
8. Make actual plans.

STEP 1. AGREE ON THE ESSENCE OF THE EXPERIENCE YOU WANT TOGETHER.

This crucial step respects the "us" of the relationship. It reflects the feeling we want to have together. It's difficult to keep people on this step because they want to get to the actual plan. Returning to Sally and Harry:

"What's the essence of what you would like to feel?" I asked.

Harry started out. "I don't want to get too frantic and try to do too much."

"Okay," I said, "could you say that in a positive way?"

With effort, Harry was finally able to say, "I want to relax and take time between doing things . . . I'd like to get outside."

Sally spoke. "I want to feel close. I'd also like to spend time with friends." Sally and Harry agreed that the essence of the experience they wanted was to be close, get some physical exercise, go at a relaxed pace, and spend some time with others.

STEP 2. BRAINSTORM WAYS TO ACTUALIZE THE ESSENCE OF WHAT YOU WANT.

The rules of brainstorming are that each person throws out ideas and no one contradicts, criticizes, or says why they wouldn't work. Each person says all the things they would like to do: "I'd like to hike up Pattee Canyon;" "I'd like to go to a basketball game;" "I'd like to play bridge with Elden and Nancy;" "I'd like a relaxing dinner and time to make love," and so on. Once the list is on the table they can move to the next step.

STEP 3. EACH PERSON PRESENTS THEIR PLAN/SOLUTION—IF THEY COULD HAVE IT ALL THEIR WAY.

Taking from the ideas put out, Harry and Sally separately described their ideal weekend plan. Sally and Harry both got excited letting themselves think of their dream day, their total heart's delight. After they put out their total plan, the next step was . . .

STEP 4. LIST THE POINTS OF AGREEMENT.

Once each person puts out their ideal plan, find the areas of agreement. Sally and Harry agreed on: eating out one night, taking a walk, calling some friends to see if they would like to join them either for the walk or for playing bridge, but not dinner. They wanted dinner to themselves, probably followed by lovemaking. Following that they went to . . .

STEP 5. EXPLORE DIFFERENCES AND GRAY AREAS.

There may be differences on the lists that could work out for both. The first step is to ask each other: Are there any things from my list that are of interest to you? Sally had listed a TV show that Harry said he could enjoy watching. Sally agreed that she could enjoy playing bridge with some friends.

STEP 6. SAY THE THINGS YOU'RE NOT WILLING TO DO.

The choice with points of disagreement is to let them go or do them separately or with others. No one is to coerce the other into doing what they want. Sally was not interested in going to a basketball game—and Harry was not interested in seeing a particular friend of Sally's or attending a Universalist Church service on Sunday. Because they had enough things they could enjoy doing together, they each decided to do one thing separately. They were then ready to move to . . .

STEP 7. ASK IF THERE ARE ANY OTHER CONSIDERATIONS TO TAKE INTO ACCOUNT.

This is where you make alternative plans. For example, if you plan a walk and it rains, what would you do instead? Sally and Harry also needed to fit in grocery shopping and doing the laundry, although they agreed that if need be, the laundry could wait.

STEP 8. MAKE THE ACTUAL PLANS WITH DATES AND TIMES AND OTHER LOGISTICS.

Talk over the plans, setting times and places. It can be helpful to write it out. Sally and Harry wrote out a complete plan, including time for quiet, time for grocery shopping, etc. The next week they came back and were very happy with the results. They felt rejuvenated by the weekend instead of frustrated that it had slipped away without their having any fun.

EXTRA GUIDELINES

1. If you get off track, go back to step 1 and talk about the essence of what you want to have happen.
2. Put everything in a positive statement. *I'd like to . . .* Don't say what you don't want to have happen or don't want to do.
3. Be honest. Do not agree to do something you don't want to do. Stay tuned into your gut and keep asking, Does this idea feel good to me?
4. When enacting the plan, if you suddenly feel overwhelmed or want to change plans, stop and talk it over. It's important to remember that nothing is etched in stone and the goal is to have a fulfilling time together.

For a couple who has been adrift or in conflict, sitting down and planning together in good faith can be a healing process in itself. If people make plans and they repeatedly fall apart or someone sabotages, it's time to look deeper and ask, What's going on here? Why do we keep pulling away? Are we being completely honest with each other?

Planning puts us in charge of our lives. It's like shoveling the snow out of the driveway so that you don't slip and slide every time you go out. It's like saying that life matters, let's help it happen. As a postscript to Sally and Harry's story, several months later, when I saw them again, Harry told me with great happiness that Sally had taken him to a basketball game on his birthday. She even enjoyed it. When I asked them about it, Sally said, "As we did more things together, I realized that Harry did want to be with me and that his love of basketball wasn't about not loving me. I started wanting to please him more and it was really fun surprising him with the basketball tickets." Planning had led to having fun together, which had increased the bond between them.

63

GETTING THROUGH CONFLICT

*I*n the previous section we talked about paying attention to details in making plans. Conflict resolution has many commonalities with problem solving, with a few additional components that I add here. If you are going to solve a conflict, read the above section and add the following steps. Sometimes if the issue is a hot one, it helps to have a third person or another couple to coach you and help you stick to the process.

In addition to the steps on problem solving you need to:

1. Affirm that no one will leave and that you will be respectful, stick to the process, listen to each other, and stay with it until you reach a win-win, livable solution. If you absolutely must

take time out, agree on a time when you will come back together.

2. Each person names the problem/conflict and includes feelings and thoughts. For example: "You have been late three times this week and I feel panic when this happens"; "We agreed to eat dinner together more often and you repeatedly made conflicting plans and I feel hurt and have withdrawn from you."

3. Own your part in creating the conflict/separateness. If you can step outside your ego and own your part in creating hurt or distance, it changes the atmosphere from combat to cooperation, from defensiveness to care. It's amazing what happens when people say things like, "I left the toilet seat up to get you" or "I stay away at dinner time because we end up arguing when we eat together." "I made a cutting remark about having sex because I was angry and wanted to hurt you." At the same time, don't take responsibility for things you didn't do, and don't manufacture something to keep things even.

4. Take time for silent reflection. If you haven't reached a point of connection or agreement, sit in silence for a few moments, allowing each person to listen internally to all the aspects of the concern. You might ask for help from the universe or pray in some way. Affirm with your whole being that there is a way to clear the air or come to an agreement and feel closer again. From that place of silence, tell each other any thoughts, concerns, or considerations that come to mind. Repeat what the other says. If nothing comes up, agree to take a break, spend time separately reflecting on the issue, and set a time to talk about it again.

5. Keep at it until a solution emerges. It may take time, but usually you will find some common ground. If you don't, you may need to agree to disagree or get professional help. There may be variations you will need to make on the above process to fit your particular situation. If you give it your best effort and reach an impasse that threatens the relationship, you are far more likely to part in peace with good wishes for the other person than if you had not gone through this process.

The main thing is to keep your mind open, continue to confront yourself, look for creative solutions, and have faith in the power of the spirit to lead you to a higher level of connection.

64

THE HANDY-DANDY CONFLICT HELPER: A QUANTUM LEAP

*H*ere's a quick helper that sometimes works wonders. I came upon it when working with a woman who complained bitterly about her life and her husband. While she was clearly miserable with him, she wouldn't initiate conversation or bring up her concerns. Any suggestion of leaving him resulted in twenty reasons as to why that was impossible. She trapped herself in a victimlike quagmire.

One day the thought came to mind, "This woman needs to make a quantum leap." So I asked her, "If you were an empowered, happy woman who cared about herself, what would you do?" She sat up erectly, and in a powerful voice I had never heard before, she said, "I'd leave the guy, get a better job, and start seeing more friends." Her eyes looked huge, as if she had surprised herself.

So I started using the approach in many situations. What would you do if you had complete faith in yourself? What would you do if you operated from your highest, wisest self? How would you two work this out if you were working together as a team? People almost always know the answer, which means that the problem is not the problem, but having faith in ourselves, loving ourselves, and allowing ourselves to speak from our wisest, highest self is the problem.

I have pondered this phenomenon from many perspectives

and keep coming back to the thought that we all know what is best for us, we all have power, and we all have God or spirit within us. We simply need to access that part of us so that we are led by wisdom and compassion.

We are moving into an era when people are able to make enormous changes by shifting their consciousness at will or by working with someone with these skills. I have seen people release trauma from childhood in a matter of hours by using Reiki healing circles—a form of channeling a high vibration of energy—trance work, and conscious breath work. I have seen miracles in healing that come from learning to transmit thought forms or transform our worries into energy. When we learn to shift to higher planes of consciousness, we begin to feel great awe as we experience the magnificent abilities we have within us for transformation.

PART VII

• • •

FRIENDS, NEIGHBORS, AND ROOMMATES

65

CALL OUT MY NAME: THE
WONDER OF FRIENDSHIPS

A faithful friend is the medicine of life.

—The Apocrypha 6:16

Good friendships are at the heart of a good life. We can live without a lover or a partner, but to live without friends is to walk a lonely journey. Good friendships can provide a comfort zone—a shoulder to cry on when we're lonely, a playmate for adventure, a hug when we've messed up, a comrade to join us in celebrating our joys. Friends can also challenge us to grow, and even though we move to different locations, sometimes thousands of miles apart, a friendship bond can remain as a warm reminder that we are loved.

Friendships challenge us spiritually, just as primary relationships do. We need to stretch our love and acceptance to accommodate each other's idiosyncrasies and deal with misunderstanding, jealousies, and divided loyalties. We need to maintain our own integrity and not sacrifice our values to preserve the relationship. Yet there is also an ease with friendships. Because they often lack the day-to-day intensity of a primary relationship, there's more time to come back and pick up the pieces of conflict and hurt. Because the commitment is less primary, we sometimes feel freer to show our vulnerability.

Like everything else, friendships can be impermanent. They begin, evolve, change, dissolve, and are sometimes reignited years later. I remember great feelings of excitement anticipating a rendezvous with my violinist friend, Henny, at the Amsterdam airport after fifteen years apart. We had perhaps exchanged three letters in all that time. But there we were, sitting in a coffee shop ten minutes after meeting, talking with excitement about our lives as if time had dissolved.

I did an informal survey with children and adults on friendship. I asked, "What comes to mind when you think of a good friend? What's it like to be with a good friend?" What struck me repeatedly was that people didn't describe friends in terms of accomplishments or riches, rather, they spoke of a special feeling they had when they were together: laughter, warmth, trust, ease, and comfort.

Here are some of the answers:

MOLLIE, AGE TEN:

"A friend makes you feel good. I can tell them anything."

SARA, AGE TWELVE:

(Pause) "I feel like going over to her house. I want to see her . . . A real friend is nice . . . and friendly—they're fun to be with."

MATT, AGE FOURTEEN:

"I think of somebody who will help you when you're in trouble. A friend will stick up for you and not talk behind your back. You don't forget them—like, if you move, you try to keep in touch."

"What's it like when you're with a friend?" I asked.

"It's uplifting, you're always having a good time. You aren't sad. You can tell things to a friend you can't tell to your family."

"What kinds of things?" I asked

(Pause, grin) "You can talk about girlfriends . . . other things."

"Do you have friends who are girls?"

"Yes . . . They're kind of the same—but they like to talk more than boys. With boys, it's more that you go out and do things. Go around and hang out. The talk is different. Boys try to be more manly and don't show their sensitive side."

"Is there someplace you talk about your sensitive side?"

"With family—and maybe a girl, sometimes, but mostly family. You don't do it around boys because you don't want to look like a sissy."

Matt was lucky, because most boys don't feel that comfortable talking to their families.

NATE, AGE FIFTEEN:

"A friend is a person who would influence you to do good. A person who cares how you feel and listens if you have a problem. A friend's a person you just like to be with—you feel like there's no care in the world, like you're free. You don't want to go home. You want it to last forever."

I asked Nate if it was different being friends with girls than boys. "You're more careful what you say around girls. It's not quite as easy." Then he laughed. "But guys change their stories more often—they're worried about their egos."

Nate said he had friends he could tell anything to. It turned out that two of his best friends were neighbors. I asked if being neighbors made a difference. "It makes a big difference," he said quickly. "It's easy to get together. You know the person better because you know how they live, what their family is like. You understand them better."

CARLA, A GOOD NEIGHBOR:

When I asked, "What comes to mind when you think about a good friend?" Carla paused and then responded.

"You know, that's really hard to put in words because it's so special . . . Let me see . . . It's someone who really sincerely cares about you and your interests. If you had a problem, they'd be there. Some people say they'd be there, but they wouldn't. A real friend would."

"Tell me what it's like being with a special friend."

"We can just talk and laugh and have fun. You can say, 'Hey, do you want to go downtown, and they say, 'Yeah, let's go.' I have a friend who lives out of town. We're both football fans. I love the Dallas Cowboys and she loves the Washington Redskins and when one's team loses the other sends a sympathy card or does something that makes you laugh. We collect little stuff for each other—little things I know she'd just love. There's a special way you know just what they like . . ." Then, as if interrupting herself, Carla said, "I'm starting to feel guilty because I just remembered I owe her a letter."

"What happens if you don't write for a long time?" I asked.

"Nothing," Carla said, relaxing. "She wouldn't say anything. She knows I'm busy . . . and how it's kind of hard for me to write."

I spoke with two adult men about friendships. They represented the changing generations although they were nearly the same age. One man, Jim, said that he didn't really get close to men that much, he found it much easier to talk with women. He'd go hunting with men and enjoy being out together, but . . . "Men don't really talk about themselves, about what they're feeling." His circle of intimacy was primarily with his immediate family. He adored his two young boys. "They just look at you and love you," he said. "They forgive you for everything." He spoke with great care about his wife, implying surprise that she loved him.

Another man, Jerry, was involved in several men's groups. He represented a new generation of men who are breaking through old stereotypes and learning to be intimate in new ways, particularly with each other. When I asked Jerry for his thoughts on friendship, he said, "I have a warm feeling in my belly. Then I think of sharing and trust."

We talked about his history with male friends. "I never used to have any," he said. "I was brought up as a narrow-minded Montana guy from the country. But I was never interested in cars, guns, and all that stuff that seemed like a male manifesto. I came across my current male friends through holistic health work. They were interested in growth and spirituality. It seemed like an unusual group, but now that I've been in several men's groups I'm realizing that there are a lot of men from every walk of life who are trying to open up and be more vulnerable and real."

As Jerry spoke I thought of the many times I had heard men bemoan not having a man to talk with in a heartfelt, personal way. My sense is that there are thousands of men longing to be more open with each other, but they're separated by the fear of looking foolish or being called a wimp or a queer.

I asked Jerry about taking the first step to open up. He said, "It really helps to have a forum to take the first step—like a men's group designed to have us talk about feelings." Jerry went on to say how good it felt not to be dependent on women for closeness and intimacy. His previously separate criteria for men and women friends had merged. "I want women friends who can be hiking buddies, and I want men friends I can talk with, no matter what we're doing."

He laughed. "I've also realized that not all women are great at talking about feelings, just as all men aren't blocked up and unable to talk about themselves. Most of all, I'm coming to appreciate how affirming and safe men can be."

Secure friendships where people "influence you to do good," as Nate said, are the building blocks of community—the connections that help us know we are not alone. This suggests that a cultural goal should be to foster communities in which children are taken care of so that they learn to trust in their lovableness. I love the African saying that Hillary Clinton used for her book title: *It Takes a Village to Raise a Child*. We could say, *It takes a good beginning in life to become a friend or to have a friend.* When we create hopelessness and despair in groups of people, we set the stage for bonding through gangs and violence.

Ultimately, friendship isn't just about finding a friend, although that's usually where we start. It's about being a good friend and then evolving into a friendly person so that we feel a sense of friendship or care for all people, known or unknown. Ultimately, being a friend means doing all we can to bring goodness into the world, and, to use a phrase from the Society of Friends, seeing that of God, in all people.

66

GETTING OVER PEOPLE FRIGHT: STAGES OF RELATING

*F*or many individuals, meeting new people carries tremendous discomfort and fear.

Will they like me? Will I fit in? If we are hoping to find a mate in life, we may be scanning all new people we meet as potential partners. Will I find Ms. or Mr. Right tonight?

There are three basic stances people take when they meet new people: victim, adult, and spirit.

STAGE 1. VICTIM STANCE. "DOES S/HE LIKE ME?"

You meet someone or walk into a gathering of people and think to yourself, "Will someone like me? Do I measure up? Am I doing it right?" You are essentially on the auction block, waiting for someone to approve of you. This stance creates tremendous anxiety, keeps us in a state of fear, and lowers self-confidence. It also leads to "performing," or possibly scarfing down too much food, grabbing a drink, or making a hasty exit. To get away from this stance, we can move to stage two.

STAGE 2. ADULT STANCE. "DO I LIKE HIM/HER?"

Instead of "Does she like me?" you ask, "Is there someone here who looks interesting to me?" or "Do I like this other person? Is she someone I want to get to know?" This means tuning into yourself, having opinions, looking around, and initiating contact. This is not to be mistaken with the predatory stance of saying, "Now who can I seduce tonight?" If this step creates fear, remember the third step.

STAGE 3. SPIRITUAL STANCE. "IS THERE A FIT?"

At this level, we surrender to the situation and let it unfold without expectations and judgment. You can calm yourself by saying, "I may meet someone here I enjoy, or I may not, and that's the way life is." This implies that we will find kindred spirits when they appear, and that nothing is do or die. Paradoxically, the more we relax, the more we will be interested in whomever we meet.

I have spent time in all three of these states. Thinking about the child state brings to mind one summer when I went to a week-long tennis camp. The first two days I could hardly hit the ball because I felt so out of place among all the country-club women with perfect fingernails, stylish hair, matching outfits, and totally clean tennis shoes. I felt acutely self-conscious in my T-shirt, shorts, and old tennis shoes. Of course, the clothes symbolized many other different values in our lives. To get over feeling self-conscious I went home, shaved my legs, and bought an outfit like theirs—well, sort of (I could never look like they did). I felt kind of silly, but at least I could relax and hit the tennis ball.

More recently, I was able to operate out of the second and third levels. I was invited to a party by some delightful people I had just met. When I arrived I didn't see anyone I knew and so I scanned the room to see if I felt drawn toward anyone. I noticed a woman in her late sixties who had a warm smile. I went over to her and said, "I don't know anyone here, and I never know what to say. . . . But you looked interesting and closest to my age." She laughed and said, "I never know what to say either." Then we got into an animated conversation and have been good friends ever since.

If you meet a friend or make a good connection, give thanks to the universe for the gift. If you don't make a heartfelt connection at any particular gathering, you can sit in silence and feel the energy or you can say hello to someone who looks uncomfortable. Remember, it's a moment in time—it's not crucial, it doesn't mean anything about your worth, and it's not a judgment on anyone else. There is total peace in this stance because you are not making any demands or judging anyone, including yourself. From this place of peace and expansiveness, it's far easier to go over to someone and initiate a conversation with them, remembering that underneath the surface, everyone has a story to tell.

67

I'M WALKING BESIDE YOU: RESPECTING OTHERS ON THEIR JOURNEYS

*V*ery often someone comes into therapy and says, "How can I get my son to feel better about himself?" or "How can I get my husband to be more introspective?" or "How can I get my wife to take herself more seriously?" The answer is, "You can't, and it's not your place to try." While it's fair game to bring up issues in relationships that affect our connection—keeping to agreements and talking respectfully—we are not here to change how others feel or tell them what to do with their lives. We are here to make our love bigger and more embracing, not to mold people to fit into our limited ability to love.

In friendships or in primary relationships, one of the biggest tangles we can get into is interfering with another person's journey. When you hear your mind start to plot changes for someone—"How can I get them to be different?"—stop and ask yourself, What is my motivation, where am I coming from? Whether we are aware of it or not, all of us are here to learn basic lessons about the meaning of life, work, love, joy, and death. Our role with loved ones and friends is a subtle dance between being a support and a helpmate but not getting in between a person and their life lessons.

The image to hold in your mind is that of walking beside another person—be it friend, lover, or neighbor. You can hold each other's hands, lean on each other, dance together, share stories, and help each other when in need, but you must not carry another person on your back. If you come across a log on the path, don't carry the other person over it. Let them use their own muscles or else they will atrophy. If a friend constantly creates financial problems in their lives, wish them luck but don't bail them out. If a loved one is going through a hard time, care for them but do not worry for them. If a person is experiencing grief, hold them, love them, but do not try to stop their tears. Just be there beside them.

Sometimes it is extremely difficult to accept people's ways of doing things. When my mother was diagnosed with angina, I wanted with all my heart for her to start exercising, improve her diet, and go to a health center to help change her negative lifestyle habits. My mother's way was to go to a traditional doctor, take increasing numbers of glycerine pills, and not change her lifestyle. I realized after coaxing and making suggestions to her that it was creating a lot of distance between us. With great sorrow I realized that she had the right to live and die her way. At first I felt abandoned, but I finally realized that it was *my* agenda that she stay alive so I could have a mother. It was *my* agenda that she exercise and change her diet because it would validate my beliefs. And, slowly, with tears, I let go. My mother died relatively young from a heart attack caused by angina, but our last phone conversation the day before she died was a happy one. She talked about her wonderful day—singing in the church choir, going on a picnic, and feeling loved. How sad it would have been if our last conversation had been tainted with me nagging her to be different and us both feeling irritated.

If you listen to your heart, you can learn to distinguish between being supportive of another person as opposed to interfering with their journey. When you are emotionally entangled with another person, you are likely to have intense feelings and be righteous, noble, or sentimental. You might think obsessively about them: "I just don't understand why she doesn't . . . " "If only he would . . . " "They'd be so much happier if they'd . . ." You might find yourself continually plotting ways to get them to follow your agenda, or constantly hinting about things they could do.

Another tip-off that you are intruding on another's journey is when you constantly worry about them. It is crucial that you not worry for another person, because the more you worry about someone, the less they will worry about themselves. If you worry for another, you are actually depriving them of the opportunity to face a tough situation and deal with it. Instead of worrying, you can pray for them, hold them in the light, as Quakers say, or offer to be of help if they need it—but let them ask.

Remember, underneath our attempts to control others is fear—fear of feelings, fear of anger, fear of loss. Controlling others by trying to "help" them when they don't want our help is usually a disguised way of saying we want or need something for ourselves: "I want you to be different so I'll feel good about myself." This reflects a lot of fusion or enmeshment in the relationship.

If your child has low self-esteem, love them with their low self-esteem. Listen to their feelings. Understand them. Don't try to change them. When you try to "help" someone feel happier so you'll feel better, you decrease their self-esteem because you are communicating the message that you don't love them the way they are. Your love is conditional upon them "doing better." It's easy to love someone who fits our models, the challenge is in loving people as they are. Letting go of agendas for other people brings us to a great "ahhh" of the spiritual journey where we give a big sigh, drop our shoulders, release our grip, and observe people with love and compassion as they tread on their path. It also enables us to bring our focus back to ourself and ask, "Why was I so busy worrying about them anyhow?"

I'll close with a story about an adventure that includes accepting differences. Last fall I wanted to learn about hunting. I figured if I ate meat, I should be connected to what it's really about. Our wonderful neighbor, Dave, agreed to take Jessie and me hunting. He was extremely helpful in loaning us guns, telling us what to wear, etc. He didn't make any cracks about us being women. We were an interesting sight on the morning of the hunt. Dave was leading us up the hill in his bright orange jacket with a patch on his sleeve saying 100% NRA (National Rifle Association). I am strongly opposed to the NRA. I was trailing behind, swinging a crystal on a chain to dowse the direction of the deer. Dowsing is about using various metal rods or a stone on a chain to divine the direction of water or anything the mind designates. Jessie went in the other direction with her rifle. I didn't bring up the topic of the NRA and Dave said nothing about me swinging my crystal. In fact, when I said, "Dave, I'm getting a reading that the deer are over the other way," he looked where I was pointing, didn't say a word and headed in that direction. We had a great day and came home with a buck. Jessie and I watched in awe at his amazing dexterity and skill in skinning the deer and getting it ready to be cut up. Gruesome, but amazing.

We'll probably be friends for a long time . . . and I may never bring up the topic of the NRA, and he may never ask me questions about dowsing with a crystal. One might say, "But shouldn't you try to talk about the NRA?" My response is, "Why?" I know what he'll say (he told me once) and I know what I'd say and that we'd butt heads and feel distant from each other. I value this relationship. If he asked, or there was an opening, I might tiptoe in. But otherwise, I think I'll just sit back and enjoy the whole show because I want to be friends, enjoy our times together, and feel love in my heart.

68

NEIGHBORS: A FRIEND IN DEED

To practice tolerance and live together in peace with one another as good neighbors . . . to unite our strength to maintain . . . peace and security . . .

—Charter of the United Nations

*W*ithin your gestures of care and love for your neighbors lie the seeds of peace for all the world. The quality of our lives is deeply impacted by the quality of our connections to our neighbors. The concept of neighborliness extends from the neighbor next door to our community to other countries. The principles are the same: cooperation, kindness, tolerance, and respect. Being a good neighbor is closely tied to many religions as a way of showing our love for God—*Love thy neighbor as thyself.* Loving our neighbors is often a reflection of our love for ourselves, although in some situations people show more respect and care for their neighbors than for their own families.

I have had neighbors who ranged from supportive to indifferent to hostile. I have lived in a boarding house, an apartment building, in working-class and middle-class neighborhoods, in racially integrated and all-white neighborhoods, in the inner city on a forty-foot lot, and on seven acres in the country. But no matter what the situation, the quality of relations with my neighbors has had a major impact on my life. Good neighbors contribute greatly to the day-to-day comfort of our lives. It's like living in a healthy ecosystem. We may not see them often, but knowing there is willing support and a friendly hello available softens the stresses of life.

There is a helpful quality associated with good neighbors—a willingness to be available. Sometimes it takes the form of tending each other's children after school, feeding each other's dogs and cats, borrowing a couple of eggs, helping push the car out of the snow, coming over in a time of trauma. I think of Carla, just down the road, a biblical scholar I have called many times to check references while writing this book.

Neighbors can play different roles in our lives. Some neighbors become longtime friends or an integral part of our lives. Others stay politely distant but let us know that we are welcome to call in time of need. Sometimes neighbors bond together, creating a sense of community by having annual block parties or celebrations together. Many have come together in neighborhoods to create social action to improve their neighborhood. And, sadly, some neighbors become antagonistic or spiteful toward each other. I'm not focusing on those negative aspects in this essay as we know them all too well. My intention is to remind ourselves of the importance of creating good-neighbor relationships.

A flood of memories pours through me as I think about the times neighbors have reached out to me. As a young child of seven, I remember a huge group of neighbors standing on the curb and waving good-bye to our family when we left Alexandria, Virginia, to move back to Montana. Years later, I remember an apartment neighbor in New York City bringing us half an apple pie shortly after I moved in with my three-year-old daughter. I remember a group of eight Quakers and their children appearing with a potluck dinner a couple of hours after I arrived at my new home in Montana. There was the man who sold medical insurance who sat at the dining table chatting for a long time about everything from pollution to tennis. This was followed the next day by a call from a man called Steve, the president of the local tennis group, inviting me to come play with them—he was friends with the insurance man and had heard that I was new to town.

When I asked people to tell about good-neighbor stories, it was like having a window opened into the extraordinary goodness of many people. I wish the principles of neighborliness and helping others would be as important in the media as someone getting shot or robbed: We need a front page *good-neighbor* column that highlights the magnificent care and support some people routinely give each other. We need to be reminded that small acts of kindness and care by ordinary people make a big difference in each other's lives.

Synonyms for "neighbors" are "to join," "to touch," or "to meet." One woman told of the neighbor across the hall in an apartment building who, like her, was a young mom. After the kids were in bed they would stand with the doors open and talk from their respective door openings. They might never have been good friends in another setting, but they shared commonalities through having children and by living in close proximity. I remember swapping child care for cooked casseroles with my neighbors in New York City. They'd arrive home with dinner prepared and I'd leave for an evening job teaching piano lessons while my daughter played happily next door.

Initiating or maintaining contact with neighbors sometimes takes effort because people tend to be very busy. In talking with an old neighbor in Minneapolis, she said, "You used to know all your neighbors because you met them when you hung out the wash. You'd chat for a few minutes and keep in touch." It's harder now to have that kind of casual contact because few people hang out the wash, and most of the women on the block have jobs outside the home. Others live in apartments or condominiums where they bump into each other at the mailbox or in the elevator, but that doesn't guarantee a connection. *Someone has to take the first step.*

It takes but one gesture of friendship to get a connection started—one phone call, one knock at the door, one little greeting card, one small present of flowers, cookies, or a small plant. Some people may reciprocate, others may not. Even so, many will be touched by your gesture. If you're uneasy about reaching out, think of it as an adventure—it's nice when it works out, and if it works out 50 percent of the time, that's not bad. If you never try, you get 0 percent.

When reaching out to connect to neighbors, a guideline is to go slowly, don't press to be close friends, talk about the things you have in common, and avoid religion and politics if you have strong differences. While it can be important to connect with close friends on a spiritual and philosophical level, it's not necessary with neighbors. We can have warm, supportive relationships without agreeing on many issues. Differences might make their way into the conversation after several years, and they might never come up. Conversations with neighbors often center more around children, the garden, how things are going on the job, the recent leak in the roof, the best place to buy tires, and the frustrations of trying to get everything done.

Reaching out is infectious. If one person reaches out to connect, it sometimes gets a chain of connections going—connections within us and between us. I smile as I remember a summer night a couple of years ago. I was trying to get the top down on my pop-up tent camper and couldn't do it alone. I called Lorraine, my neighbor up the hill, and asked, "Do you have some kid power around to help me get my trailer top down tight?"

"Do you need one or two?" she said, laughing.

"Well . . ." (I didn't want to seem greedy) "Two would be nice, although I could probably do it with one." A few minutes later, in the warm dusky evening, I could hear laughter and footsteps coming down the dirt road to my house. As their forms came to light, there were five kids and four dogs—the Moe Road neighborhood gang. They were laughing and joking. They jumped on top of the trailer and it was down in a minute. It was like having a party of elves come to take care of me. We gabbed about new bikes, camping, and other stuff for a while and then they ambled off down the drive—the little enclave that had brought my heart delight.

Neighborliness is a metaphor for creating peace and bridging differences. Peace on the planet is a grassroots effort that we do day by day, one by one. One time when I was in a Vietnamese grocery store near my house in Minneapolis, I took a moment to look at the woman at the checkout counter who apparently owned the store. I looked at her and wondered what it would be like to come from such a different culture.

"How is it going for you here?" I said.

"Pretty good," she said with a smile, looking right at me.

"It must be something to move here from so far away. Do you mind if I ask you what's it like to be here for you?" I said, moving beyond the usual parameters of our contact.

"It is something!" she said with a burst of energy. "I'm like two people—the one who lived over there and the one who lives here. I lost my sister, my mother, my father, and my brother. But now I am here and we are doing well." She continued talking about her past. I was stunned inside, almost breathless imagining what she had endured. After a few minutes, a new customer walked in the store. There was a pause as she smiled at me.

"I admire your courage and wish you all the best," I said as our eyes caught each other's for a fleeting moment that signified our recognition that we had crossed a bridge together. Those moments with her—the words and the feelings—are with me today. Connecting with people in a caring way can turn any day into a special day. The jewels of life are right here, in the grocery store, the waiting room, at the bus stop, next door.

69

THE FLEETING FAMILY UNIT— ROOMMATES AND HOUSEMATES

At one time, having roommates was thought of as something for people just out of high school or college students. With the rising cost of living and the shortage of living space, the prevalence of people having roommates and housemates has expanded to include couples, professionals, divorced people,

and older people who want to stay in their homes. This sometimes includes friends buying a home together to have a sense
of community and ease the stresses of home maintenance. A
friend of mine, a widowed woman in her sixties who bought a
house with two other women, said it has been the happiest
time in her life.

I have shared a duplex or had roommates numerous times
my adult life. It's been a way to share child care, pay the bills,
and have someone around to say hello at the end of a day. Just
hearing the familiar noises of someone climbing the stairs to
their apartment above is comforting to me. Occasionally roommates or housemates have become good friends. Other times it
doesn't go deeper than being pleasant or okay, but it means
having company, someone to feed the cats and water plants
while I'm away. Every roommate has given me a window into
another person's life. It's fascinating to me.

I asked my roommate Mary why she likes sharing a house
instead of living alone. "It feels stable," she said with a laugh.

"Stable?" I asked

"Yes, you're . . . normal."

"Normal!" I said with surprise. "How so?"

"You eat and sleep. . . . You're steady, which helps me feel
more grounded." She went on to explain that in her family
there was a constant threat of people falling apart and going
crazy at the slightest provocation. Along with rarely having
been called "normal" before, I like living with Mary because of
her friendly nature, openness about her life, ability to talk politics and feminism, and dazzling, creative outfits. I like it when
she joins us for soup on a chilly winter evening.

Coming together to be roommates is quite amazing when
you stop to think about it. In many cases, deciding to share a
household is based on a half-hour meeting and checking out a
few references. It's a great test of intuition and judgment, and
the willingness to make a mistake. It also takes the strength to
be able to say, "This isn't working," and agree that someone
needs to leave.

One reason I like the idea of housemates and roommates is

that it's ecologically friendly. We save resources when we share a kitchen, washer, dryer, furnace with four people rather than with two. It also contributes to the community by providing a nice place for people at a reasonable price. When we cluster together, it leaves more room for natural, open spaces.

Beyond efficiency and companionship, for me, having housemates is like a spiritual practice. It's about knowing myself, being clear, and learning to value relationships above material goods. For example, I happen to own a lot of nice dishes—it's a strange story and I'll spare you the details—and I decided some time ago to put them in the everyday cupboard and use them regularly. That means that every now and then a beautiful dish gets broken. It's been a good step for me to use them, enjoy them, share them, and let them go when they break.

The spiritual practice of sharing space is also about learning to be true to oneself—to listen, be open, be respectful, and set limits. It requires the discipline of keeping communal space cleaned up, of ending a conversation and getting to work, of going to one's room and having quiet time when needed, of reaching out for kindness and support on occasion. It requires being clear about expectations, which means being clear about oneself.

Another crucial aspect of sharing space—be it lover, house-mate, or friend—is to be aware of our issues with authority figures so we don't project them on to each other and act like defiant adolescents by not cleaning up the kitchen, paying the rent on time, keeping track of phone bills (everyone has their own phone line here), and being respectful.

A good roommate is usually someone with roommate experience. It's the same as having practice with anything else. At best, people learn to be comfortable around others, sensitive to others' needs for space and quiet, and able to set limits for themselves. People learn to negotiate space, time, and having friends over. Good roommates understand the roommate contract, which is a bit tricky because it's partly a business deal but very intimate at the same time. We'll be sharing a kitchen, and possibly a bathroom, laundry, etc. We'll be talking with each other and getting acquainted, yet we deal with finances together.

If you are going to share space with people, you need to be able to make mistakes, own up to it, and move on . . . or out. Deciding to share space with someone is like many decisions we make—we don't have sufficient data until we've tried it. It's not a personal failure if it doesn't work out, it means we have something to learn. I've certainly made my share of mistakes, yet looking back, every one of them related to not listening clearly to myself.

Many people have extreme fears about sharing their living space with a stranger—you never know who you'll get. What if they're dangerous? It can be interesting to explore these fears. Often they come from the small person inside us who fears being overwhelmed by others and has no confidence in his ability to make clear judgments or set limits—such as saying, "No, I don't think we'd be a good fit." When you meet people and talk for a while you usually have a good idea if they feel right, especially if you listen to yourself. The challenge is to follow through on your feelings and not move in with someone if there is doubt.

I referred to this section as "the fleeting family unit." With the frequent disintegration of marriages, families, and extended families, people are often isolated and short of money. While we cannot replace our original family, and many of us wouldn't want to, we can have a family feeling with others, even if it's for a short time. We can have someone to talk to, learn how others live, cook, and deal with life's problems. It's a good practice ground for intimate relationships and living in community. It helps us expand our world, learn to define ourselves, be good at sharing space, negotiating our needs, letting go of control . . . and expanding our love.

70

AM I BEING A BOTHER OR A FRIEND?

*H*ave you ever said to yourself, I don't know if I should call so and so because I don't want to bother her. Or, you call wondering if the other person really wants to talk with you. The solution is simple—ask them.

While asking others what they want may seem simple, it often eludes people. It's as simple as saying, "Is this a good time to call?" "Are you up for helping me think through a problem I'm having?" In times of birth, death, sickness, or celebrations, people often withdraw, not because they don't care, but because they feel awkward and don't know what to do. Because you can never know for sure what different people want at a given time, the only way to find out is to ask. You can even tell the other person of your fear: "Hi, Aya, I feel awkward calling because I don't want to be a bother—but I heard you were going through a hard time and I wondered if there was anything I could do." At that point, Aya can pick up on the conversation and lead it forward.

I had a very touching exchange with my neighbor Carla on this subject. Shortly after her daughter's boyfriend had been killed in a car accident, in which her daughter and son were injured, I went to their house with some flowers. Carla's bright, warm greeting came as something of a surprise because I was expecting everyone to be morose. "I've sure learned a lot from this," she said. "When friends of the kids were in the hospital or having a difficult time and my kids wanted to go, I used to say, 'Now don't go bother them, they're going through enough right now.' Well, I feel badly I ever said that, and I'll never say it again. It's been awesome with all these kids stopping by. It's great seeing them together talking it out, and it's been a comfort to me. I'm the kind that feels better if I talk about things."

Several months later Carla talked about how the experience had helped her step through her reticence and call a woman who had just lost her son. "I used to hesitate, but now it's easier to call. You know that boy who just got killed?" she asked. "I called his mother and we went out to dinner. I started talking about how Daniel's death felt to me, and then she started talking about her son. She said, 'It's so comforting to talk to someone about all my memories of him and all the neat things he did.' She was really glad I called."

One of the biggest blocks to reaching out is our own lack of self-confidence: "They don't need me. I'm not important enough to be of help to someone." "What if they're busy?" "What would I say?" We get lost in our own fears. If you get locked into fear, think of times when people have reached out to you, or imagine how you might feel in their situation. If you can reach through the boundaries of your own fearful world, you will learn that you have much to give others. You don't have to be polished or know the right things to say, you simply need to speak simply from your own heart and ask them what would be helpful.

When my sister, Lenore, was dying, I was feeling morose and sad. When several of us were in her room at the hospital, I asked her what she wanted and she asked us to sing "You Are My Sunshine." That was helpful to me because I was feeling full of grief and sadness, which wasn't what she needed to hear about. She wanted songs, stories, jokes, and playfulness, which brings me to the other side of the equation.

If someone asks you if they are being a bother, be honest and give specifics. "I'm glad you called but I'm busy right now, can we set a later time?" "Yes, I've got about ten minutes to talk." "You're no bother, I'm honored that you called." If you are going through a trauma or a change, you can help your friends by letting them know what you need. When I got divorced, I let my friends know I loved to hear from them, I enjoyed being included in dinner parties even without a date, it was okay if they mentioned my husband's name, and, no, I didn't want to be at a small party with him.

You can also let your friends know there are areas of your life you don't want to discuss. "Please don't ask me about my troubled daughter, I'm trying not to dwell on her." Often a troubled or bereaved person doesn't want us to be heavy and deep with them. Two children whose mother died suddenly said, "I hate it when people keep saying in a heavy tone of voice, 'I'm *so* sorry for you, how *are* you doing?' I just want to be treated as normal." We talked about ways in which they could tell their friends not to ask about their mother. Which brings up one last example—the negative impact of saying nothing because you fear being a bother. It came to light in a therapy session with my mother. I told her I felt hurt because she rarely invited me to visit her—although she always seemed glad when I came for a visit. My mother looked astonished. With a bit of work, the therapist figured out the misunderstanding. She said, "I think I've got it. Here's Mary on one end of the phone, not wanting to seem pushy or like she's intruding on you. There's you, Charlotte, on the other end of the phone wondering if she even cares. Mary, why don't you tell her what you would like?" At that point, my mother burst into tears and said, "How could you ever think I don't want you to visit?" But I honestly couldn't tell. Misunderstandings like this abound in the world. People make assumptions about others, try not to be a bother or a bore, and, as a result, people feel left out, hurt, or abandoned.

While you can never know what people want, it is far better to call someone and have them say "I'd rather be left alone" than have someone feel left alone and abandoned in a difficult time. It will also help you learn that you are of value to others just the way you are.

71

ON THE OUTSIDE LOOKING IN: THE PROBLEM WITH "WHAT HE/SHE DID" STORIES

When someone disappoints us, doesn't fulfill our expectations, or has hurt us, we sometimes want to retaliate by telling stories about them—depicting them as the jerk, the fool, the selfish or crazy one. We might roll our eyes behind their back, mock them or gossip about them to others. It can feel especially delicious to draw people into our sorry plight and hear a sympathetic "poor you." While it's understandable to want compassion when we feel hurt, if we repeatedly say, "Can you believe what s/he did (to me)" stories, we will stay stuck inside ourselves and in our relationship. We are essentially posturing ourself as a victim when we act as if we had no part in creating a situation and have no power to change it.

Mocking someone or feeling righteous about their behavior is usually an indirect way of expressing irritation, anger, and fear. Looking beneath our impulse to tell "Can you believe what s/he did" stories can bring a wealth of inner growth. Almost always we will find that we did not take care of ourselves, set limits, or express our feelings honestly.

To explore your motivation, you can ask yourself: "What am *I* feeling about this situation?" "What fuels my desire to talk about this other person or put them down to others?" "Why do I keep acting surprised when they do the same thing over and over again?" "What is my fear of being direct and honest?" Our self-exploration will almost always involve an investigation of our own dependency. Why are we staying around someone for whom we have so much disdain? At the depth of the exploration we might well see ourselves in them. So often the behaviors that irritate the most are the parts of ourselves we reject.

It's important to realize that when we repeatedly talk about another person or fear talking to them directly, we are the one with the problem. We are upset, afraid, and lacking faith in ourselves. It's our gut that is aching, our sleep that is being interrupted, and our body that carries the anger and resentment.

Once we have done our inner exploration, our growth lies in becoming honest with ourself and with the other person instead of talking behind their back or mocking them. It may feel like stepping into a fire because it challenges the part of us that played it safe by avoiding direct confrontation and honesty. Yet only by passing through this fire can we again break bread together with compassion and care for each other. Otherwise we remain as a frightened child.

Often the walk through the fire of honesty means ripping through profound layers of guilt. We were taught that speaking our displeasure or taking care of ourselves is mean or selfish. Yet, in reality, being directly honest protects the relationship . . . or helps you find out if it has a foundation for growth. It takes courage to be direct and stop sidestepping issues. It also takes faith to believe that by being honest you can live with the outcome, even if it means the collapse of a relationship. If you have done all you can to be honest and speak from your heart, you will be more able to wish each other well and go on your separate journeys.

If you are on the receiving end of *what s/he did to me* stories, remember that colluding will drain your energy and perpetuate the other's victim stance. You can put the responsibility back in the other's lap with messages that convey that they have the ability to deal with the problem: "That's tough, I sure wish you luck in dealing with that" or "Have you thought about what you are going to do?" You might decide you no longer want to hear about this problem. "I care about you, but I don't want to hear about what X is doing anymore." In *Daughters of Copperwoman*, Anne Cameron talks about a Native

Women's talking circle. After someone had brought up the same tired old story three times and done nothing to make change, the women simply got up and moved the circle. This gave the message that the person had taken enough of everyone's energy and it was time to *do* something rather than complain. *Remember, when you keep listening to tales of woe, you are as stuck as the person who continues to complain and do nothing.* You are in a symbiotic, enmeshed system that will prevent both of you from growing.

Staying honest in our relationships is core to the spiritual path. If you continue to be a sounding board, or feign friendship when you feel resentful, ultimately you may want to slam the door. It is far kinder and truer to your own heart to be honest along the way—risking conflict, difficulty and pain—than to stay in the false comfort of calm waters while below the surface you turn into a shark wanting blood.

72

BREAKING IN AND SIGNING OFF . . . OVERCOMING PHONE TYRANNY

*T*he phone was invented as a convenience. Unfortunately, it sometimes becomes a tyrant because we allow ourselves to become slaves to it. People play out their lifestyles in relationship to the phone—constant interruptions, not setting limits, and always waiting for the next call instead of living now.

A common scenario: Jan and Ellie are spending an evening together having dinner and catching up on old times when an old friend of Jan's calls. Without checking to see if it's a good time to talk, Melba launches into the unexpurgated details of her new love life. Jan gets paralyzed and doesn't say anything. She makes faces at the phone while Ellie looks on, amused at first, then irritated after twenty minutes go by and dinner has gotten cold. After Jan finally gets off the phone, she apologizes but says lamely, "Well, what could I do? She just kept talking."

There's a lot she could have done. The answer is interrupt, cut in, and take care of herself—or else don't answer the phone in the first place. It's like a chain of people being inconsiderate—it was inconsiderate of Melba to start talking without checking to see if Jan was free, and it was inconsiderate of Jan to take so much time away from Ellie during dinner. Jan could have cut in and said, "Melba, excuse me for cutting in. I'm glad you've called and I'd love to talk to you sometime, but right now I have company. Can we set another time?" No one has to be a victim to the phone.

It's amazing how many people feel that they absolutely must answer the phone if it rings. I was talking with a client who said she was exhausted because people kept calling as late as eleven and she needed to be asleep by nine-thirty. "Why don't you turn off the phone?" I asked.

"If one of my kids [all over thirty] had an accident and called—I'd want to be there." This belies a worried mind and heart living in fear rather than feeling a right to take care of herself. It also belies the illusion that you have control over situations.

My thought is that if someone dies, they'll still be dead in the morning. I need my sleep. I can't live my life wondering *what if*. People lived without phones for thousands of years. And for the most part, people don't want to wake you up or disturb you.

I remember another time when a group of us were sitting out in a friend's backyard on a heavenly summer day talking and eating together. There was wonderful chemistry between us and we were in the middle of a real conversation when the tyrant bells beckoned from afar. My friend, who had invited us over, leapt out of her chair as if summoned by God and completely broke the ambiance as she rushed to the house.

Later, when someone asked, "Were you expecting some-one?" she said, casually, "No." It's as if people turn into little children when the phone rings. I wonder who they think is calling. Their fairy godmother? Someone giving away a million dollars?

Breaking a connection with someone—or yourself for that matter—to answer the phone reflects our linear lives, which stay on the surface and seldom go deep. Our phone habits become a metaphor for our lifestyles. We make our lives breathless with constant interruptions and keep our minds pointed to the future for the "next call," the better lover, the new friends, or winning the lottery. We forget to treat the cur-rent moment as if it truly matters. It reflects a fear of connec-tion and intimacy that come from being completely present in the moment, allowing ourselves to go deeper and deeper into our hearts.

I remember coming to the dinner table with two room-mates who both brought their portable phones with them—so they wouldn't miss a call. My phone line was nearby. At one level, I can understand this, and we even laughed about being the modern family, but it definitely put others ahead of our shared time having dinner. I felt reticent to engage in conversa-tion because there was always the threat of being interrupted by a phone call. It's as if any conversation we might have had was not as important as someone who might inadvertently call.

There are also times when we're just not in the mood to talk to anyone. We can turn on the answering machine and wait until a time that feels right to call back. Keep remember-ing, the phone was created to be a convenience, not a tyrant. And many of the phone calls people get don't ever need an answer. "Your order is in at Sears;" "The community meeting is at seven-thirty Wednesday."

If you have a good friend who is seriously hooked on answering the phone, don't expect them to change—people who have this malaise usually have a strong case of it. If some-one repeatedly interrupts your visits to their home with phone conversations, ask them to come over to your house, take a hike together, or go to a restaurant so you can have their undivided attention.

Imagine what it would be like to give your family and friends your complete attention when you are with them. What would it be like to forget about the phone when friends are over or you are spending time with your children? (You can turn it down or put on the answering machine so you don't hear it.) If it's important, people will call again. If you have an answering machine you can call back later. Life will become less frenetic and your connections will deepen. It meant so much to my daughter when I turned the phone off at her bedtime to read a story and chat without interruption. "My time," she would say happily.

73

STAYING AS A PEER WITH PARTNERS AND FRIENDS, OR, WHY RESCUERS GET CLOBBERED

To have fulfilling, enjoyable relationships we need to meet each other as peers. Being peers means that we meet each other eye to eye, speaking from our heart, saying what's true and listening to the other without taking a one-up or one-down stance. We operate from the center of our being, giving and receiving without expectations and demands of each other.

Our sex role stereotyping sets heterosexual couples up for the rescuer-rescued collusion. Men are conditioned to be the knight in shining armor—the rescuers—and women are conditioned to be the princess in need of rescuing. While we have moved away from this stereotype to some degree, the residual programming from thousands of years lives on. This results in symbiotic marriages that reinforce people denying aspects of self: The knight in shining armor hides his fears and dependency needs and the fragile princess hides her power and strength. This results in a conscious marriage between the strong knight and the fragile princess, and an unconscious marriage between the dependent prince and strong princess.

EXAMPLES OF BEING ONE UP.

We take a one-up stance when we give advice, pontificate, make patronizing remarks, analyze others, defend ourselves, announce the rules, refuse to apologize, or act as if we're above life's problems—"I've never felt that way" or "I got over that a long time ago." The one-up person rarely exposes their vulnerability or talks about feelings.

EXAMPLES OF BEING ONE DOWN.

We position ourselves as one down when we ask for advice, pet the other's ego, feel guilty, be sweet and charming or super helpful, always listen but don't talk about ourselves, blindly follow the rules, make excuses, avoid conflict, don't ask for what we want or don't say how we feel—particularly when we're angry. We might also act like a chameleon, trying to fit the other person's desired image.

It's easy for our egos to get snookered into being either one up or one down. Thoughts of being admired as the wise one draw us into the one-up stance. Being one down brings the illusion of safety and security—someone to protect us and take care of us. Assuming a one-up position is really a smoke screen for our fears of being vulnerable and open; being in a one-down position is a fear of our self-identity and power. The starting point is to observe ourselves kindly when we take on these roles, having mercy for the wounds that send us fleeing from our authentic selves. We can become aware of the temporary comfort of playing a role and the long-term sense of separation we feel.

When we take on a one-up role as advice-giver or wise one, we place the other person in a double bind. If they accept us as the seer, they deny their own wisdom. If they don't want to play one down to us, they need to defy us to assert their autonomy: "Don't tell me what to do." This usually leads to conflict. Likewise, when we take a one-down role, we ask the other person to assume a wise, parental role with us, or risk our well-honed ability to cause them to feel guilt for leaving us to confront our pain or be responsible for ourselves.

When we play one up or one down with others, it's like sitting on a teeter-totter: We meet eye to eye for a flash before going up or down in opposite directions, constantly keeping distance from each other. If we know how to play one role, we usually know how to play the other. It might switch throughout the day as we act subservient to our supervisor at work, then come home and boss our partner around. In either role, we end up being lonely.

To be a peer, we need to stay focused on our feelings and hopes, speak truthfully, and let go of the outcome. From this position, we can speak as a peer. For example, if your partner drinks a lot every evening, a one-up stance would be to give a lecture on the perils of alcoholism. However, as a peer you might say, "When you drink, I feel left out and cut off from you. I feel jealous of the alcohol. I want you to be here with me."

A peer stance always includes your feelings and your needs rather than lectures about what's good for the other person. If we have a strong reaction to what someone says, instead of telling them what to do, we could say, "I'm having a huge reaction to what you're saying. Do you want to hear it?" or "Do you want my thoughts on the situation?" In this way we are not barging in without permission. We are speaking as a peer.

When people try to entice us into being the wise one or seer by asking advice, we can say, "I don't have any advice, but I'd be willing to explore that with you" or "What have you thought about as possible solutions?" In the process of moving toward this place of intimacy, we can note how it feels in our body and in our heart.

If you tend to take a one-up position and rush in and rescue people, assume that you need some rescuing yourself. It is likely, very likely, that you have a little hurt person hidden inside that needs some tender, loving care. Ask yourself: What am I giving the other person that I really need for myself? Rescuing people serves the purpose of denying our needs and keeping our focus on others, thus staying in hurtful relationships. I can't leave because s/he needs me so much.

People who rescue can be very indignant if you suggest they might have a hidden agenda underneath their magnanimous exterior. "Well, aren't you supposed to reach out a hand and help people!!" "Isn't that the Christian way?" The answer is yes and no. Sure, we need to reach out a hand to others, but rescuers look for frogs to rescue. They are doing it for their own ego needs, and are actually encouraging the dependency of others. That's far different from giving the milk of human kindness from an open heart.

If you seek to be rescued, remember that no one can give you power and strength, you need to find it for yourself. You may attract a lot of rescuers when you transmit a sense of being fragile and needy, but you won't create peer relationships. Within you is a well of wisdom waiting to be tapped.

If the only way you've ever gotten attention is by being needy or subservient, you may have to learn by experience that you can get attention as a powerful, strong person.

If either person in a relationship stops playing the one-up or one-down role, the system will have to change. That's because by changing, you break the symbiotic tie and take away the role of the other person. This forces them to confront themselves or leave. For example, instead of the one-up person saying, "You should get exercise, eat better and get a better job so you won't feel so depressed," he might say, "I'm lonely in this relationship. I want to live with someone who isn't depressed all the time, who's fun to be with, someone who contributes to the marriage." This challenges the other person if they want to keep the relationship. Likewise, if the one-down person starts to find interests of her own and says no to advice, the one-up person loses his or her teacher/rescuer role and has to confront his or her own emptiness.

Being a peer doesn't preclude teaching each other, being helpful, or sharing our wisdom. From a peer level, our motivation is to connect as equals, with open hearts. The ego does not have a covert agenda. For example, my partner, a geologist, often explains rock formations and the history of the land when we're hiking or canoeing. She has taught me how to canoe and backpack. I am in awe of her knowledge. Similarly, I might teach her how to cook. The stance of one up or one down is often determined more by our motivation than the actual act. If someone is ill or hurting, we take a one-up stance when we give to them while feeling noble or superior, and a peer stance when we simply *be* with them in their pain. It's the difference between doing and being.

Now to explain why rescuers sometimes get clobbered . . . or left. The one seeking to be rescued unconsciously wants the other to play a parental role. But what do kids do when they grow up? They rebel against their parents and leave home. Deeper than our fragile victim side lies a human spirit that wants dignity and self-respect. The compliant side may listen intently to the rescuer's pearls of wisdom, but sooner or later their defiant side is likely to surface with a roar: *Don't tell me what to do!!* If the rescuer and rescuee are in a primary relationship, this symbiotic type of parent-child collusion results in an incestuous feeling. This often kills off sexual desire.

In response to the roar of "Don't tell me what to do," the rescuer feels shunned, gets angry, or lays on the guilt. "After all I've done for you, how could you do this to me?" The answer is, "Easy, it happens all the time."

LIFE LESSON 101:

Don't rescue people. Don't fix people. Don't be a martyr.

Be a friend, buddy, playmate, peer, a fellow seeker, and another imperfect person dancing with your loved ones and friends on the path.

74

ALLOW RELATIONSHIPS TO FIND THEIR OWN LEVEL

When allowed to unfold, relationships each have their own special nature. The art of creating friendships is allowing them to evolve naturally, finding out what we have to offer each other, how we best connect, and what nurtures our affiliation. With some people, we're more likely to play and laugh, while with others, we feel a deep level of understanding. Some people are buddies for adventure, while others can relate to our spiritual journey. Most of our friends combine many aspects of things that are important to us. But each friendship is like a different entity with its own qualities.

It is an act of faith to allow friendships to find their own level and not try to force or control them. Some people we meet will respond and become our friends, others will not and it's up to us to accept this. Some people will be casual friends we see a few times a year, while others become part of our intimate circle. One way to allow a friendship to evolve naturally is to stay tuned into the rhythm of give and take. If you initiate contact with someone several times and they don't respond, then wait a while, particularly if you are starting to feel resentful. You can ask them if something is wrong so long as your motivation is to clarify the situation, not to cause them shame or guilt. Noticing the flow of give and take isn't for the purpose of scorekeeping or proving anyone wrong, it's to be aware of a natural evolution.

If someone reaches out to you and you want to be their friend, reach back and do your part to help the relationship along. Instead of *allowing* relationships to find their level, you *help the relationship find its true level.* Many people want friends and connections but don't reciprocate when people reach out to them. It's not that they are selfish, it's that they feel undeserving, unimportant, or unconsciously want friends to be caretakers. It's our ability to push through our fears and enter the flow of give and take that nourishes friendships—otherwise we attract rescuers into our lives.

To help friendships find their *true nature*—that special chemistry that lies between us—we explore various ways of being together. We also learn the logistics of staying connected. Some people like frequent phone calls while others would rather be called only on occasion, and not at the children's bedtime! Some people are open to spontaneous plans, some like a lot of advance notice. Beyond finding the nature of a connection, we can also help each other open new horizons by inviting them to join us for something they don't usually do.

The concept of letting relationships find their level is a guideline, not a rigid rule. In an established relationship, there may be an ebb and flow to the giving and receiving over long periods of time. When someone is new to town, is shy, or has been hurting, we might reach out to them more often. When I was new to one place I lived, several people repeatedly included me before I was settled enough to give back. Years later I passed this kindness along to an older woman who loved getting together but had great difficulty in asking.

Allowing relationships to find their own level often means that there will be some empty spots in life. In my own life, when I started "letting relationships find their own level," I had many lonely hours to contend with. But I also stopped feeling as if I betrayed myself by initiating contact too much with certain people, or was dishonest by calling someone out of neediness when there wasn't a genuine connection. I had a growing sense of self-respect and a fascination with the future as I trusted that following a natural process would be best. Over time I naturally gravitated toward people who were more active in initiating contact.

Allowing friendships to find their own level is woven into our spiritual journey because it means giving up control and allowing evolution to take its course. The focus shifts to becoming authentic and natural—in touch with the beating of our heart and the softness of our belly.

75

ASK SOMEONE TO BE YOUR SPIRITUAL FRIEND

*T*he concept of spiritual friends is based on the belief that when you focus on the spirit, or the light within, transformation occurs. When two people agree to be spiritual friends, they enter into a special trust, offering each other a safe haven where they periodically get together to talk about the evolution of their spiritual journey. This can include ways in which you are growing. It can be about inner leadings that suggest a certain direction in your life that feels both exciting and scary.

Talking about spirituality is personal and uncomfortable for many people. It's not something we regularly do in many circles, although it is commonplace in some groups or communities. That's why having a place to focus on our spiritual journey helps us ponder our journey more consciously. Once two people—possibly three—agree to be spiritual friends, they might get together for an hour or two, either weekly, biweekly, or monthly.

Making a commitment to be a spiritual friend implies a commitment of time together either on a regular basis or when one person is in need. When you get together for a meeting with a spiritual friend, you can take a few moments of silence to center yourselves, then start by one of you asking the other, by name, "Where is the spirit leading you in your life?" The listener might ask a question for clarification, but the primary role is to listen as deeply as possible, sending love and compassion through the heart and breath.

There is a special quality to a spiritual friendship. Because we are reaching for spirit together, we enter hallowed ground. As Jesus of Nazareth said, "When two or more people are gathered in my name, I am there also." It is a connection both intimate, special, and sacred. It is also a model for being in relationship with all people—regarding each other with feelings of care, love, and compassion.

PART VIII

◆ ◆ ◆

ESPECIALLY
FOR COUPLES

Come live with me and be my love,
And we will some new pleasures prove
Of golden sands, and crystal brooks,
With silken lines, and silver hooks.
                            —John Donne

To rage, to lust, to write to, to commend,
All is the purlieu of the god of love.

—John Donne

*T*here is a mystery to attraction. How is it that of all the hundreds of people we meet, we find a path to that one special person? Some would say that self-esteem levels attract, or that it is lust at first sight, or that we are meeting what needs to be healed inside us. Some say we are attracted to people who are equally autonomous or equally able to differentiate. There is also a spiritual aspect to attraction, the sense of finding a kindred spirit, a soul who seems to resonate with ours. When we meet a kindred spirit, our connection runs deeper than values and beliefs. It's as if our spirits have met in another realm. There is a sense of something eternal.

Even when the spiritual and physical attraction is strong, we have the task of living together on this earth with all our conditioning, programming, and the primitive longings of the human heart and body. Every one of us is a package deal, a mixed bag of humanity. When there is a powerful attraction, the joys are profound, but the hurts and anguish can also be intense. Sometimes we feel as if our life gets absorbed in the relationship. In other situations, people make a "head" decision to be together and the chemistry develops. Other times it doesn't.

This section is especially for couples, but is applicable to all people. It's an invitation to nudge yourself, go deep, and work close to the fire of your inner world, to heat up the chill inside that comes from denying, hiding, and playing it safe in relationships. This doesn't mean jumping into the fire and getting burned, as people do in highly addictive relationships, it means doing the disciplined, conscious work that opens our hearts to the wonder and magic of a deep and abiding human bond.

Committing to a primary intimate relationship is like embarking on a major voyage. As we each change, grow, create, and re-create ourselves, the relationship fluctuates and shifts, taking on new forms. We are constantly challenged to let go of past expectations, accept the imperfect present, and be authentic. Our relationship becomes one with our spiritual journey.

Moving toward deep levels of intimacy carries the potential for love, healing, closeness, and joy, along with pain, loneliness, depression, and violence. We often replay the intense conflicts between oneness and separateness that mark the early years of life. Maggie Scarf writes in *Intimate Partners*, "It is in marriage that we resurrect not only the intensity of our first attachment feelings, but the miseries of old frustrations and repressed hatreds as well. What is so frequently sought in a mate—and then fought out with that mate—is some unresolved dilemma about a parent."

If we unconsciously live out patterns from childhood, we run the risk of re-wounding each other, living parallel lives, or creating great distance in order to prevent our old goblins from getting loose and being seen. If we dare to be close, to strip away the facade and stand vulnerable before another person, the buried, disowned parts of ourselves that are sometimes called our "shadow side" are torn from their hiding places and brought out in the open. This face-to-face meeting with our shame, hurt, and grief provides the merciful possibility of healing and transformation.

Nothing is a greater challenge in life than to commit from the heart to be true and honest with another human being. It's like accepting an invitation for a carousel ride in the cosmos— we see it all, feel it all, and are challenged over and over again to let go of the armor covering our heart. Sometimes we feel as if we're going in circles. Most of all, we invite into our lives the possibility of knowing humor, joy, unity, and oneness as we find our power and allow our boundaries to melt into each other, into love.

76

THE DAILY PRACTICE OF LOVING RELATIONSHIPS

Creating deep levels of intimacy is a spiritual practice that takes daily commitment. Here is a list of some fundamentals for intimate relationships to have available as a daily reminder.

1. *Be on your own spiritual journey: know yourself.*
   Have your own daily spiritual practice that brings you into conscious contact with God, Goddess, or spirit, and keeps you centered in your heart. This can also include learning to define yourself. Who am I? What do I think, feel, dream, and desire?

2. *Honor your commitments.*
   As far as is humanly possible, keep the daily commitments to be on time and do the things you say you will do. The deeper commitments of being true and honest are a lifetime commitment that continue to unfold as you deepen your level of self-awareness. At a spiritual level, a commitment to another person is a commitment to spirit/God and to yourself—a commitment to truth and love.

3. *Seek your own purpose in life.*
   No matter how wonderful a relationship may be, you need to live in the center of your own life, finding that which gives meaning on a daily basis. Central to anyone's spiritual journey is to discover one's strengths and talents and seek our life's purpose.

4. *Know that you can support yourself financially.*
   When you know you can earn a living, it brings a sense of inner security and lessens your dependency on your mate.

It also creates a sense of equality in a relationship and frees you to leave if need be. This doesn't mean that both people need to be working if there is an agreement that one stays home to care for children, go to school, or take some time off. It means that both people know they can make a living if necessary, and no one feels trapped in the relationship because they have no ability to support themselves.

5. *Explore the parts of you that feel dependent/addicted to having a relationship.*

If you go from one relationship into another, or stay in harmful relationships because you are afraid to leave, there is something in your heart that needs healing. *Becoming addictive in relationships is usually rooted in our desperate child part seeking the all loving, all caring father or mother figure. It is also a longing for spirit.* Treat the desperate parts of yourself with great compassion and kindness, grieve the past, and meet your beloved as an equal, fallible person who can participate in your healing but cannot fill the longing for a loving parent.

6. *Seek equality.*

Equality in a relationship is not only about equal child care and doing the dishes—although these are important. It's about equal vulnerability—bringing up conflict, initiating lovemaking, letting your beloved know they are in your heart. It's also about equal responsibility for the concerns of the household, money, and planning time together. So bare your heart to your beloved *and* pitch in with the daily household chores.

7. *Accept the dance of change.*

Leave the fairy-tale books behind that talk about living happily ever after, and know you are two people with lumps and bumps who are coming together in body, mind, and spirit to grow and learn to love. A partnership can provide a shelter from the storm, but it won't take away the storm. You are two people going through the journey of life together. Bring fascination and wonder to the unfolding of your beloved and of yourself. The question to remember is: How do we dance together on this journey side-by-side?

8. *Remember to apologize, and own up to your unconscious or hurtful behavior.*
   An apology is an invitation to forgiveness and reconciliation for ourself and our beloved. It opens the way to building back the bridge we have broken, and invites us to reflect on our own behavior. An apology is sincere when we are willing to look underneath our behavior and make changes.

9. *Be willing to put time and energy into the relationship.*
   A relationship needs tending, just like a garden. It takes a daily commitment to keep the air clear between you so that the time you spend together brings pleasure. It is also important to get beyond serious discussion, voice your appreciation for each other, and take time for pleasure.

10. *Understand the goblins of your past.*
    Pay attention to your fears, knee-jerk reactions, and intense responses. They often signal that you are reacting out of past wounds, which blind you from seeing your beloved for who they are. Explore your intense emotions with kindness and compassion, seeing them as a wounded part of you needing your help to become a wise adult who is able to see clearly and to create a healthy relationship.

11. *Let go of excuses and "deliver the goods."*
    At some point, regardless of our past, we need to behave as a responsible adult and "deliver the goods." We're either on time or we're not. We either initiate conversation and lovemaking or we don't. We need to stretch and expand ourselves so we don't ask for special rules, or take without giving. Phrases such as "It's hard" or "I'm afraid" need to be expanded to say, "It's hard, but I can do it," "I'm afraid, but I can walk though the fear." We need to nudge ourselves to grow, expand, say what's on our mind, and give to our partner.

12. Practice a big-mind perspective: Enjoy the whole show.

The more you are in touch with big mind and big heart, the more you can observe yourself in the middle of your ongoing saga—the drama of your life—with a light heart. You can keep your perspective broad and large rather than narrow and intense. From the perspective of big mind, you can grasp that you are experiencing the common threads that run through all relationships—*the* relationship challenge of having different habits; *the* relationship challenge of supporting each other in hard times; *the* relationship difficulties of keeping sex alive. Seeing with a big-mind perspective can be a daily practice that lifts your spirits, adds humor to life, and reminds you that you are one of many couples struggling, loving, and sometimes gnashing your teeth in relationships.

77

LOVING IT ALL: A TOURIST'S GUIDE TO RELATIONSHIPS

*L*ast spring I looked through numerous tourist guides to Montana in anticipation of a summer of hiking and camping. The pictures of mountains, rivers, and campgrounds were shown against a bright blue sky, sunshine, and an occasional picturesque cloud. People were camping, hiking, fishing, and boating with happy smiles and no signs of sweat, as if it were a 75- to 80-degree day.

By contrast, imagine a tourist guide made of images from my summer of canoeing, hiking, and camping in Montana with my partner, Jessie. On the north fork of the Flathead River, we are standing in two feet of water, chilled by the pouring rain, pulling the canoe around the rapids which are dangerously low. There's a scene where the boat jerked and I fell backward into the water. The massive mountains behind us are almost completely covered by dark rain clouds. In one scene on a Missouri River canoe trip, the sky is a strange, musty, gray blue due to smoke from forest fires. Our eyes are red, our throats irritated, and we both wake up in the mornings coughing. On another day of a canoe trip we are carrying our packs far from the river to make camp because we are overwhelmed from the stench of a dead cow lying at the edge of the river. Then there's the time we are standing by the Missouri River, looking at a map, arguing over where we are just after I got stung by a bee. I'm mad because I think I deserve more sympathy for the bee sting. Oh yes, and there I am on what started out as a beautiful fall day, leaning forward, hiding my face from a snowstorm, hiking toward St. Mary's Peak. The anticipated view from the top is reduced to ice-covered windows in a fire tower as we eat our lunch. And yes, there are pictures of comfortable 70- to 85-degree days sitting with friends on a ridge, looking at wildflowers, feeling awe at the breathtaking 360-degree views—but they were the exception, not the rule.

One way to reflect back on the summer would be to say that there were good days and bad days. Another perspective is to embrace it all as a feast, none of it better or worse than another day, just all part of the great, big, tossed salad of life—climbing, stretching, sweating, relaxing, and experiencing sun, rain, cold, snow, clear air, smoky air, high winds, and the stench of dead cow. Yes, some days were easier and more relaxed, but that doesn't make them better or worse. They all leave their imprints in different ways—some days were a quiet time for the soul and spirit, while on other days we stretched our endurance and our relationship. Some days we felt close, some days brought up tensions; sometimes we laughed in the rain and argued in the sunshine. What binds all these events together is the shared sense of Jessie and me intertwined with the vastness of nature and human experience.

To have a rich, lasting friendship or partnership, imagine accepting all human experience and feelings as part of the whole—not something to be feared or medicated, but like rivers, streams, mountains, clouds, rain, and sun, all part of the natural order. Our ability to immerse ourselves in this vast, ever changing river of life is the source of spirit and intimate relationships.

Relationships get advertised in our society a lot like the tourist's guide, with Cinderellas, knights in shining armor, and everyone "living happily ever after." No serious fights, sickness, screaming children, unemployment, belches, wrinkles, or loneliness. To have intimacy, we need to surpass this narrow view and embrace with all our heart that intimacy includes living through all kinds of situations together—talking, arguing, planning, and holding each other's hand. It also means meeting all that is buried inside—our wounds and fears. The wonder of intimate connection evolves as we slip out of the cloak of fear that says: Be careful, don't say that, no one would understand, that's too shameful, it's too scary to be alone. We drop the cloak and speak our truths, perhaps awkwardly at first, but with an authenticity that rises up from inside. It might start with simply saying, "I feel that we've gotten distant" or "I really care about you." No matter how afraid, halting, or clumsy we are, when we speak truth we open our hearts to connection.

Walking the path of committed intimate relationships is a spiritual practice because it requires reflection and self-awareness. It takes great faith to speak the truth and trust the outcome, to expose our frightened, tender side, to sometimes give far more than we get. Yet as our love deepens we become able to let go of expectations and love the other as flawed and amazing—a mirror of ourselves. We become more able to stay grounded through the difficult times instead of letting them rip us apart. An intimate connection brings the possibility of dissolving our boundaries and feeling unity with another, a unity that reflects our relationship to spirit, or God. But how do we do this?

Most of us have a dual image of relationships: We have the model from our original family juxtaposed with a dream or illusion of something better, which is highly influenced by fairy tales and the mass media. Most frequently, our families taught us a few things about what we wanted in adult relationships, and a lot about what we didn't want. As a result, we went on a search to find something to fill our inner emptiness. In our desire to find something better, we cast about for models.

What did we find? In sitcoms, people are like comic-book characters, always joking through conflict, which always has a happy ending. In romance movies, we see kisses that melt our socks off, and lovers always ready with quick repartee. In classic literature, all true love in tragedies ends in death, and in comedies it ends in marriage. In women's magazines there are skinny, beautiful women pictured in clothes that would look silly on us next to pictures of chocolate tortes that would make us fat. The images of men are tough, tall, square-jawed, drinking, or standing by a fancy car.

We are led to believe that we can find fabulous passion, unending romance, freedom from loneliness, a permanent Band-Aid from hurt, and a partner who never changes. We are hard-pressed to find models of ordinary-looking people who have caring, affirming, affectionate, sexual, loving relationships. Most of us know the high of first romance, but what a jolt to find that romance doesn't have a picture-book, happy ending. In fact, there is no ending—relationships aren't fixed. They go on and on and change and change.

We don't think of falling in love with someone who is thoughtful and fun, but also gets scared meeting new people, has trouble being on time, and is allergic to our cat. When we stare deeply into the eyes of our new beloved, we don't imagine him or her losing interest in making love, clamming up when angry, or being grumpy or detached for hours or even days. And we certainly don't imagine violence, battering, and screaming.

Yet, quietly in many homes across the world, there are people whose eyes light up at the sight of each other, who support each other as they grow and change, who laugh and accept the other's foibles, who after many years still have a conjugal sexual relationship, a true marriage of body, mind, and spirit. We often don't recognize them because they appear to be so ordinary. But if you are in their presence, you will feel a warmth and charge of energy that reflects their love and acceptance for each other. In the following sections are some of the basics that happy couples seem to practice either consciously or unconsciously.

78

INTRODUCE YOUR FEARS, FOIBLES, AND QUIRKS

When we first meet, we tend to show our best side. That's fine for a while, but it's important to introduce the whole of our being, including our foibles and quirks. It's like saying to each other, *Here we are, you and me—each of us a maze of qualities. I have my talents, strengths, and preferences along with my own special quirks and foibles. You, my partner, have all of these things as well. We are imperfect, funny, and wondrous at the same time. Let's get to know each other—all of us, so we can play together, unafraid, with nothing hidden from each other. Let's introduce our quirks and foibles to each other.*

Our strange little habits do not need to block the path to a heart connection if we bring them out in the open and introduce them to each other. It's a way to say *I'm imperfect and I know it, and I expect to be accepted this way.* Quirks are part of the package deal, part of being human. Openness and acceptance are the keys to deflating the power of these human but troublesome parts of ourselves. I remember one time when Jessie and I stayed at a little cabin. She insisted that we move the bed tight against the wall which I found rather pointless—I mean, it was only three inches away. When she gave up arguing her point, and said with a sheepish grin, "I'm afraid of falling through the crack," my heart melted.

"Oh, in that case," I said, "let's get it good and close to the wall; I wouldn't want to lose you."

When we introduce our quirks *as* quirks, we no longer need to defend ourselves or feel as if we are hiding a part of ourselves. I remember years ago when my mom and dad visited me and I offered them my loft bed. My mother got halfway up the ladder and looked scared. With panic in her eyes she said, "I'd rather not sleep up there," and came down. I could see her feeling troubled during the day. When I asked her about it she said, "I'm afraid you think I'm stupid because I'm afraid of going up the ladder into the loft." I felt a pang in my heart seeing such fear in her eyes. "Oh, Mother, I don't think you are stupid. It's all right. It doesn't matter." Her worry didn't go away easily because she had broken the family code that said, Hide your fear. Paradoxically, when she revealed her fear, I felt much closer to her.

It's crucial that when someone reveals a foible to us that we receive it with kindness and compassion. It's often a scared part of the person, revealing his or her needs. It may not make sense to us or seem rational, but it doesn't have to. It's just there. We don't need to argue over it any more than we argue over someone's favorite color. We simply open our heart to each other's little stuff and create a safe haven.

In telling each other about our quirks, we take them out of the shame department and make them another part of ourselves. We're not thrilled about them, but, oh, well, they are a part of us. It's just the way we are. This helps prevent sudden surprises later on: "You what!!!—but you never told me!" or "I wish you had told me, I could have helped you."

Another aspect of introducing ourselves to each other is revealing what we do when we're afraid: If, for example, our partner sees us chattering constantly, it may seem like an irritating trait. If we can find the words to say, *When I'm afraid, I tend to chatter* (clam up, get bossy, and so on), we take our partner into our confidence. By exposing the fear beneath our protective behavior, we are saying, *I have this wound and it hurts sometimes. I get afraid. I act it out.* In the very act of owning our fear, we release its intensity and allow the possibility of healing. If our partner is willing to smile at us or tenderly take our arm when we manifest our fearful behavior instead of re-wounding the cut by showing irritation, our partner helps us start to heal.

In an ongoing workshop for couples, I had each person introduce both their foibles and the subtle ways in which they punished their partners when they were mad. People sat, spellbound, listening intently as the level of honesty went deeper and deeper, opening up the hidden covert behaviors that blocked connection in the marriages. By looking underneath these unskillful, camouflaged ways of communicating, each couple reached a new level of vulnerability and understanding. There were astonished reactions: "You knew you did that to get me! It always felt that way, but I kept thinking I was making things up." Relief, release, laughter, and a deeper sense of being on the journey together emerged as couples bridged their sense of separation and became allies to each other.

79

BECOME ALLIES TO EACH OTHER'S WOUNDED PLACES

*L*earning to be allies to each other's wounded places is a way to meet the wounds of our beloved with compassion and caring. This process is not so much about getting rid of troublesome behavior as it is a joint effort to stop re-wounding the old hurts, and open the possibility of transformation. By engaging in this process, we tap into the vast healing power of two people aligning their hearts.

Our childhood wounds often got buried under layers of unexpressed grief. We often cover these heartaches with behavior that seems "childish" and unskillful. While the inner goal is self-protection, the outer behavior is often irritating to others. We get afraid, needy, jealous, petulant, bossy, demanding, or withdrawn. Our relationships get stuck in patterns of acting and reacting in some of the following ways:

1. One gets needy, the other withdraws or feels obliged to caretake.
2. One withdraws, the other tries to force them to talk and then feels hurt or mad.
3. One is scared, the other puts them down.
4. One person bosses, the other snaps back.
5. One gets demanding, the other withdraws, won't talk, or gets hostile in return.
6. One often breaks agreements, the other is constantly mad or retaliates.
7. One wants to be sexual, the other withholds.
8. One wants to spend time together, the other is always busy.
9. One person withholds love and care, the other engages in addictions or gets depressed.
10. One person starts growing and getting strong, the other sabotages or becomes violent.

When we become allies to each other, instead of reacting unconsciously to each other in these dysfunctional ways, we recognize the underlying wound and become an ally in healing.

There are five stages to the process of becoming allies to each other's wounded places:

STEPS TO BEING ALLIES TO EACH OTHER'S WOUNDED PLACES

1. Agree to help each other heal and grow.
2. Recognize and list your wise adult and wounded child states (including behaviors, thoughts, and feelings).
3. Tell your partner about your child states and pick one or two to heal.

4. Tell your partner what would be helpful when you fall into your child state (start with one or two items).
5. Agree to stick to the plan and give it a chance to work.

AGREE THAT YOU WANT TO HEAL AND GROW TOGETHER.

Sit down together and make a commitment to engage in this process. The commitment implies that both partners acknowledge their wounds or imperfections and are willing to give and receive help. Ideally, it is entered into as an experiment in loving each other. In the beginning of working with this process, it can help immeasurably to affirm the commitment to each other on a daily basis. It can be a simple as saying, *I am committed and open to growing together. I offer my support to you and I am open to receiving your support and care. I will bring my love and awareness to this process.*

RECOGNIZE YOUR WISE ADULT AND VULNERABLE CHILD STATES.

In this step we make separate lists titled "wise adult" and "vulnerable child."

Core to the "wise adult"—which could be called your higher, compassionate self, your wise woman/man—is having your self-esteem rest comfortably within you, grounded in the knowledge that you are a child of creation, sacred because you are alive. In this state we observe our childlike traits from a wise adult stance, seeing them as part of us but not central to our spiritual being. When we are able to witness and embrace them, we can soften their edges quite rapidly.

Typical aspects of being in an adult state are: feeling centered, flexible, open, reasonable, and seeing both sides of a situation. We are able to negotiate without becoming defensive and listen carefully to others. In this state we also have a sense of humor and can see the big perspective of a situation. We can protect ourselves and set limits, but we don't do it with hate or violence. In an adult state we are able to take action to improve our situation as opposed to complaining and whining and taking no action. We can feel compassion without being sucked into people's drama and chaos, and feel joy from simple pleasures.

Typical aspects of being in a childhood state are: being afraid, whiny, needy; complaining (but not taking action); being hostile, blaming; stonewalling; being withdrawn, dishonest, petulant, demanding; holding on to grudges, retaliating, controlling others; being passive-aggressive, violent, or manipulative. In this childhood state we may also feel chronically guilty and shameful, have worrisome thoughts about "doing it right" or "saying it right," or feel like a victim—everyone is doing it to us and we have no power to take charge of our lives. Most addictive behavior comes from a childhood state. What I refer to as childhood states are also called our narcissistic, victim, shadow, reactive, or unconscious sides.

Here's an example of the lists made by a couple I worked with, Nancy and Frank. One common pattern was for Nancy to get irritated and start snapping at Frank: "Why didn't you fix the faucet last night?" "Hurry up. We've got to get going now so we'll be on time." "You never do what you say you will do." She'd sound like a military sergeant. Frank's automatic response was to become sullen and withdraw or counterattack: "Well, you didn't keep the dogs in the house last night and they got loose. " Underneath, he was saying to himself, "You're such a bitch, I'll never fix the damn faucet." He was often passive-aggressive by making them late to appointments and breaking agreements to do things.

In making their lists, they were to include specific behaviors as well as the underlying feelings.

NANCY'S CHILD LIST

Behavior:
    bossy
    must have my way
    strategizing how to say it right
    demanding

start losing my temper
whining
flirt with (or fantasize about) other men

Underlying Feelings/Thoughts:
very hurt and very little
wildly angry, as if I'll blow up and scream my head off
panic about everything falling apart
afraid I won't be heard and our relationship will fall apart
do or die feelings about getting my way—I must win
shame attack—I'm bad, I'm no good, I'm defective
lonely

FRANK'S CHILD LIST

Behavior:
sarcastic
quietly defiant/passive-aggressive
won't talk
counterattacks
withdraws to woodworking shop or to play with dogs
explodes in anger
flirts with other women
very important someone say he is right

Underlying Feelings/Thoughts:
fear of being overwhelmed or swallowed up
intense anger and hurt
fear
hopelessness
shame
loneliness
this is never going to work
I'm incompetent
I'm unappreciated
I can never do enough

When Nancy and Frank revealed the feelings underlying
their behavior, there was a shift in energy from judgment to

compassion, from irritation to understanding. If we know someone is getting bossy and demanding because *they are scared,* we can realize they're not doing it *to* us. They're doing it because that's how they are wired.

The next step was to make their adult lists.

NANCY'S WISE ADULT LIST

I stop to think over what I am saying before I say it.
I don't see Frank as the enemy who wants to hurt me.
I remember that we love each other, and it feels good to stay connected.
I stop to think about how Frank might feel.
I see it as a problem to solve.
I listen and don't argue back or get defensive.
I can let go of having things my way.

FRANK'S WISE ADULT LIST

I take a moment and react slowly.
I don't see her as this bitch who's trying to control me (I asked him if he could say this in a positive way. He progressed to, "I see her as someone who is not very good at asking for what she wants," and finally to "I see her as someone who cares about me and is scared.")
I listen to what she says and try to repeat it back to show her I understand.
If I'm upset, I call a time out and say when I'll be back to finish the discussion.

TELL YOUR PARTNER ABOUT YOUR CHILD STATES AND PICK ONE OR TWO TO HEAL.

Each person reads their list to the other, and then picks out one or two aspects they want help with. It's important that you start with something that feels manageable. Both partners can take part in deciding which items feel useful to work on together, but it's important that each person want to change something for themselves.

To continue with our example of Nancy and Frank. After reading her list, Nancy decided to work on her tendency to get bossy and critical. In exploring the underlying feelings, Nancy realized that her bossiness was paired with old memories of trying to be perfect to keep her drunken mother from beating her. She owned that she had been venting her anger about this at Frank. He listened with great care as she spoke about her underlying pain.

Next, Frank read his list and decided to work on his response to Nancy's bossiness, which was to retreat and clam up. With reflection, he was able to see that he was triggered into feeling like a bad kid when she got bossy, just as he had felt when his mother or father had berated him and put him down. He was withdrawing in an attempt to shut out the voices that said, "You're bad, you're a fuckup. You're nothing."

As a word of caution, I encourage people to pick one or two items and work on them until they feel an inner shift. When we go deep and heal in one area, the message is sent to the whole of our being. Once you have accomplished this, other changes will come much faster. If we stay on the surface doing a little of this and a litle of that, we never penetrate our deeper resistance and we're likely to feel stuck, or say to ourselves, "I've tried all these things and nothing works."

TELL YOUR PARTNER WHAT WOULD BE HELPFUL WHEN YOU FALL/SLIP/CRASH INTO YOUR CHILD STATE (START WITH ONE OR TWO ITEMS).

Take one behavior you would like to change, and think of a response from your partner that would be helpful when you do this behavior. This can involve brainstorming and experimentation until an idea feels right.

Returning to our example with Nancy and Frank, the discussion between myself, Nancy, and Frank went something like this:

CK: Nancy, how can Frank be helpful to you when you get bossy?

Nancy *(after pondering a bit)*: Last week at work, when I started snapping at people, one of the other people saluted and said, "Aye, aye, Captain," and I just cracked up.

CK: So would you like Frank to say that to you when you get bossy.

Nancy: Yeah, that would be great. Then I'll just laugh.

CK: Ask Frank if he's willing to do that.

Nancy: When I get bossy, I'd like you to salute and say "Aye, aye, Captain." Is that okay?

Frank: Yes. . . . But I wouldn't want you to do that to me.

We now have an agreement. When Nancy gets little/bossy, Frank has a way to stay in an adult place and lighten the situation by saying "Aye, aye, Captain." She will not be shamed or re-wounded by his withdrawing or lashing out at her, and he has a way to stay centered as an adult.

Frank's last remark, "Yes, but I wouldn't want you to do that to me" reflects an important point. What works for one person won't work for another. It's up to each person to say what will be helpful. To salute and say "aye, aye" to Frank would have been infuriating for him. But for Nancy, it worked. This is the essence of creating intimate relationships: We develop the language that works for each person. We went through a similar process with Frank, who asked Nancy to touch his arm and say gently, "What are you feeling?" whenever he withdrew.

STICK TO THE PLAN AND GIVE IT A CHANCE
TO WORK. *I'LL SAY THAT TWICE. STICK TO THE
PLAN AND GIVE IT A CHANCE TO WORK.*

Eventually it will be absorbed into your way of relating to each other. It's good to check in every couple of weeks to talk about how it's going. Slowly, you can add more items to the agreement. If you can push through and keep at it for a few months, exploring various ways in which to be allies to each other, your compassion will grow immeasurably and you will feel the stranglehold of old patterns slipping away as you feel a new freedom inside.

Some people have commented on the fact that this process seems codependent—that it's Nancy's responsibility to stop getting bossy, and Frank's responsibility to stop withdrawing. That's true at one level, but it lacks comprehension of the wondrous ability of genuine human interaction to create healing. It is very difficult to do for ourselves what was never done for us.

Ultimately, we do want to be able to pull ourselves onto center when we are slipping. Being allies to each other can facilitate this. Over time, by hearing the voice of our beloved partner repeatedly bringing understanding where there was negative judgment, we can internalize their caring words. Eventually we recognize when we are falling into a vulnerable child state and elicit our own wise adult—the voice of our beloved within us—and bring ourselves back to center.

80

MAKE 'EM PAY: A QUICK METHOD FOR BEHAVIOR CHANGE

I learned this concept first from my father, and later from Albert Ellis, a pioneer in the field of cognitive therapy and author of *Rational Emotive Therapy*. My father didn't call it cognitive therapy or "Make 'Em Pay," but he applied the principle in a beautiful way. The point is that you learn to control a behavior that feels out of control by making it cost you something . . . for example, money.

The phrase "make 'em pay" comes from a tennis teacher, Todd Curtiss, who would tell us, "When they give you a powder-puff ball, hit it! Make 'em pay."

My father voluntarily played "Make 'Em Pay" when we went camping. I wish he were alive so I could ask him why he did it, but I suspect he wanted us to share his love of the woods and not dampen our experience with his volatile temper. He told us on the camping trip that any time he lost his temper he would put a dime in a box. He called it the "no expostulation box." If he started to snap at us or get hot under the collar, we could say, "Put a dime in the box, Dad," and he would. It took the sting out of his temper. At the end of a trip we went out and had ice cream with the money he'd put in the box. Unfortunately, the contract ended when we got home, but it left me with a lot of admiration for my father who, at least for a short time, owned up to the destructive power of his temper and provided a means of controlling it.

Most of us have habits or traits that block intimacy and connection. They are the little irritating monsters of relationships that get in the way of feeling close. Playing "Make 'Em Pay" with a partner involves both people owning a behavior that is harmful or hurtful to the relationship and agreeing that they want to change it. It needs to be agreed upon in the spirit of good faith and with a light touch—we all have these traits. The essential ingredient is to shift the internal resistance to something so noxious that you will stop and think about what you are doing. The maxim is this: *If something costs you enough, you will change it.* For example, with people who plead forgetfulness in relationships, I have seen their memory improve immediately if it costs them five or ten dollars to forget.

When clients feel discouraged about changing a behavior, they will sometimes say, "I'd do anything to change this."

"Anything?" I often say with a smile. "Well, I know something that usually works."

Here's an example with Ruth and Sam, a couple who faced many struggles together but dearly wanted to maintain their relationship. Each one started by picking a behavior they wanted to change. Ruth decided to work on her rage explosions. She would build up tension and then blast her partner, hitting below the belt: *You this, you that. Why don't you ever . . . ?#@* You never . . .* Her partner, Sam, would just stand there and take it, feeling paralyzed and hurt. They both wanted this to change.

Here's the contract we made: When Ruth lost control and started screaming, Sam was to put out his hand and Ruth had to give him $5.00 on the spot. (They were both directed to carry $5.00 bills with them at all times.) This symbolized Ruth taking responsibility for her behavior. It also helped Sam to not feel so afraid of her outbursts because she would own it as her problem . . . and he got five bucks out of it. Because he was emotionally distant, and often hid behind a newspaper or his computer, Sam agreed to initiate conversation about his day and ask Ruth about hers. If he hadn't done this by 7 P.M., he had to pay her $5.00.

I knew it was working because they came in together smiling the next week and Ruth said, "Well, it helped, but I think we'd better up the ante to ten dollars because I started thinking, 'For five dollars, it's worth it.'" She was showing her commitment. The cost has to pinch enough to get your attention.

There are many helpful aspects to this type of contract. First of all, each person has to admit to their own tacky or destructive behavior. This is always music to their partner's ears. Second, each person makes a clear commitment to changing their behavior—they literally put their money where their mouth is. Third, by making the consequence immediate and expensive, it shows people they *can* control or change their behavior. Fourth, the one who is victimized or intruded upon gets an energy return in the form of money, which sends the message to the brain: You don't deserve this. It helps them learn to stand up for themselves. Most of all, it makes people laugh and gives them an immediate experience of making change and seeing the positive consequences in their relationship.

81

KIND WORDS AND SWEET SURPRISES: 365 VALENTINE'S DAYS

Let the beauty you love be what you do.
There are hundreds of ways
to kneel and kiss the ground.

—Rumi

*L*ike a garden, relationships need tending. Making love isn't just something to be done at night in bed. With our touches, looks, thoughts, and words not only do we make love to our partner, we make love to life. In this way we bring an ever expanding, vital, alive presence into our relationships.

When we hear "How did your day go?" or "It's so nice to be with you" or "Is there anything I can do to help?" accompanied by loving looks, tender touches, or warm hugs, every cell in our body is soothed and nurtured. This is in direct contrast to hearing a sharply spoken, "Where the hell is the newspaper?" or "Didn't you get the bills sent off?" or "Are you talking on the phone again?!," where our body is likely to click into a defensive, protective mode.

I'm writing this piece on February 14, 1995, Valentine's Day—a day set aside to tell people you love them. This strikes me as kind of odd, like having an Earth Day. What about the other 364 days? Considering the way some couples treat each other, it probably is good to have one day to be nice to each other, but what good are flowers when no one has looked into your eyes with longing and tenderness for months?

Let the beauty you love be what you do—in hundreds of ways every day. In a life that flows with spirit, our love flows through every day. Every day is Valentine's Day. The people who will buy the biggest bouquets and spend the most money on lavish presents are often operating from a sense of guilt or duty or from a desire to make a connection that isn't there. The people who make love through the day might send flowers or a small remembrance, but they won't need to prove their love with a lavish present because their love is felt and needs no proof. Like a song in the heart, their love sings like a celebration on a daily basis.

There are hundreds of ways to show care and affection with notes, phone calls, and the giving generously of our heart. We become the valentine—a loving, radiant person. Becoming the valentine doesn't mean we are dishonest, gushy, or overly sentimental. It means we live in a state of gratitude for what we have and what our partner brings to us. It doesn't mean there isn't conflict, but rather that we operate from a deep state of integrity, honoring ourselves and honoring our beloved. In our culture we are taught in hundreds of ways that you must prove your love with diamonds, cars, trips, and cards. But true love never needs proof. It will be felt as a warm heat in the belly and a light, happy feeling in the heart.

As daily practice in becoming a valentine, when you come into the presence of another person, bring your complete presence and willingness to both reveal yourself and understand the other. Show your care with warm smiles and soft eyes. With all your heart, think of that person as the same as you—wanting love, care, purpose, and freedom from pain. Breathe deeply, relax for a moment, and think the word *"Namaste,"* or I honor to the light/divinity in you. Then ask, with an open heart and mind, "How are you?" And when they respond, listen.

82

WHOSE FEELINGS ARE THESE ANYHOW? RECOGNIZING PROJECTIONS

In the mirror of our projections, we don't see our spouses; we see ourselves.

—Maggie Scarf

*I*n the next four sections I explore projections. Understanding this concept is core to understanding intimacy and creating loving relationships. The more people own and articulate their feelings directly, and stop projecting buried feelings on the partner, the greater the differentiation between them. The greater the differentiation, the more we have the ability to be intimately involved with another person without losing our sense of self.

Although poets and philosophers have alluded to the need to maintain our separateness in order to love, the connection between being well differentiated and creating intimacy was originally written about in psychological literature by Murray Bowen, a marriage and family therapist. David Schnarch, in *The Sexual Crucible* talks about differentiation as related to high levels of sexual desire and the ability to sustain passion in long-term relationships.

Differentiation starts by being separate from one's family, not just having broken off and moved far away, but, as Maggie Scarf writes in *Intimate Partners*, "Being truly separate from one's parents and not experiencing that differentness as a loss or a betrayal of what has been." Differentiation is about an internal, psychological separateness and is not necessarily related to physical proximity to one's family. Differentiation also means sorting through the teachings from institutions of church, school, government and finding one's own internal values based on experimentation and exploration.

Some traits of differentiation are: not having your self-esteem tied to other people's feelings, thoughts and behaviors, not violating your integrity to please or accommodate others, being able to stay centered when others are anxious or upset, being comfortable with differences, not needing people to validate your worth, not personalizing what others say or do, taking responsibility for one's feelings—i.e., not blaming others for how you feel, and being able to see all people as having their own separate and sacred journey. Put another way, you become able to trust your own reality, stay centered in highly charged situations, stop overreacting or giving yourself away, and become an amused and loving observer of your dramas.

In intimate relationships, we become like energy channels, unconsciously sending our inner feelings back and forth to each other. A negative projection arises when one person disowns a part of him or herself and attributes it to another person who often starts feeling it or carrying it unconsciously. We disown what we feel ashamed of. Instead of having an internal struggle with our shameful parts, we create a conflict between ourselves and another person. This often results in one person carrying the depression for two while the other expresses the anger for two.

Patterns of projecting start in childhood. If, for example, Mark is repeatedly called stupid, he externalizes the unwanted feelings by calling other kids stupid. It's a way of managing the overwhelming feelings: Get them out of me and dump them on someone else. Over time, we learn to disown anything we think is "bad" and present ourselves from our "good" image. Projecting keeps us deeply ensnared with our partner through unconscious power struggles and trade-offs, creating a highly conflicted, unconscious marriage. An unconscious trade-off might be: "I'll let you appear strong and not expose your fear if you'll let me look sweet and not expose my anger." Of course, it never works.

Maggie Scarf writes in *Intimate Partners*:

> Although it is true that projections of the internal self . . . are probably always going to play some role in close, emotional attachments, the degree of mutual gratification that a couple experiences will depend greatly upon how much of the personality of each partner is being disposed of in this fashion.

In Western culture, sex role conditioning contributes greatly to our tendency to project on each other because women are systematically taught to deny their power, anger, intelligence, and leadership skills, and project them on to men. Men are systematically taught to deny their fear, insecurity, uncertainty, incompetence, and neediness, and project these traits on to women. Other factors such as culture, temperament, and one's particular family also play a role.

There is an important paradox to projections: *What we disown in ourselves, we will initially be attracted to in others. However, after time, when the trait we once admired starts to remind us of our disowned part, we will feel repelled by it.* This sets up some common scenarios with many couples—heterosexual, lesbian, or gay.

Here is a common example of a woman projecting her anger. It follows a predictable set of steps.

Jane, who presents herself as very charming and disowns ever being angry, was initially attracted to Al because of his forceful personality: "He says what he means, he's assertive." As the relationship progressed, whenever Jane got bothered by something, she disowned her anger and projected it on to Al. Here is the process:

1. *Disown the feelings.*
   Jane felt angry at Al for dominating the conversation when friends came to dinner. Her internal anger censor leads her to deny her anger out of shame, fear of Al "being upset," or his possibly calling her a bitch. She attempted to maintain her self-image as good and kind.

2. *Project the feelings.*
   Instead of expressing her anger directly, she made a seemingly innocent comment—a sugar-coated dig—at her hus-

band, Al. "You certainly had a lot to say to our friends."
(She is sending the projection.) Al feels the underlying sting
of the remark and gets angry. This provides relief for Jane,
because he is now exploding with her anger.

3. *Feel relief and put down the person expressing the projected feelings.*
    In the ensuing argument, Jane stays calm and cool, feeling
    a vicarious thrill as Al loses control. She adds to the insult
    by saying, "Why do you always have to get so angry?" She
    has now completed the cycle by putting Al down for her
    projected trait. Instead of struggling within to reconcile
    herself with her anger, she has created a struggle between
    herself and her partner.

4. *Polarization increases.*
    Al, who is unaware of the projection, gets more angry and
    they end up more deeply entrenched in their roles, with
    Jane as the angel (read "martyr") and Al as the angry one
    (read "bad guy").

Here is a common scene, when a man projects his vulnerability and neediness. (We'll use Al and Jane again for our example.)

1. *Disown one's feelings.*
    Al got a mediocre evaluation from his boss when he was
    expecting to be congratulated on an excellent job. He
    quickly disowned his feelings of hurt and sadness and felt
    angry. After leaving work, he had a couple of drinks before
    heading home. Jane picked up on his distraught mood and
    asked, "What's wrong?"

2. *Project the feelings.*
    In response to Jane, Al staunchly replied, "Nothing," as he
    headed to the TV room to be alone with his wounds.
    (Through his denial he projects his hurt on to Jane.)

3. *Get relief and put down the person expressing the projected feel-
    ings.*
    Jane felt hurt after Al said "Nothing" and left the room. She
    started wondering if she had done something wrong—the

same thoughts Al was having about his work performance. She followed him into the TV room and said, with her voice cracking, "I feel so bad when you shut me out." Jane's sadness started to get too close for Al's comfort. To fend off his disowned feelings of sadness, he said with a sharp tone, "Why do you have to get so upset all the time?" Al's derision of Jane for what he was unconsciously feeling completed the process of projecting.

4. *Polarization increases.*

In feeling rebuffed, Jane got even more insistent on getting Al to talk. When he repeatedly refused, Jane felt hopeless and went to the bedroom sobbing while thinking to herself, "This relationship is hopeless."

As you can see from these examples, some projections result from what we do say and others come from withholding our words and feelings.

Another form of sending projections is done slowly, over time: A person in pain maintains a happy exterior while silently hurting inside. In these situations it can be very difficult to realize what is happening, but the people nearby might start feeling drained, fuzzy-minded, or somewhat depressed. This happened with a family member who was visiting me for a few weeks.

Allie was being chipper and active—up early doing exercises and being unusually cheerful. At some level this didn't compute with several previous phone calls when she had talked about money and marriage problems that sounded extremely troublesome to her. Without any precipitating event—we weren't arguing, or having difficulty being together—I started feeling absolutely drained and exhausted. I could see myself getting depressed, yet I knew I wasn't really depressed. But knowledge didn't relieve the exhaustion. I went to have an energy-balancing session and a massage thinking it might help. Then, a few days later, the thought started flickering through my mind, This is about Allie. So I asked her, "Allie, have you been depressed lately?" Tears welled up in her eyes, and she said, "Yes, terribly." As she started talking about her problems, I felt an instant surge of energy. I realized that I had been carrying her depression for her (as I had done for my mother and father throughout most of my childhood). It was amazing to me that as soon as she started owning her depression, I no longer felt it. That is the power of owning a projection. (We'll talk about my role in taking on the projection later.)

Another means of projecting anger and hurt is through withholding and "forgetting," sometimes referred to as passive-aggressive behavior. We are likely to be projecting our unconscious anger or fear when someone reaches for a comforting hand and we hold back, or limply take their hand; when we say, "Don't call the plumber, I'll fix it," and six months later the faucet is still leaking, causing distress to our mate; when we withhold sex or won't give our partner what we know they enjoy.

I discussed the concept of passive-aggressive behavior with several therapists. Psychologist Sigurd Hoppe, my co-family therapist in Minneapolis, who saw passive-aggressive behavior as a learned part of male culture, said:

> The learned behavior is not to know certain parts of oneself or what it means to be in a relationship. It's about a way of escaping personal responsibility. This allows us to say we're innocent when we hurt someone, but the cost is the ability to be deeply engaged with someone. To give up our innocence would require a deeper level of commitment, which often creates the terror of feeling inadequate. The thought is, "If I really invest myself fully, then the pain and loss is so much greater if it doesn't work out." Becoming vulnerable is harder for men because they have so much more performance anxiety. They're so preoccupied with their own fear of rejection, they defend themselves rather than saying, "I really want to know what that other person is about."

In talking with friend and counselor Jean Templeton, there was agreement that women also engage in passive-aggressive behavior, sometimes in the same way as men but often with a different character. A woman might make indirect remarks, withhold sex, cook fattening foods the partner can't resist and smile when they put on weight. Passive-aggressive behavior comes from people who feel deeply disempowered, so they express their power and anger in silent ways, not owning what they are doing. In most cases, people who are passive-aggressive will staunchly proclaim their innocence—that's what makes it feel so crazy to the people around them.

Passive-aggressive behavior also involves feeling powerful by causing others to feel pain. If we don't feel powerful enough to love, we know we have an impact when we hurt others. For example, when a father is late picking up his daughter at a day care center, the teacher and staff (and their children waiting at home) are inconvenienced and upset, the mother waiting at home is worried, and the child feels abandoned and forgotten. More confusing, the person who is passive-aggressive often has a litany of excuses and appears completely surprised when people are hurt and angry in response to their behavior: "I didn't go to the store because I didn't have enough money with me," or "I forgot what you wanted," or worse, they blame: "You didn't say it was important to go to the store," or "You didn't give me money," or the problem is reframed as a "communication problem"—"You didn't make it clear when I should pick up food for dinner." There is no expression of empathy. The person seems incapable of saying, simply, "I'm sorry, I was inconsiderate and caused you pain."

People usually feel a lot of resistance to owning projections because it rips open the door to their shadow side—their shame, fear, hurt, and capacity to inflict great pain on others. It also means we give up the comfort of someone carrying our disowned feelings for us. Yet, if we don't deal with projections, they may become more deeply entrenched. Maggie Scarf writes:

> Predictably, the more he projects his repudiated, intolerable feelings of dejection and sadness on to his wife, the more he is likely to dissociate his own self from them—and from her as well. She will, then, not only be carrying the depression for the pair of them, but the more she does what he, at an unconscious level, *wants her to do for him*, the more their mutual estrangement and tension will grow.

SEXUALITY AND PROJECTIONS

Projections are extremely common and troublesome in sexual relationships. Sexual shame, which is projected through nearly all advertising, most religions, and in our educational system makes its way into the bedrooms of many couples. Childhood sexual abuse also spills over into adult relationships. The woman who believes that nice women are passive is initially excited by her aggressive partner, but eventually projects her disgust on to him, saying, "All you want is sex, you're so crude." The man who has been taught that men are beasts becomes unable to feel sexually aroused with a loving partner and instead has affairs or seeks out women in prostitution. The fundamentalist preacher, who constantly warns about the evils of sex, seduces young women or boys in his congregation. What we resist persists.

Sexual energy is powerful energy. Thus, it takes a lot of our life-force energy to repress and disown our sexual shame. It's easier by far to project it on to others. A crowning example of our country's projection about sex as dirty/shameful was when the surgeon general, Jocelyn Elders, was fired for mentioning that we might consider talking about masturbation in sex education classes! Several righteous politicians hurled accusations at her of "going against family values." Don't people in families masturbate? We all come from families. What got hurled at her was people's collective shame about masturbating. She broke a taboo. While most people masturbate, or at least have thought about it, few people talk about it. It was not long ago that masturbation was said to drive people crazy or make them sick. Looking at the drama from a distance, it seemed almost funny, like a cartoon. It was sad, however, that a fine woman with great compassion and an understanding of oppressed people got fired. (For a more detailed discussion on the various permutations of sexual projections, the reader is referred to *Women, Sex, and Addiction: A Search for Love and Power.*) Suffice it to say here that it is important for couples to explore their sexual history and talk about the feelings and thoughts that were paired with sex. There are some excellent books on the subject; *Intimate Partners* by Maggie Scarf is a favorite of mine.

83

"I TAKE IT BACK": OWNING OUR PROJECTIONS

A conscious union depends upon both members of the couple exploring and owning their disowned parts. The more we do this, the more potent and powerful we become as human beings. We learn the true meaning of honesty and integrity. It is not an easy path because it invariably taps into our feelings of shame.

When I first learned to apologize for hurting people with sideways expressions of anger, it felt like pulling a fish hook out of my throat. I was terrified to say, "I wasn't honest with you, I was angry and I hurt you. I'm sorry." I feared people would hate me and say, "You're terrible, I never want to see you again." Yet it almost never happened. To my amazement, people usually thanked me for telling the truth. For myself, when someone owns up to a passive-aggressive act, I admire them for having the guts to be honest because I know how hard it is.

To move beneath projections, we need to give up fighting over superficial concerns and look at our underlying fears, which center around questions such as: Do you desire me sexually? Do you think I'm lovable? Do you respect me? If you feel a wave of fear thinking about a discussion at this level, remember that it's the only way to intimacy. We often spend more energy avoiding the conversation than having it. Besides that, we probably know the answers already, we just don't want to feel them or face them.

To overcome projections, we need to step back from our polarized stance and realize that when we point our finger at another person, we are probably pointing it at ourselves. Fortunately, it takes but one person to start breaking the pattern, either through blocking the other's projections or owning our own projection. When someone throws a wrench in the system, it has to change.

Being upset or feeling depressed doesn't necessarily create projections, it's repressing our feelings and cloaking them with shame that leads us to hide them and dump them on someone else. If you can say, "I'm upset and hurt about my lousy evaluation at work," the feelings have been named and owned. They have an identity, a form that makes them manageable. They are no longer an unconscious energy force transmitted through the channels of withdrawal, moodiness, or faking a happy exterior. We bless ourselves and everyone around us when we learn to talk about what is going on inside us.

Here is an exercise to help you get at some feeling you might be projecting on to your partner or family members.

1. Think of people who have had a major impact on your life.
2. As you think of these people, make a list on the left-hand side of the page of all the traits in them that "get on your nerves"—traits you scorn, fear, or are relieved that *you don't have* (this gives you cues as to what you might be projecting).
3. Go through the list of disliked traits, checking for the following:

> Ways in which you have been the same.
> Ways in which you have feared being the same.
> Behaviors you no longer do, but have done in the past (you may still need to forgive yourself).
> Feelings of righteousness: "I'd *never* do that, I'd *never* be like that."
> Ways in which you are the total opposite. We often cover one behavior with the total opposite: dependence—independence, disobedience—obedience, etc.

The similarity may not be concrete. They might be parallel or capture the essence of the experience. For example, the parallel to feeling scorn for someone who is needy in a relationship could be a deep need for status or money. Just remember that righteousness or disdain usually signals a disowned part of oneself.

In case you didn't think of anything or would like something to stimulate your memory, here's a checklist you can use:

Do these traits get on your nerves or cause you to feel judgmental/scornful, or would you "never be like that"?

whining	staying in an abusive
complaining	relationship
interrupting	compulsive eating
forgetting	(look at all your
being irresponsible	compulsive hungers)
passive	being judgmental
assertive	withdrawing
bossy	not talking
outspoken	withholds love and care
taking charge of a situation	independent
acting clueless	successful
dependent on relationships	powerful
helpless	brazen
always helpful	sensuous
martyr	seductive
know it all	acting like a baby

Note which item brings up the strongest reaction in you and then entertain the possibility that you are looking at a rejected part of yourself. If, for example, you scorn people who play a victim role, always whining, complaining, and wanting others to take care of them—look at how you may secretly feel like complaining, whining, and wanting someone to take care of you. If you feel that this isn't a current problem, ask yourself if you have forgiven yourself for the times in the past when you whined and complained and acted "like a baby." Or look to the opposite— how you've become a competent loner, denying your need for care or help. Another approach is to explore what attracts you to people: *If you repeatedly attract people into your life who have traits you disdain, there's a good chance you have similar traits you need to explore in yourself.*

As you engage in this exploration, remember to have kindness and compassion for yourself. You dissociated from parts of yourself because they were the source of pain. In order to survive, you felt you had to commit emotional suicide on aspects of yourself to fit in or be accepted. In daring to touch what was once so painful or forbidden, you tap into the experiences that led to your internal splitting. This can feel extremely painful and can trigger grief, anger, guilt, and shame. The more you are able to embrace these feelings as both human and healing, the more you will give birth to the lover and friend you have wanted to be.

84

NO THANKS! BLOCKING A PROJECTION

*L*earning to block projections is central to the spiritual path because it requires a strong sense of self-worth, self-definition, and a protective psychological barrier that comes from building self-identity, healing childhood wounds, and engaging in a spiritual practice. Projections can feel like a shot out of the blue: Someone makes a remark, or lets you down, and you have a sudden change of mood, a strong flash of hurt or anger. In graduate school, we used to talk about the flash of the chocolate-covered stiletto. You're in a conversation and all of a sudden, zap, ouch, you feel stung, wounded, or knocked off center while the other person sweetly smiles at you. You're so stunned, you don't know what to say.

For a projection to work, there needs to be collusion between two people: a sender, and a receiver who "accepts" the projection. The difficulty lies in having a conscious mind that doesn't want to accept the projection and an unconscious mind that allows it in, either because there are no well-constructed barriers to others' feelings, or because there is an unconscious belief that the price of a relationship involves carrying the feelings for another. In either case, there has to be a place inside that is vulnerable to the projection. People can't project on to you if the projection has no place to go. Unfortunately, when the part that accepts the projection is unconscious, it doesn't feel like a choice; therefore, it's important to have mercy on oneself in the process of learning to recognize and block projections.

Childhood abuse, neglect, or overly intrusive parents set the stage for being vulnerable to projections. It's as if your psychological skin has been punctured, allowing other people's energy to seep in. If we are easily affected by others, we need to be aware of our limitations and not shame ourselves or set unreasonable expectations. It's better to acknowledge that we feel hurt than to fake a happy exterior to prove how detached we can be. We can use our strong reactions as lessons for our growth.

The area of projections is fraught with my own personal struggle. I have felt guilty or irritated reading teachings in the addiction and spiritual literature that say, "No one causes your feelings." While I know this is essentially true, it has a "just say no" ring that is simplistic and doesn't honor the impact of projections. Developing the ability to be involved with others, yet not continually infiltrated by their emotions, is a life journey. I had a father whose feelings were totally enmeshed with mine. A typical adolescent remark from me would "give him" a headache for two days. He was like a child, wanting my acceptance. I felt as if my psychological skin was severely punctured. Fortunately, my mother was far more impervious to other people's feelings. As a result, some things roll off my back easily and other times I struggle not to take on the depression of others or personalize what others say or do.

Having said all of this, I will talk about ways to block projections, or at least recognize them and take care of yourself. All of these approaches come from personal experience and teachings I've learned along the way, particularly from Ken Keyes.

PREVENTION.

Look at the parts of you that are touchy and defensive, and the things you tend to "take personally." Explore them: Where did they come from, what is the underlying wound? Even if the wound isn't healed, you can acknowledge that the wound exists. We mend our Achilles heel with self-acceptance. Go through all the parts of you that you chastise and say, "That's just the way I am. It doesn't mean I'm bad."

Explore your primary relationships and look at all the extremes in behavior. If one person is deeply depressed and the other happy and chipper, entertain the possibility that an unconscious trade-off has occurred. Maybe the happy person has underlying depression. Underlying addictive behavior, we often find projections. One person buries their fear and despair with alcohol and appears happy, while the partner or other family members become depressed.

We also immunize ourselves against projections as we build up our psychological skin so people's stuff doesn't infiltrate our emotional body. Here are some thoughts for daily practice that will help you build a psychological barrier to fend off projections, or at least diminish their power. You may want to pick a few that connect for you, write them down, and keep them handy. The more you internalize them, the more you will have a shield around you to protect you from other people's unexpressed emotions.

I'll start with one of Ken Keyes's Twelve Pathways to Higher Consciousness; it helps to repeat it over and over. "I feel with loving compassion the problems of others without getting caught up emotionally in *their* problems that are offering *them* messages *they* need for *their* growth."

Whatever anyone says or does means nothing about my worth. (This was voted the most popular phrase by my therapy clients.)

People are acting our of *their* conditioning and programming—it means nothing about me.

No matter what I have done, I deserve respect.

I can handle someone saying yes and I can handle someone saying no.

Some people will like me and some people won't and that's the way it goes—I am a child of the creator, worthy of compassion and mercy no matter what.

I get to make mistakes. It's okay to make mistakes. Everyone makes mistakes.

I get to define myself—my wants, needs, and values.

People can be different and still get along.

(Make up your own.)

If you have a sudden shift in mood and suspect you have taken on a projection, think of it as an infection that needs to be tended. Be fascinated with the process, not self-absorbed by the momentary feeling. First, acknowledge when you've taken on a projection, then track back to exactly what was said or done. What is going on with the other person that you might have taken in? At what point did your mood shift? How did you personalize the remark or behavior to say it meant something about you?

A technique that is useful when you feel that someone got "under your skin" is to literally pull the feelings out of you. Pull out the energy from your feet to the top of your head as if wiping off something that got spilled on you. Then throw the feelings out the window. A big hoot or howl can help. So can blowing out and clicking your fingers as if to break up the energy. This may sound a bit silly, but it works extremely well and is something children easily learn to do. Another method is to relax, focus on your feelings, and breathe into them. Give them your complete attention and either draw what they look like or picture them having shape, color, or texture. As you do this, take your mind off the event or thoughts you have about it, and stay aware of the energy you feel inside. Sometimes this will diffuse the feelings. We can also send back projections with verbal responses.

POSSIBLE VERBAL RESPONSES TO PROJECTIONS

If you feel zapped by someone, you can simply say, *Zap! That hurt!* You don't need to know why, you can simply state your experience.

If someone makes a statement that feels like a disguised jab, such as, "Gee you're slow at that," you can reply, "Yes, I am. Is that making you uncomfortable?" In other words, if someone puts you down for trait, don't buy into their shame, simply own it. Yes, I'm depressed, slow, tired, overweight, not a good dancer, etc. *If you start getting defensive, you've taken on the projection.*

If you start to feel intense guilt because you want to say no to rescuing someone or bailing them out of trouble, say so out loud: "I'm feeling guilty for saying no. I'm worried that you will be mad at me." You can also say kindly, "That sounds tough, I wish you the best in figuring out what to do."

We can also learn to fend off projections through body work. The more you center your energy in your solar plexus and belly, and feel the energy pulsing inside, the more grounded you become. The martial arts help people ground themselves and feel their center—so do yoga and meditation. Walking around a room feeling fierce, like a mother bear protecting her cubs, can help. Another approach is to stand, and with the palms of your hands, "draw" a large imaginary space around you, defining your boundaries. You can imagine it filled with light or an energy force that protects you as people's hurtful remarks and thoughts bounce off it. As described earlier, you can make great big belly sounds of "no" as you stand firmly planted on your feet, knees unlocked, pushing your palms out in front of your heart and solar-plexus region. This helps set a neurological response in motion that eventually goes on automatic, even under stress.

In refusing a projection it's important to distinguish between defending ourselves and becoming defensive. Part of blocking a projection can be to rationally defend ourselves by presenting our reality of the situation. "No, I'm not mad at you, I was thinking about a problem at work." "I didn't say I'm going to leave you, I said I wanted to spend some time with friends by myself." If they disagree, drop it and trust your reality. Defensiveness often signals we've dropped out of our neocortex into our limbic system. We're in survival mode and feeling threatened.

If you are able to block the projection or get it out of you quickly, it will change the dynamic of the relationship. Here's a personal example of refusing a projection. Early in our relationship, my partner, Jessie, and I were preparing to load the canoe on the car. To get closer to where the canoe was laid on the ground, I backed up the car and accidentally drove over a five-inch log, which made the car bounce. Jessie grabbed her head in the "yikes" position and had a look of panic in her eyes.

"It's okay, I'll just drive back over it," I said as Jessie lunged out of the car yelling, "No, no, I'll get the log out." She moved like wildfire to pull it out. A few minutes later, she appeared to be irritated with and disdainful of me. Her projection was her internal judgment that I was stupid and incompetent for driving over the log. Fortunately, I didn't get hooked and start apologizing or worrying that she'd leave me—which I would have done some years back.

I said in a relaxed way, "Jessie, it wasn't a big log. It didn't hurt anything." She was still upset. "You think I'm this incompetent flake, don't you?" I could see the edge of a grin emerging. "Look," I said, "I spill milk, I run over logs, I make mistakes . . . so get used to it. Do you want to see me do it again?" I said as I revved up the engine.

"No, no," she said.

It then occurred to me to say, "Your family sure didn't give you much slack, did they?" On the ride home, Jessie pondered her intense reaction, and then talked about how spilling milk or breaking a glass was cause for a beating by her father. If she had driven over the log she would have called herself a stupid flake and feared her father's belt.

My refusing the projection and Jessie's ability to reflect on the incident was instrumental in healing both of us. First of all, I felt good for sticking up for myself and not groveling as if I had committed a crime. Jessie's willingness to reflect and talk over the situation gave her insight into her reactions. We both appreciated how quickly the conflict passed. Handling projections involves a balance between learning not to absorb the negative projections of others, and deciding what we can't handle. I don't choose to spend extended time with people who are chronically negative, depressed, or pessimistic because I lose energy. Maybe someday I'll be able to handle it better, but for now, it's too much for me. If someone is depressed, owns it, and is doing something about it, it's not a problem, I can stay separate and feel care and compassion. If we decide to keep distance from people whose projections we can't handle, we don't need to cast them out of our heart. We can care for them and respect them . . . from a distance, and hope that others will do the same for us. Likewise, we need to remember to hold ourselves in our heart, making nothing bad or wrong, simply seeing our strong reactions and fears as part of our unfinished business.

We can also look for people who send positive projections.

85

YOU MAKE ME FEEL SO GOOD: THE POWER OF POSITIVE PROJECTIONS

*S*everal years ago, in the hope of getting an endorsement for a book, I called Ram Dass. We had exchanged one or two letters, but I had never spoken with him personally. Although we talked for less than ten minutes, when I got off the phone I felt infused with a sense of happiness and peace. It was as if I had absorbed some of his loving energy. On another occasion, while practicing tennis on a backboard, a man came along and hit the ball so fast I was amazed. As I watched him, it was as if I absorbed his ability, and was able to double the pace at which I hit the ball . . . at least for a while.

In the psychology field, we talk about people being able to borrow on the ego strength of others and finding the strength to do what we couldn't do alone. The more we are centered in spirit and have internalized a sense of strength, optimism, and creativity, the more we will transmit this power to others. It is far more through our actions and loving presence that we communicate strength and spirit than by words. We don't "work" on doing this, it will happen automatically as we become increasingly centered in our spirituality and circle of power.

It has often been said that world peace starts with each of us. This is far more true than we often realize. Simply staying peaceful and calm in a traffic jam makes the road safer for everyone around. Warmly greeting our beloved with an open heart transmits love and kindness.

My father projected the sense that I was intelligent and "quite a trouper." From my earliest days, he told me I was a born teacher. My mother projected a sense of humor about making mistakes by laughing when she sewed a zipper in backward or forgot the baking powder in the cookies. While I may have innately had some of the abilities my father projected on to me, they were certainly strengthened by him. In any case, being around people who transmit a joyful spirit and affirm our strength will affect us deeply and will help us grow.

I've often believed that the greatest strength I give my clients is my abiding belief in people's ability to heal, no matter how deep the wounds and heavy the grief. I don't say anything about it. It's just there. Belief isn't even the right word, it's more than a belief—it's a profound sense of knowing in all of my being that healing is possible.

There are conscious ways in which we can practice both sending and receiving positive projections. We learn to envision people as they wish to be.

Creating people as they wish to be is based on the principle that arose from quantum physics, namely, that the observer's perception affects the person or thing being observed. Gary Zukav wrote in *The Dancing Wu Li Masters,* "The new physics tells us that an observer cannot observe without altering what he sees." If we see someone as loving, they are likely to become more loving. If teachers see students as intelligent, they often function in a more intelligent way. In a couples workshop, people practiced consciously changing perceptions of each other for a six-month period and found it to be extremely helpful.

Here's how the process works:

The two people agree on who will start out as the sender and who will be the receiver. The receiver tells the sender how he or she wants to be envisioned/created (I want you to see me being easy on myself when I make a mistake. I want you to create me as stopping myself before I explode with anger). When you are the sender, it is extremely important that you create the other person as *they* wish to be, not as *you* wish them to be. You are strengthening their vision of themselves, not imposing your own.

As the sender, take a few moments to breathe, relax, and tap into your whole being and create the image the sender requests. Some people will see the image, others will simply feel it. Either way works. Imagine the person being as they wish to be. You can also send them the message in words. Start by saying their name, and with all your being, say what they want to hear. "I see you as stopping yourself before you explode with anger." Interspersed with moments of silence and time to breathe, continue to send the image to the receiver.

As the receiver, imagine the cells of your body, your heart, and your spirit opening up to receive the new image of yourself. Notice any blocks to receiving the new image of yourself. Don't give them energy, just note them in passing and return to receiving this new image of yourself. Know with all your heart that you can be different, that you can accept this new image and let the old ways slip away.

The receiver can signal when it's time to close or you can use a timer. If the sender has finished before the receiver feels ready to stop, s/he can quietly sit and meditate or send light energy. Afterward, bring your eyes back to each other and thank each other. You might want to bow to each other and say *Namaste.*

I have often done this form of creative visualizing in group healing. One person is the receiver and everyone sends to them at once. Often, the group energy becomes very powerful and everyone drops into a deep sense of relaxation and peace. In many cases, they will feel shifts in their own self-concept happening inside themselves.

Couples in the workshop found it helpful to do a brief version of this at bedtime, using the same affirmation or image over several weeks or months. They would look each other in the eyes and say, "I create you as . . ." Take a short pause to breathe and switch rolls. For many people this provides a longed-for healing voice that eventually became their own.

Envisioning each other as we wish to be is really a form of prayer, a blessing we give to each other. As we bring the energy of our love, spirit, mind, and body to focus on each other, we invoke the power of the universe/God to send the energy of transformation.

86
SEXUALITY, SPIRITUALITY, AND INTIMACY

Resolve to be always beginning—to be a beginner.
—Ranier Maria Rilke

*S*exual energy is powerful. To allow it free rein in our bodies is to open ourselves to be moved and transformed. This requires that we be willing to suffer discomfort and anxiety, as well as experience joy and ecstasy.

Feeling the arousal of our passion and sexual energy and dissolving into our beloved, allows the power of the universe to unfold within us. If we allow our sexual energy to expand and move upward into our heart, we heighten our intimacy with each other. As we melt into each other, flesh to flesh, and heart to heart, we create a connection with both spirit and flesh.

At the other extreme, sex can hurt or feel cold and exploitive. Sex can be a form of violation—emotionally, physically, and spiritually—another form of taking a drink to ease life's pain, another rote act performed to prevent abandonment. Sex without love can create a momentary high, usually followed by a chasm opening between two people as they roll over and feel an emptiness quake open within them . . . or they take another drink to numb the pain.

In between these extremes, a lot of sex feels more like cold oatmeal or going over a speed bump (as a friend put it), than having an intimate, affirming experience. It's not bad, it's just routine and uninteresting. Who cares? If this is the case, it's time to explore our sexuality—our fears and insecurities. It's also time to explore the areas of the relationship that have been shut down or avoided. If we have retreated into our isolated corners for protective safety, we need to come back into the playing field and allow ourselves to give and receive pleasure. Our ability to be sexually intimate is a mirror into our individual selves; whatever is missing, withheld, or unexplored may manifest in our lovemaking . . . or our attempts at lovemaking.

The path toward sexual intimacy can merge with the path toward spirit if we are willing to open ourselves to all we are and to knowing another person. This path is not for the faint of heart. It takes discipline and courage. Some would say our sexual energy and our spiritual energy are one and the same—our life-force energy, the chi, the prana, the pulse beat of the universe manifest in us.

When we release sexual energy and let it flow through our body, it searches out anything that hides and brings it to consciousness. To open ourselves to our sexual energy is to say, I open myself to knowing myself. I open myself to life. For most people, sex starts out feeling unnatural and anxiety-producing, just as any new venture does. Unlike media images of young, beautiful people having passionate sex, deep sexual intimacy evolves over the years as a relationship deepens and the individuals grow.

I've often been amazed that few people talk about practice and experience as important to evolving sexually. As a piano instructor who taught courses in performance anxiety, it was obvious that people got more proficient with practice, and that the level of performance anxiety diminished as people gained experience performing. Rainer Rilke writes in *Love and Other Difficulties*, "Young people . . . must not forget, when they love, that they are beginners, bunglers of life, apprentices in love— must *learn* love, and that (like *all* learning) wants peace, patience, and composure!"

To enter into an authentic sexual union is to expose our tenderness, passion, and wild side, along with our wounds and fears. Sex will vary with the fluctuations in our lives, sometimes being sweet and tender, other times feeling powerful, like the roar of an ocean wave. Like any energy force, it waxes and wanes and changes with the seasons. When it is paired with spirituality, it is a reflection of our inner worlds meeting one another. When two people first feel the electricity of sexual chemistry and attraction, sex may take center stage. Enduring, happy couples have different levels of sexual intensity, but, for the most part sex plays an important role in the relationship. Sexual chemistry and attraction isn't a guarantee of a healthy, intimate relationship, but it can be an important spark that helps keep relationships vital and alive.

I am troubled by spiritual literature—from Christianity to various Eastern religions—that position celibacy as somehow higher and holier than sexual intimacy. While for some, celibacy helps deepen spirituality, more often it is imposed because sex is feared as a huge force that will run rampant. This often leads to people becoming obsessed with *not* being sexual. When sex is forbidden out of fear, it often becomes the desired fruit and implies that sex is shameful or dirty. *To bring sexuality and spirituality together, it's important that loving God and loving someone in a physical way feel unified in our hearts and minds.* I have also heard teachings that say we should save our sexual energy so we have more energy for serving others. It has not been my experience that people who don't have sex are any more enlightened, generous, or open-hearted as a group than people who are in sexual relationships. On the contrary, I have seen people who, thinking it is required for enlightenment, have strangled their impulses and stopped the flow of their warmth and energy as a result of living an austere, sexless life. Sexuality, when combined with love and spirit, can open our energy, help us expand, and bring us closer to our partner and to the work we are doing in the world.

We need to be aware of when sex brings us closer to love and when sex blocks intimacy by becoming rote and detached. The sexual act needs to include giving and receiving love and being genuine with each other, not just having a physical high. To sustain long-lasting sexual intimacy, we need to be able to discern when we are sexual from an adult state rather than from a needy child state. In the section on being allies to each other's wounded places, we explored the ego states of child and adult. We are likely to be operating from a child state when we use sex to show we are important, to prevent someone leaving, as a disguised way to vent anger, or when we see our partner as the all-protective father or the nurturing mother. Sexual expression from a child state eventually creates an incestuous feeling that can lead to withdrawal of sexual attraction and can create intense ambivalent feelings about our partner.

We need a great deal of gentleness with ourselves in exploring our sexual beliefs, fantasies, and experiences. Western culture has taken sex from the spiritual realm and made it a commodity—an aspect of domination, control, and violence. Without developing a spiritual connection—seeing sex as spiritual union—sex remains superficial and keeps us from connecting at the level of essence. Sexuality *is* tied to spirituality no matter what we have been taught to believe.

Keeping the sexual connection alive in a "marriage" is like keeping water flowing in a streambed. We need to stay alive, open, creative, and growing. It is crucial that we maintain our separate identities and not let go of our values and passions. Ranier Maria Rilke writes in his essay, "Learning to Love":

> When two people both give themselves up in order to come close to each other, there is no longer any ground beneath them and their being together is a continual falling.

Many of the problems of aging and loss of sexual desire are not about lines, weight gain, and thinning hair; they are about a spirit that goes dull, and a heart that feels weary from routines and lack of passion.

In our busy lives it is easy to let sex slip into a rare or rushed event—something we do on vacation or every now and then. In general, if you keep the sexual part of your relationship alive, you will enjoy sex more and increase your desire to be sexual. As Debra Rein said at a couples' sexuality workshop, "It's like exercise. When you're out of practice, you have to drag yourself out the first time, but once you get started, it feels good. It gets easier every time you go and eventually you look forward to it and are eager to go." Sometimes we need to get in the habit of having sex—without being sexual in a habitual way.

For many it helps to make dates to make love. It's a matter of putting our relationship on the calendar and making it a priority. It can be wonderful to set aside a lengthy time in which there will be no interruptions. Some people argue that you have to wait for the mood to come. While this might be true on occasion, it might also be an excuse to avoid facing uncomfortable feelings. It implies that we don't have the power to formulate an intention and follow through with actions. Part of having ego strength is the ability to set a time to be sexual and then get ourselves into the mood. Making a date together takes away the stress of someone being turned down. It becomes an "us" commitment that two people make together. One of the main ingredients is allowing enough time and getting in the mood together.

If sex has dried up or if one person is feeling afraid or has performance anxiety, some people suggest taking a break from explicit sexual contact and doing massage, and sensual touch, followed eventually by sexual massage. Sometimes these forms of physical contact stimulate the desire for sex. Other times, however, we may need to move through our anxiety and forge ahead by being sexual. This may involve facing the discomfort of someone getting numb, falling asleep in the middle, or getting scared. It may entail explicit talk about what each partner likes and doesn't like. It may bring up our insecurities and all kinds of fears. We may feel like nervous adolescents, which is not surprising, because most people have not fully allowed themselves to experience the power and breadth of sexual intimacy. To become comfortable with anything unknown or challenging, we need to go there again and again. We need to become more present to each other, tune into the physical sensations, and allow our bodies to feel pleasure and intensity.

Deepening our sexual intimacy includes deepening our honesty in the relationship. When we start to open up sexually, our mind may be barraged with thoughts of irritation and anger from issues left unresolved. The parts of us we are holding back and protecting will be felt during our lovemaking.

If the aversion to sex comes because it reawakens memories of abuse, then take time to find a healing group or therapist to release the wounds and allow you to define your own sexuality and sexual relationship. Otherwise, you stay a victim to whoever harmed you. I discuss this at length in *Women, Sex, and Addiction*.

Here are some affirmations that help us create a spiritual sexual union:

I am open to knowing myself and my beloved.

I am open to pleasure, joy, intensity, and eroticism.

I am committed to my spiritual journey—to deepening my ability to love, speak the truth, and feel compassion.

I am open to allowing my playfulness and creativity to come alive with my partner.

If coming together in an intimate sexual relationship is difficult, have compassion and kindness for yourself and for your beloved. Sexuality taps into our deepest feelings and fears. It can take a lot of effort and personal growth to love with an open heart. We need to validate our desire for love, passion, and ecstasy, but remember that the journey to finding these things is long and composed of many small steps. Blessings on your journey.

87

UNDER THE CARE OF US ALL— SUPPORT FOR COUPLES

Couples and families need support within community. Intimacy doesn't happen in a vacuum, it happens in a system that creates a foundation of support. Stress and strain have an immediate impact on couples and families, particularly when there are no outside resources to take up the slack and ease the burdens. Stress from long work hours, lack of good child care, health care, mental health care, working different shifts and minimum-wage jobs without benefits often leave people frustrated and exhausted at the end of the day. When a couple has chronic stress, both the individuals and the relationship bond are deeply tested. The more stress each person has to deal with, the harder it is to give to the other. Instead of their cups overflowing, they drag themselves to the marriage table or bed with an empty mug, hoping that the other might fill it up.

In the United States, the situation for couples and families is becoming more and more stressful. Few families can exist with one wage earner, and people are now required to do 1.3 times the amount of work, on the average, than they did twenty years ago. We often hear the phrase "family values," but if we don't enact policies that support families, the rhetoric about family values is nothing but empty political posturing.

Historically, people have had extended family around to call on in a myriad of ways. I think of my grandma Emily, a widow with a fourth-grade education and seven young children who made it through with hard work, seven day boarders, the help of relatives and friends, and her profound belief in God. My mother, the seventh child, recalls a happy childhood, singing and reading together as a family, and enjoying extended family gatherings with numerous aunts, uncles, and cousins who lived in the neighborhood. Two of her brothers worked at the Star Garage run by her uncle Will. Although Hershey bars were split eight ways and my mother tells of keeping her piece still on her tongue so the taste would last, she never had a sense of deprivation because there was a profound spirit of cooperation—everyone pitched in and helped. Everyone was of value. Her older brothers helped her go to college before them because she was gifted for playing the violin. They were poor in money, but they had support and community.

One avenue of support for couples is being intimate with other couples so they can give support, have fun, and talk honestly about troubles in the relationship. Many couples keep up a protective cover even when there is a lot of pain and confusion beneath the surface. My experience is that many couples are willing to talk if someone breaks the ice. When I led a six-month couples' workshop, each couple paired up with another couple for the duration of the workshop. The couples got together for support, going over homework and practicing consensus problem solving. Part of the process was to get to know the inner workings of the other couple. For many, this was a new experience and one they treasured. Several of the couples remained friends.

When a couple argues, fights, and hits an impasse, both are likely to shield their hearts, retreat, and lose energy unless they have an outside resource to help them. It can be profoundly helpful if each person can call on a trusted friend to help them process their inner feelings and gain clarity in the situation. It's also helpful if the couple has an organized form of support. I would love to see religious organizations, mental health clinics, and community agencies provide more support groups for couples for both social connections as well as places to learn communication skills and talk about sexuality and parenting. The sense of isolation abates and people feel reassured when they realize that others have the same concerns or struggles. It also gives people a window into other couples' lives—of what's possible or how others deal with problems. This also paves the way for individual members of couples to call on others for help in troubled times.

Because calling an "outsider" to process feelings is a foreign concept for many people, particularly men, teaching people these skills in support groups for couples would help them experience the relief of opening up and talking. It would help people lower stress, lessen abuse, and make homes a kinder place for children.

There are training programs set up to help individuals give each other peer support in the form of cocounseling and reevaluation counseling. This can contribute greatly to individuals and can help them with their relationships. We need to develop the same sort of program for couples so that they are supported by the community, not just left alone to struggle with one of the most difficult tasks in life—being mated to another person.

In the Quaker community, a couple goes through a process of meeting with a clearness committee before marriage. There might be several meetings. When the committee feels clear that the decision to marry is grounded and led by spirit, they agree to take the couple *under the care of the meeting*. It gives the couple a permanent shelter, a group committed to their support, for better or worse. I have been through this process and it is a comforting feeling in the center of my heart to know that there is a group of people committed to support our relationship and help us through the hard times. I wish every couple could be under the care of community and have a special group committed to their support and care.

PART IX

...

WHAT THE WORLD NEEDS NOW: COMMUNITY

I commit . . .
to become the best version of myself
to make and keep agreements with great care
to be constant through conflict
to give myself fully to the process of transformation through the expression of love
to trust the good intentions of each of us
to relate with respect and acceptance
to enter fully into life's experiences
to awaken to my awareness of my unique role in the universe
to acknowledge the inner and interconnectednss of all creation.
So be it!

—Covenants of the Goodenough Community

*S*o far we have talked about ways to clear out negative influences from childhood, define ourselves as adults, create a circle of friends, focus on communication skills, and deepen our intimacy in relationships. When we bring these skills and abilities together, they create a synergistic energy that feeds into the well-being of community. We are better able to work together, respecting differences, handling disagreements, and following a process for decision making. Likewise, when we have a healthy community, it provides a multitude of avenues for people to evolve and develop skills for intimacy and caring. Community is much more than the sum of its parts. It is a felt sense of unity that permeates our daily lives. It is the spirit of love manifesting itself on earth.

Healthy community is guided by wisdom that emanates from the heart. We collectively move toward love through an abiding commitment to the well-being of each other and to all that sustains life—air, water, earth, natural habitat, and love. We find a home for our heart when we are safe and know that our voices will be heard. We also accept that as humans we are flawed and imperfect, capable of wounding each other deeply. In healthy community, we learn how to live together with our imperfections, accepting them and controlling our capacity for harming each other. *Healthy community is inclusive of all, a mosaic of many colors, shapes, and forms. It embraces a philosophy of abundance, not scarcity; of love, not fear; of inclusion, not segregation; of sharing, not hoarding; of peace and joy, not endless suffering and pain.*

Even though Western society has created separation and alienation by stressing rugged individualism and material wealth, we are, essentially, tribal people meant to live together, share the load, and care for one another as we pass through the many phases of life. In a healthy community, everyone has a role to play, from the child who brings delight, to the young adult who needs mentoring and guidance, to the adults—the builders, artists, teachers, musicians, seers, cooks, healers, clowns, crones, and elders who impart their wisdom. In healthy community, our personal and community lives are fused together.

When we use the phrase "finding ourselves," it also suggests that we are finding our role in community. We find our
special gifts, talents, and strengths to feel whole *and* to become
a contributing cell in our community. The two are inseparable.
Because our personal joys and strengths are synonymous with
the strength and joy of the whole, healthy community supports
whatever feeds the spirit and helps people's talents and skills
flourish. This is the most economical use of energy, for when
people are valued and encouraged to develop their potential,
they are most likely to be healthy and happy and enjoy giving
their very best to community.

People are often seeking a lover to fulfill what only community can provide—support, companionship, safety, excitement,
adventure, and help in sharing the load. Attempting to meet all
our needs for intimacy and understanding from a primary relationship puts too much pressure on our partner or children. As
we are nurtured and cared for in community, we feel a sense of
abundance within that spills over on to those around us. We
naturally want to give back to others. It becomes a big, intertwined circle of energy where we give and take freely, knowing
there is enough for all.

88

A WHEEL IN A WHEEL: THE MANY CELLS OF COMMUNITY

Ezekiel saw the wheel, way up in the middle of the air
Ezekiel saw the wheel way in the middle of the air.
And the little wheel run by faith
And the big wheel run by the grace of God.
It's a wheel in a wheel, way in the middle of the air.
—Religious folk song (The Book of Ezekiel)

*C*onnections create spinning wheels of energy that bring us alive—like two energy circuits coming together. It starts with connecting to ourselves—our love, power, wisdom, feelings, and perceptions. And then, like dropping a pebble in still water, the circles of our lives expand to include connections with family, friends, and neighbors. Beyond this it reaches out to community, country, and, eventually, the universe. The energy is strongest in the center, but the ripple effect is infinite, just as love is infinite. The more powerful our love, the greater the depth and power of our connections.

Community is comprised of many circles connected in different ways—the wheels in a wheel. We can talk about living in a community as well as feeling the spirit of community—of connection, ties, and commitment to each other.

People form a community identity in many ways. There are intentional communities in which people live together based on a belief system or a common purpose. Their ties are often intense, and people pay a great deal of attention to community process. There are communities in which people do not live together but are bound to each other in an ongoing way through religious or community organizations. I think of my Quaker meeting, the Unity churches, and the Peace Dance Community. These communities are not as intense as living together, but the ties run deep through a shared belief system as well as spending time together in a variety of ways. They provide a safety net, a spiritual home, and a system that has a structure for helping people.

Sometimes a neighborhood develops a sense of community through having block parties, crime prevention groups, or working together to solve a neighborhood problem. One group of neighbors, for example, worked together to convince an apartment owner to evict the drug dealers from the adjoining apartment complex.

Some cities and towns create a spirit of community when their policies reflect the best interests of people as a whole, not just a privileged few. This often leads to a sense of community pride and generosity between people.

People also talk about a sense of community with professional or work colleagues. These connections might operate on different levels: Some might limit their relationships to the workplace, others might socialize occasionally, and some become close friends. People who work independently might get together with colleagues for occasional support. For years I was part of a network of community workers and therapists in Minneapolis who got together monthly to talk about working with incest and abuse. We all learned from each other.

Groups of people often create the spirit of community when they bond together for a common goal. In working together for labor unions, women's rights, civil rights, peace, land preservation, or to create low-income housing, large groups of people have felt linked through time and space with other like-minded people. If you visit a similar organization in a different city, or even a different country, it would have a familiar feeling. I remember the incredible sense of connection I felt with women all over the world when I attended the International Decade of Women Conference in Nairobi with 14,000 women from all over the world.

Other cells of community are the myriad interest and support groups for adventure, recovery, hiking, bowling, and studying books that bring people together in circles for enlightenment, adventure, exploration, or healing. By looking at the list of community announcements in any newspaper, one can see numerous ways in which people gather together to fulfill different needs.

Each of us affects the spirit of community in everything we do. Supporting good public schools affects not only the children who attend, but their families and, ultimately, the whole community. The happiness and well-being of any one person affects the well-being of all. The care we give to our jobs or volunteer activities becomes part of the connective tissue of community. If you work at a checkout stand and are warm and friendly to customers, that will affect their feelings and their connections with others. If you manage a business, your treatment of your employees affects their mood, and that of the people they serve, as well as their families and friends. Whatever you do ultimately has an effect on others, probably far more so than most people realize.

While we often hear about the troubles in communities— and there are many—there are also hundreds of thousands of people generously volunteering time at nursing homes, hospice centers, shelters, as big brothers and sisters, at schools, painting old houses, facilitating groups for abused women, and so on. There are also many people in their sixties and seventies relinquishing their retirement years to bring up grandchildren. There is an extraordinary amount of care and giving that we don't hear about because people who give from the heart are often quiet about it and the media pays little attention. This is the spirit of community in action. We are here to love and serve others, and in doing so we find our own spirit and meaning in life.

The image of the little wheel run by faith suggests that we need to trust our hearts to lead us to circles that welcome our true nature, embrace our power, and encourage us to grow. When we put ourselves in situations that are dynamic, changing, comforting, supportive, and expansive, we nourish our passion for life and charge our wheels within—our energy vortexes, or chakras. When we are supported and fulfilled and our cup overflows, we naturally contribute to our loved ones and the community as a whole. By collectively joining together in community we experience the big wheel—the grace of God or the presence of love in us and around us. It's not that we submit to others or give up our integrity, rather, we surrender our rigid ego boundaries for the mystical wheel in a wheel, allowing us to intertwine our energies with each other's and raise our collective consciousness to embrace love as the greatest force in the Universe.

89

COMMUNITY IS GOOD FOR YOUR HEALTH

Stress, one of the leading causes of illness, is often created by a blockage of energy flow within us. Fear, worry, and pain narrow our vision and constrict the systems of our body. They are hard to overcome alone. People talk of feeling drained, depleted, fatigued, or just plain blah. They are low on energy— the fuel of life and vitality. Our minds and bodies alone cannot bear the pain of life's losses, but in community we can share the pain. And when we share the pain, our body releases tension and stress.

Connections are a profound source of healing and help overcome stress. Connections to self, spirit, and others help us open up and ignite our energy. When our energy flows, we are more likely to be healthy—emotionally and physically. When we connect to ourselves, we feel the pulse and energy charge of our emotions and feelings along with the joy of our strengths and talents. This inner connection is embedded in our outer connection to All That Is—the wisdom, wonder, and awe of creation, the mystery of what it is to have a life. The interpenetration of our inner world with spirit helps us feel the presence of big mind and big heart. This, in turn, helps us see our problems within the broad context of life, not as isolated problems we are experiencing alone. This openness leads to healthy give-and-take connections to others, which forms the bedrock of our experience here on earth. *The capacity to connect authentically with another human being is perhaps the most sustaining ability we can develop.* Healthy community is an integral part of this process when it assures us of a support network where we can make connections and celebrate our joys.

Community building starts with getting to know each other at a personal level. As we build, repair, celebrate, create safety, tell our stories, deal with conflict, and work toward our dreams, we get to know the details of each other's lives and personalities. As we make these connections, we learn a basic truth: namely, that when we truly know someone well, we feel caring and compassion for them. As part of a Quaker meeting I attended in St. Paul, Minnesota, someone would tell the story of their spiritual journey at the adult education session prior to the meeting for worship. I never ceased being amazed at the roads people had traveled. I always left those gatherings feeling more love and compassion for the individual who had spoken.

As we open our hearts to each other, we open the healing forces within us. We don't need to like someone's personality or want to be close friends to include them in the wider embrace of compassion—we see them as another person on the journey, hungering for love, understanding, and purpose. This broad sense of compassion helps us stay connected to them in spirit and in supporting them in community.

When Dr. Dean Ornish created a program for reversing heart disease, he set up groups to help people motivate each other to exercise and follow proper diets. He writes:

> Over time, I began to realize that the group support itself was one of the most powerful interventions, as it addressed what I am beginning to believe is a more fundamental cause of why we feel stressed, and in turn why we get illnesses like heart disease; the perception of isolation . . . Anything that leads to real intimacy and feeling of connection can be healing: to bring together to make whole.

Likewise, in another study, researchers explored a community in which the levels of illness, including heart attack, and cancer were significantly below the national average even though there was apparently no difference in the diet, alcohol consumption, type of work, or external stress. Eventually, the researchers found that the community thrived because of the close ties among people. As an immigrant community of Italians, they were deeply involved in each other's lives—talking, helping, keeping up to date with each other. When the next generation started moving away and people lost their community ties, levels of illness rose toward the national average. Health is a combination of mind, body, and spirit flowing together within us, stimulated by adventure, joy, connection, and purpose. Healthy community is a combination of minds, bodies, and spirits coming together in the name of support and care for each other.

90

CREATING RITUALS IN COMMUNITY

Rituals bring a spiritual dimension to familiar experiences and bestow protected time and space to stop and reflect on life's transformations.
—Evan Imber-Black and Janine Roberts, *Rituals for Our Times*

Community comes alive through rituals to honor passages of birth, puberty, adulthood, marriage, birthdays, death, or any significant change. Rituals have the ability to connect us to our inner world, to spirit, and to each other. They can be joyful, playful, serious, secular, or sacred. All cultures and religions have rituals that center around everything from food, to greetings, to ceremonies and holy days.

In Western culture, our separation from meaningful rituals often leaves us feeling that life is empty and bereft. We eat dinner separately, watching TV, we come and go without making eye contact or acknowledging each other's presence, holidays focus on gifts instead of the intended spiritual meaning, we are semiconscious of the changing of the seasons. Rituals help us stop, breathe, take note, and connect us to life's passages.

Most of us are familiar with traditional rituals: a prayer before meals; a secret wish before blowing out the birthday candles; a knock on wood when we make a strong assertion; an exchange of rings in marriage.

Daily rituals are involved in saying hello or good-bye. Other daily rituals center around eating and sleeping. Bedtime for children, for example, might include a story, a drink of water, a favorite stuffed toy, a prayer, or a kiss good night. With eating rituals, we not only eat different types of foods in different combinations, but, depending on our culture, we also have different ways of eating.

Rituals come alive when they are personal and heartfelt. Daily blessings before meals can have special meaning if we create them in the moment, as we listen to our hearts. Rituals risk becoming rote and empty, however, when we forget their symbolic meaning. We sit through worship services intoning prayers in a trance and all of a sudden wonder what we were saying. The healing power of ritual comes alive when we connect symbols, our inner world, and the world of spirit. For example, when people do the dances of universal peace, they usually have a cloth centerpiece symbolizing the world's major religions, flowers for beauty, and rocks or shells symbolizing our connection to the earth. Before going into a sweat lodge, people place symbolic articles they want blessed near the opening. They also string together prayer bags with small pieces of cloth and tobacco, saying a prayer as they make each one to prepare themselves spiritually for the sweat lodge.

Ultimately, ritual is a form of living consciously throughout our days, bringing our heart and care to all we do, consecrating life as sacred and wondrous. In *Mutant Message Downunder*, Marlo Morgan talks about the aboriginal tribe that was able to live totally off the land:

> The Real People explained how absurd it appeared to them when the missionaries insisted they teach their children to fold hands and give two minutes of grace before meals. They wake up being grateful! They spend the entire day never taking anything for granted.

Whenever a ritual takes us into the heart and spirit, it becomes sacred. It awakens us, stimulates our consciousness, makes us more tuned in and alive. Secular rituals like watching sporting events can be pleasant but may do little to raise our consciousness if we satiate ourselves with food and drink and our mood depends upon who wins. On the other hand, watching some sporting events might stimulate our spirit if we watch in awe as we see the amazing strength, agility, and beauty of the human body, and the dedication of people to excellence.

When rituals lack a purpose beyond immediate gratification, they often descend into an excess of food, sex, drugs, or sedentary behavior. One summer, when driving from Minnesota to Montana, Jessie and I started seeing thousands of motorcycles swarming together on the highway. I learned that they were heading to a motorcycle gathering in Sturgis, South Dakota. I was so amazed by the numbers of people involved—an estimated 400,000—I started asking the bikers what drew them there. The most common answers were to drink beer, get smashed, have sex, and hang out. Some people said, "It just feels good." While I admit to feeling glad when I saw a woman driving her own motorcycle rather than hanging onto a man in the driver's seat, and I was impressed with the spit-and-polish shine of the many motorcycles, I kept thinking about what would happen if all these people got together for a higher purpose. When we reached the Black Hills State Park, I spent some time walking through the parking lot, entranced with the different models, ages, colors, and designs of so many motorcycles. I found out that the gathering had originated some twenty years earlier as a way to raise money for an adolescent boy's medical expenses. I was glad there was an altruistic origin although few people knew about it. As I chatted with some of the men, the Peggy Lee song, "Is That All There Is?", kept going through my mind. She talks about going to the circus, riding the carousel, eating cotton candy, and then wondering when it's over ". . . is that all there is?"

Before I understood ritual, I used to think it was some mysterious event with incense, icons, and special incantations. Rituals can be simple and personal. They are a way to heighten awareness as we consciously share an experience with others. For five years I've had my annual postcancer mammogram ritual, in which friends come with me to look at the X rays and join me in celebrating one more year without a recurrence of cancer. On the fifth anniversary, three of us went together and all had mammograms. We then went home and were joined by another friend for sparkling cider, snacks, and a soak in the hot tub, where we talked about our lives. We called it the "breast party." When we bring completion to an event by having a ritual, we let go of it in our psyche and make room to live in the present.

Rituals that are alive invite people's individual expression or contribution, even if there is an existing structure or leader. This shifts the dynamics from leader and followers to a facilitator who is part of the circle. Whenever the circle invites all to share, we learn about each other in a personal way.

Rituals can connect us to the earth's cycles as well as to each other. This can include drumming, singing, and dancing. The drumming connects us to our heartbeat and a sense of pulse in the belly that symbolizes the greater pulse of life. Singing helps connect us with each other through the breath, the sounds, and the words. As our voices become as one, we feel unity, we transcend our separate selves. Dancing also brings our bodies into a shared rhythm and flow, just as there is rhythm and flow in life and in the earth's cycles.

Rituals can help bring closure to situations. Too often we glide over a painful experience, numbing our feelings and toughing it out. We can create small personal rituals for the end of a relationship, having a miscarriage, leaving a job, getting over an illness, or having the children leave home. When we provide a time to stop, gather together with friends to share our experience, reminisce, and grieve, we release our pain rather than storing it away to haunt us in a thousand ways.

Rituals can tap into our creativity. One time, several women had a ritual to let go of negative ties to parents. One woman brought ropes, symbolizing the negative connections between herself and her parents, and laid them on the floor. As she cut each rope she said things like, "I am letting go of believing I am unlovable. I am letting go of abusing myself because you hurt me."

Another form of ritual is helping people when they are confused, trying to make a decision, or having a difficult time with children. A model I mentioned earlier is what Quakers call "clearness" committees. They can be used and adapted by anyone. The goal is to help a person become clear on whatever problem they are facing. We come together and collectively tap into the leadings of the spirit. A small group, generally from three to eight people, convene. After a time of silence to help us center, we listen to the concern, and paraphrase what we've heard to make sure we understand. Then we often ask questions to flush out the deeper levels of the problem. We operate in the spirit of exploration and do not give advice. Sometimes we pause for silence to let the thoughts deepen or listen for guidance or insight. After the silence, people say what has come to them. Then we explore solutions or ways to resolve the problem. This helps people make a decision, have a new way of understanding a problem, or have greater clarity on the path they want to follow. The person having the clearness meeting may feel better simply by feeling understood and knowing that they are not alone in a difficult time.

In reflecting on clearness gatherings, we often speak with wonder at the miraculous sense of spirit that is ignited by this simple act of bringing our wisdom and hearts together to minister to another person. I also like clearness meetings because we give to each other as equals and friends without pathologizing the stresses and struggles of life. Instead of denying our problems, suffering them alone, or feeling that our only recourse is going to a counselor or psychologist, we come together in community, invoking spirit and love to guide us to wisdom. I would love to see some form of this process available to all people through religious organizations, community clinics, and in schools.

From the blowing out of birthday candles, to the symbolic cutting of ties, to the celebrating of a success, to the saying of thanks for food and shelter, to dancing under the stars to a drumbeat, ritual is taking time to stop, breathe, and connect ourselves to the wonder of All That Is. The more our rituals connect us to gratitude, wonder, and an open heart, the more they bring healing energy into our lives. The more we bring conscious awareness to eating, waking, coming together, and going apart, the more our lives take on a rhythm and flow that brings sustenance to our souls and fills us up.

91

SO WHAT ABOUT THE CYBERSPACE COMMUNITY?

(I am focusing this discussion on cyberspace, but it could also apply to TV and other technological inventions.)

I love sending E-mail to friends. I've probably exchanged more letters with my brother and his wife in the last year than we did in the past ten. There's something relaxing about sitting down, typing a letter, and knowing it has arrived in less than a minute. I don't have to look for stationery, and the loose ethics of E-mail allows me to be brief, leave in the typos, and not worry about the literary quality of my writing. E-mail has gotten people to write letters again.

The Internet has an incredible capacity to help people to connect around the world, to talk, share ideas, and disseminate information. My roommate Mary got help on a crocheting project from a seventy-six-year-old woman in New Zealand. My other roommate Annie was able to find a guide to guitar chords. A friend met her future husband. The possibilities are infinite.

The Internet also gives people a way to converse. People who are alone can connect via the Internet. I heard the story of a woman who came home feeling terrible after losing a job. She told her story on the Internet and many people responded with kindness and sympathy. She felt much better. The potential for talking with people around the world has many implications for improving our understanding of each other.

So why am I so uneasy about cyberspace within the context of creating healthy communities for us to live in?

Forging intimate relationships is one with the spiritual journey—a process that takes time, effort, and the willingness to suffer our mistakes and learn from them. It is an ongoing process that challenges us to grow and become vulnerable—to look each other in the eyes, speak honestly, and touch appropriately. One of the great lessons of life is to realize that there are no quick fixes. Technological wonders or artificial highs cannot substitute for a loving connection with another human, a sense of purpose, and the ability to be sustained by the beauty of the natural world. I worry that cruising the Internet, just like any other compulsive behavior, often becomes one more escape hatch from being present and facing life's struggles.

Over and over again, when I ask people to recall their happiest times, they talk about giving birth, seeing their children grow, feeling at peace, being intimate, being in nature—or a combination of these things. How does cyberspace help bring us closer to our spiritual nature and connect us in community?

The trip through cyberspace can be linear and superficial. We can cruise around, check out information, have an exchange with a person, and if we get bored, we can disconnect. There is little responsibility or accountability in clicking people on and off, in never having a face-to-face encounter. We run the risk of becoming more and more removed from the challenges and rewards of human interaction or of stretching our minds in a creative way.

Going beyond the concept of cyberspace to TV, computer games, and other examples of technology, I am also concerned that their extensive use contributes to a culture of restless people dependent on external stimulus and modern technology for meaning or entertainment in life. I am concerned about the time it takes from other endeavors, and its addictiveness. As we adapt to speeding images, it becomes more and more difficult to slow down, watch a sunset, read a book, or take on a creative project.

Creativity is deeply connected with spirituality because it represents the ongoing creation of the universe coming through us. For hundreds of years children have broadened their creativity through playing together outdoors, making up games, and exploring nature. In learning to play a musical instrument, children develop discipline and a trust in the learning process—if you persist, you improve. In spite of children today having five times the toys and technological resources that people of my generation had, kids repeatedly complain of being bored. A friend of mine said that her ten-year-old son's first comment when she said they were going to take a vacation was, "Can I bring the computer?" He simply couldn't imagine life without it.

When people become dependent on constant external stimulus, they have difficulty entertaining themselves. This starts with children and carries over to adulthood. I have been fascinated by watching various children who come to a lake where I often stay. Some of them watch the turtles, sit on a dock looking for fish, paddle around in inner tubes, stack rocks, and never want for something to do, while others ride four-wheel-ers or motorcycles in circles for hours, play loud music, and then wander around looking bored. What was once a quiet refuge full of loons, turtles, birds, beavers, deer, and other wildlife is becoming overrun to a large degree by people who appear to be dependent on motorized toys—for big people and little people.

One of the great challenges of life that leads to becoming a mature and integrated person is learning to push through frustrations and challenge ourselves. We need to experience our restlessness and go beneath it. Anyone who has taken part in meditation in its many forms knows that there can be times when you get bored, restless, feel uncomfortable, and want to quit. If you persevere, however, and tolerate the restlessness, there will come a moment of letting go in which you sink into a peaceful state that removes all wants.

We need to look at our priorities and note how we spend our time. Time, for many of us, is the most valuable commodity in life. People talk about "downtime"—unplanned time in which you can putz around, relax, fix something, sit and read a book, or stare out at space. Most of us are overloaded with responsibilities and information. In his book on meditation, Ram Dass speaks of "information overload." He talks about being away for six months meditating in India, never seeing a paper or hearing the news. He said it took a day or two to catch up on the news. What do we do with all the information we gather on the Internet or, for that matter, from magazines and newspapers? What potential for walking in nature, seeing a friend, meditating, or learning to go deep inside ourselves is lost by cruising the Net?

One fascinating aspect of this technology is the sense of anarchy it has created. This is not all good or all bad. On the one hand, people are free to create and invent to their heart's content. On the other hand, they are also free to disseminate pornography, hate mail, racist and sexist propaganda, and use any form of language they like. There is no censorship. The rebel in me feels a sense of pleasure in knowing that there is something beyond the control of the federal government and righteous right-wing politicians. On the other hand, I think of children who are vulnerable and easily influenced. Having worked in the field of sexuality for many years, I know how easy it is for many people, particularly teenagers, to become obsessed with pornography, phone sex, and the like, particularly when they are alone and unsupervised. More than once, a teenager has gotten ideas for molesting children, or self-destructive forms of masturbation from pornography or phone sex.

A good aspect of anarchy is that people are challenged to censor each other and discuss moral standards. There are already many instances of people responding negatively to the hate and prejudice being disseminated in cyberspace. But where will that lead? It seems far more important that we talk face-to-face within our local communities, get to know each other, and take action to improve the well-being of all of us. Cyberspace primarily takes us into our heads instead of leading to love in action—love that will help improve our community relationships. People talk about the plumber in Michigan talking with a professor in Moscow. At one level, that's incredible. If making these bridges between people continents away helps move toward doing the same in our own communities, that's wonderful. But if talking to someone in Moscow precludes making connections at home, then we are, in essence, going into an illusory world, almost a dream state, that keeps connections safely at a distance—manageable and unreal.

While cyberspace, TV, and other examples of technology are used in a balanced way by some, for others they can become an escalating compulsion, a way of having serial, shallow relationships, a way of hiding out from the world and becoming more and more dependent on external stimulus.

Cyberspace is here to stay and gives us yet another balancing act to challenge our lives. We need to pause and reflect on the role it plays in our lives and in our communities. To me, it's another invention that tests us in a fundamental way and makes us look at our values, our relationships, and our ability to combine head and heart and work for the good of our communities.

92

PROTECTING THE HEALTH OF COMMUNITIES

Communities can heal or harm. In this section, I refer to communities that range from groups within a community to whole countries. While there will always be tyrants, demigods, and charismatic people seeking power, their success depends on the collusion of masses of people. It is our responsibility to not collude or give power to destructive people. With politicians and charismatic leaders, we need to be alert to superficial promises, slick rhetoric, and unsubstantiated emotional incantations that trigger and manipulate our buried fear, anger, and prejudice.

On a more daily level, we need to be attuned to people who are disruptive or drain the energy of the various organizations and groups we belong to. We need to set limits in a respectful way. We also need to reflect on our own behavior in groups. Do we listen, give energy to others, talk about ourselves personally (as opposed to preaching and pontificating), and help keep groups on track?

It is difficult talking about people who are destructive in groups because such a discussion invites us to create a sense of I and other instead of a sense of us. The way to bridge this is to find our compassion and see all people as living out their journey the best they can.

In difficult situations, we need to summon the courage to speak up rather than slink away in fear. Many groups dissolve or become dysfunctional because no one takes action to monitor someone who dominates, takes center stage, is divisive, or attempts to control others. Remember, it is as dysfunctional to let a group or organization disintegrate from lack of courage to meet a difficult situation as it is to be a difficult person. We don't need to attack or be rude, but we need to collectively find our voices, take compassionate action to protect the group, and offer assistance and feedback to the other person—always remembering that the "other" person could be us, or is a part of us.

Sometimes communities form around charismatic leaders who operate from a narcissistic, self-serving perspective, but appear as the benevolent leader—the one who knows all and saves all. Charismatic people can be wily and cunning as they lull people into submission and dependency. Our buried emptiness, fears, anger, and longings are fertile ground for the charismatic leader seeking to seduce us en masse, to embed in us their personal pathologies. Like a father (or mother) tapping into our longings for eternal care and protection, the power-hungry leader may assure us s/he knows all the answers and will take care of us. This false benevolence often entices people into a system that slowly erodes their self-trust, quiets their voices, and envelops them in a dependency on the leader, government, or organization.

The charismatic leader or seducer may appear charming and brilliant and may appear to care about people. S/he manipulates followers into feeling prejudice and hatred by using the tactic of reframing political issues to seem like self-care or self-protection. For example, racism gets reframed as protecting people's jobs, keeping the race pure, or as pride in one's ethnic group; sexual promiscuity and abuse are framed as free love or rebellion against the prudish restrictions of patriarchy; homophobia is reframed as protecting the children; sexism and controlling women's reproductive rights is reframed as following the Bible or being pro-life; neo-Nazism is reframed as defending oneself against the government; taking away social programs and protecting the interests of the wealthy is framed as wanting to reduce "big government."

We need to look beneath impassioned rhetoric and ask, What is the goal of these people? How big is their vision? Is it their personal pathology being projected as political theory? The strategies are similar whether it be an individual, a political party, or a fundamentalist organization seeking to control people.

Here are some of the signs of perpetrators of abuse, charismatic leaders, and tyrants:

1. The leader knows all and promises to save everyone. This plays on people's unconscious need for the benevolent, loving father or mother to take care of and protect them.

2. Manipulation is accomplished with the use of emotional rhetoric. Speeches and slogans are aimed at tapping into the buried emotions of fear, insecurity, and hatred in order to manipulate people to the leader's or organization's way of thinking. Phrases are highly charged, and people speak glibly of right and wrong and usually have some form of enemy.

3. The will of the members must merge with the will of the leader. Charismatic leaders and cults attempt to co-opt the will of their followers so that they can manipulate them for their personal needs. Individuals are not invited to think for themselves, rely on their internal wisdom, or express their opinions if they conflict with the prevailing belief system. Genuine intimacy between followers is discouraged or blocked to prevent people from reflecting, sharing their perspectives, or challenging the leader.

4. Control is accomplished by fear. There is a covert or overt threat: If you don't follow the rules, something bad will happen to you. This could include exclusion, punishment, death, or other covert tactics, such as being demoted or shunned.

5. No questioning is allowed. Questioning is reframed as disobedience, arrogance, or attacking the leaders. Punishment may be swift if questioning continues.

6.   Paranoia, hatred, and prejudice are common. It's us against others, and others against us. Perpetrators, tyrants, and fundamentalists always need an enemy, whether it is sin, ethnic groups, or laws. There is a sense of being better and more enlightened than other people—the poor, foreigners, people of a different religion or color, people wanting certain rights. There is also a sense of being victimized by others. "The government is doing it to us. They're out to get us."

7.   There is little sense of personal responsibility. Blame is rampant. Everything that happens is someone else's fault. There is no sense of needing to take responsibility for one's life. This often reflects the deep personal wounding of the charismatic leader, which is projected on to all people as opposed to the person or people who initially abused him or her.

8.   There is small-minded thinking. The motives of the leader(s) are always self-serving: to maintain power, vent hatred, get rich, or have control. There is a lack of big-picture, big-mind thinking that involves compassion or understanding for others. There is no overriding spiritual value, such as caring for people or being concerned for the future. There may be rhetoric and dramatic speeches that pretend to care, but there is no evidence in behavior, legislation, or practices.

9.   Leaders deny their power and self-interest. They assure followers that they are operating for their own good while they often implement practices and policies that drain people financially, spiritually, and emotionally.

10. There is a certainty of being right. There is no objective examination of beliefs and practices because there is certainty that the leader's way is aligned more with goodness, the right way, and the only way. This is used as justification for violence against those who differ.

11. A fear of differences often leads to violence or control. If I think my way is the right way and you are different, then one of us is wrong. Since I'm not wrong, you must change your mind and agree with me. I will start by trying to convert you. If you won't convert, I will put you down, ridicule you, and get rid of you. I don't want anyone to make me think or reflect on what I am doing.

12. There is reductionistic and simplistic concrete thinking. Things are good or bad, right or wrong. You are with me or against me. There is little room for statements such as "I'm not sure," or "We can look at this from many perspectives," or "What do you think?"

13. There is an inability to reflect or laugh at oneself. Righteousness abounds. Because charismatic leaders and fundamentalist groups are operating from a very primitive psychological stage of development, they have little ability to reflect and understand paradox and metaphor. Everything is intense, serious, and of do-or-die importance. Laughter is absent because there is no ability to stand back, see the big picture, and be amused by our foibles, the games we play, and the ways in which we trip over our own feet.

14. Lies are pervasive. Tyrants often say exactly the opposite of what they do. The fundamentalist preacher emotionally entices people to give money for God while taking the money for his own selfish purposes. The imperialist tells a foreign community that they're building factories to benefit the poor while their only interest is in making money. The sexual perpetrator tells the child he is loving her by sexually using her. The medical establishment says pills and implants are totally safe and subvert research and anecdotal data showing them to be harmful.

Our job as part of community is to be wary and wise. That doesn't mean we can't have fun and be spontaneous, it means we give up our naivete and our desire to have someone take care of us, and instead become the keepers of our community. *We realize that the community is us.*

To protect our groups or community we must learn to listen to ourselves and keep counsel with others when we feel uneasy or have a sense that something is wrong. Common symptoms of being caught or enmeshed in an oppressive or exploitive system are confusion, loss of energy, depression, anxiety, denial, troublesome dreams, and an increase in compulsive behaviors such as eating and drinking, gambling, and angry outbursts. We don't have to know why or know the solution. Some peers are likely to try and silence us, particularly if their will has merged with the prevailing belief system of the leader.

Common forms of silencing people who have doubts and raise questions are: *You're exaggerating. You're so critical. Give it time. He seems friendly. I don't think they mean to hurt anyone. But she said she cared.* If a person continues to question, he or she is called a troublemaker and is shunned by their group. Because people are conditioned to experience a deep sense of fear at the thought of being disobedient or questioning authority, they often suffer serious internal consequences such as major depression or anxiety before they realize that someone is exploiting them.

If you are in a situation that feels manipulative or dangerous, listen to yourself and try to believe yourself before you become ill or depressed. This is a time to gather together with other people who feel similarly, create a strategy, and make your feelings known. There is power in numbers. It is up to all of us to be the keepers of community.

Being a keeper of community starts with being tuned into others and being present to our inner experience. We are keepers of community when we look people in the eyes and listen carefully to what they say. We are keepers of community when we ask to be treated with respect, speak up against racist or sexist remarks, and work against all forms of injustice. We are keepers of community when we acknowledge disagreements, stop pointing fingers from a distance, put away the platitudes, and sit at the table together. We don't have to like each other or agree with each other, but we need to talk honestly from our hearts with equal vulnerability, sharing our fears and concerns. From this point of vulnerability, we need to make peaceful coexistence the goal.

The absolute core of coming together in community is realizing that people can be different and still get along. No one needs to be converted to a single belief system. There can be more than one set of values so long as they don't endanger the well-being of anyone or the community as a whole. Even when people seem diametrically opposed, there is usually some point of common ground that can serve as a starting place for discussion. The most important aspect of bringing our differences to the table is to talk from a personal, feeling stance, be willing to enter into the reality of others, let go of the ego's desire to win, and bring a fundamental belief that unity and care for each other bring us home to our hearts.

93

GRIEVING AND DYING IN COMMUNITY

*M*y only sister, Lenore, died at her home in the summer of 1995, nearly three months from the day she was diagnosed with pancreatic cancer. I had recently returned home from New Zealand and was at the end of a workshop tour when I got the news. Jessie and I were able to drive over to be near her when she had surgery. As I write this, a strange sort of tingling starts in my body. I am not over the loss or through grieving, but I did have the relief of seeing her die with grace, at home, cared for by people she knew and loved, assisted by a hospice program. I also had the help of people in my own community with my grief and sadness, both for the loss of Lenore and the sadness about my family, so disconnected that we were unable to support each other in sharing our grief except in very distant ways.

In healthy community, we allow the process of death to be a natural part of our lives. Instead of making death a medical procedure, something to overcome, it is met as part of life, part of community. As Lenore's friends flew in from all over the country to say good-bye and help care for her, there was often a joyful, festive feeling interspersed with tears that erupted at moments when the reality of her imminent death shot through each of us with its own kind of rhythm and sting.

Lenore talked warmly about all her visitors. "Everyone's visit was different," she said. "Everyone gave in their own way. One person got the visiting schedule organized, someone else would sing to me, and someone else would clean, weed the garden, or give me a bath." In the times I spent at her home, I was aware of the people who could crack jokes and lighten up the atmosphere and the others who stood at a distance, wondering what to say or do. It was clear that for some people there were no memories to call on to help them know how to deal with death. I smile as I remember Lenore's best friend, Arnelle, and I hugging, crying, laughing . . . and then going to Lenore's favorite thrift store to help each other pick out clothes.

Lenore died with the help of a hospice program that enabled her to be at home. She was able to be with loved ones, avoid unnecessary surgery and procedures, and regulate medications to remain as comfortable as possible. This lent great dignity to her journey of leaving us and going to whatever lies beyond death. It was also helpful to me. The hospice nurse was there for all of us: Dying became a family affair.

We need to include children in bringing meaningful rituals to death. For many children, the first death they experience is a pet or some other animal. When Lenore and I were between

the ages of four and nine—she was two years older than me—
we created an animal cemetery in the woods. When we found
a dead bird or snake, we would bring it to our animal grave-
yard, bury it, and decorate the grave with flowers and twigs or
a little cross. I remember feeling almost sick when burying a
turtle that had been partially smashed, and I remember that we
had a discussion about the place the turtle would like best to be
buried. A generation later, when my daughter, Janel's, hamster
died, we lovingly put it in a shoebox with food and straw. We
stood by the grave, sang songs, and Janel read a poem she had
learned in school before bursting into tears.

When children are deprived of knowing about a death
because "We don't want them to be upset," what we're really
saying is that *we* don't want to feel upset. When we have the
family dog disposed of in secret and tell our child, "He disap-
peared," or say, "It was only a dog, we'll get another one," we
are showing a tremendous lack of empathy and understanding
for children and give them no model for dealing with death. I
remember when my mother died and we were creating various
rituals around the burial, my two nieces suggested that we put
M&M's in her casket because Grandma sure liked M&M's. I
remember the sweet feeling in my heart as Alissa and Danielle
walked up to the casket gingerly, but with fascination, and
made their contribution to her passing.

Funerals and partings should be a time to reminisce and
honor the life of the person going on the trail of death. We
need to meet our personal needs for saying good-bye, and create rituals that reflect the person who is departing. Lenore was
great at orchestrating rituals and parties. This held true for our
mother's funeral. We personally arranged most of the flowers
as she had done for both of our home weddings. I played a
Shubert impromptu she liked on the piano and we found a violinist to play some old sentimental pieces my mother had
played as a young woman. Each of us four children spoke and
reminisced about our mom at the service and together carried
her coffin in and out of church. When it was over, Lenore came
out of the church smiling. "Good press on the funeral," she

said. "Best one they've had in a long time." And that's how it should be—a good funeral, one that celebrates the person's life.

After my first visit to Lenore when I found out that she hadn't long to live, a woman named Ruth in Missoula offered to bring her harp to my house to play for me and comfort me. I took many pictures of Lenore and myself off the walls, along with paintings and objects Lenore had created, and arranged them in an open, carpeted space by a huge glass wall that faces the mountains. Several friends came over to join us. I lay down on the rug with my head in the lap of my dear friend, Jeanine, who stroked my hair and gave me the warmth of her loving presence as I let the tears flow. When one is immersed in the middle of loss, it's so hard to believe you'll ever get past the grief, but the more we let it flow, the more we can release the sting. I think of the phrase, "Weeping endureth for the night, but joy comes in the morning." I can't say I felt joy afterward, but I did feel an easing in my heart, and now when I think of Lenore's death, I also remember the embrace of my friends as I was comforted by Ruth's beautiful music.

I don't want to romanticize dying. There is physical pain in dying and there is pain in saying good-bye. In Lenore's case, medications would work well to alleviate the pain, and then all of a sudden various symptoms would flare up and there would be a need to adjust them. Mercifully, with hospice care, there was no withholding of medication or using of rote formulas. There was careful attention to the relief of her suffering.

Any death magnifies and intensifies the buried pains in a family. One time, when Lenore's husband and I had a tense encounter, he called a friend to come over and help us out. I admired his goodwill and was thankful for Janice, who came right over to be of support.

Lenore and I did our best to clear the air between us, but I can't say it was done completely. There was no dramatic scene of perfect forgiveness, but there were wonderful moments when love permeated our connection. Shortly before she died, she said, "You know, you've sent a lot of that . . . energy to me . . .

that healing you call Reike. I'm going to have to learn about that, because I've never sent any to you. I'll be doing that." And then there was the last day, when she sat on the front-porch swing smiling faintly as her husband, Bill, looked at her with a smile and a tear, as he held a great, big, red tomato in his hand as if offering it to her.

I need to end this piece of death in community because my tears are blocking my vision. This very ritual of talking with you, my unknown reader, about a very personal death is helping me with my grief, and it's important to move through grief because life is here to be lived.

The more we bring meaningful rituals to death and grief, the more we are free to live without great fear of death. I believe the extent to which our culture and media focus on violent death reflects our actual distancing and fear of death. And the fear of death is really a fear of life, a fear of facing on a daily basis all the losses we suffer as life changes. If we make death part of life—something to be shared in community—it can become a process to behold and not fear, to heighten our awareness, rather than leaving us numb and afraid. As we learn to bear our grief together, we also make room for new birth.

94

GOOD LOVERS, EARTH LOVERS

*B*eing a good lover helps us care for the earth. In *Lucky in Love, the Secrets of Happy Couples,* Catherine Johnson writes that with happy couples "two souls become one . . . they drink each other in," often becoming telepathic, knowing what the other wants and feels. The sense of two becoming one is not two people enmeshing into one person, it's two spirits that intertwine and experience a sense of oneness. They feel each other's joys and sorrows.

What's a good lover? Along with the ability to become as one with another, a good lover creates an ongoing flow of give and take, allowing himself to be known, seen, and connected. She is sensitive to her effect on others. A good lover wishes the best for another person, and doesn't dominate, exploit, or mold others to fit her needs. Rather, s/he stands back and looks at the marvel of what it is to be a human being, perfect in our imperfectness, amazing with all our fears and foibles. A good lover loves well in a thousand small ways on a daily basis. A good lover is versatile emotionally—a person who can be as strong as a lion and as tender as a sapling, as quiet as a snowfall and as wild as a river in spring. In short, a person who is full of life and compassion.

Now let's apply these characteristics to our relationship to the earth. An earth lover has a soul merger with the natural habitat and all sentient life. S/he basks in the wonder of earth's beauty and feels her pain when gouged, poisoned, and exploited. An earth lover is aware that we cannot take more than we give without damage to the ecosystem, an ecosystem that includes us. An earth lover is conscious of the impact of her daily habits on the earth and has an inner alarm that goes off to prevent throwing anything that can be recycled in the trash, or realizes the relationships between excess material possessions and the quality of air and water. A good lover wishes the best for the earth and knows that we have a finite amount of resources. S/he takes care of the earth in a thousand small ways on a daily basis, recycling, bicycling, picking up litter, not using more than he needs to be comfortable.

An earth lover brings skills to community to help all of us do our part to preserve our greatest gifts—clean water, air, soil, and food. It takes many of us doing small, creative projects to preserve our natural resources. One such trend is for Community Supported Agriculture (CSA). I spoke to my friend, Jeanine Walker, who has been involved with a local group. "I love it." she said. "Everyone is on an equal footing—you all do the work and you all enjoy the food. Every CSA that I know of is based on using organic gardening principles. We are a diverse group of people who share the common desire to have good, safe food and participate in growing it. We get to know each other out weeding onions. We hire a grower or farmer to do some of the primary work and see that he (or she) gets benefits and is well paid, even if the crops fail—if the corn blows over, everyone absorbs the loss. It's been a lesson in abundance, because so far, there is always more food than we can eat, so we make contributions to the food bank or the homeless shelter. When you focus so much good energy on a piece of ground and take good care of it, the abundance is amazing."

As another example of a community project, two men started a "Free Cycles" (drive no more) project to park 100 bicycles in racks around town for people to use and leave anywhere else. It was based on a project originally started in Portland, Oregon. They collected the bikes from local residents and asked businesses to sponsor a bike for $50.00 so they could have them repaired and painted. In return, the sponsor's logo appeared on the bike. Free Cycles also sponsors seminars on bike safety and works with the city to improve bike corridors. When someone asked the organizer, "But what if someone steals the bike?" he said, "You can't steal these bikes because they belong to the whole community. As long as you're using the bicycle, you're all right. That's the whole idea." This is a win, win, win situation. We need thousands of them.

The mistaken attitudes we have about the great lover who fulfills our needs reflects the same mistaken thinking that we have toward the earth. It is one of taking without giving back. It is the epitome of narcissism—seeing the world through our own eyes and having no awareness of our impact on it or the ecosystem that supports life. It's the same self-centered attitude that often results in separation or divorce. Couples are splitting up in increasing numbers as we are divorcing ourselves from natural laws of give and take and being connected to the earth.

Currently in Montana, Women's Voices for the Earth and other organizations interested in protecting our natural habitat are protesting the creation of a huge open-pit gold mine proposed nearby. The mine is likely to upset the economy of the area, change the nature of the community, and leave a huge gouge in the earth where chemicals will run off into the rivers, destroying the fish habitat, poisoning the water, and putting poisonous toxins into the air. What is the purpose of digging up gold? To have gold jewelry for the most part. Women are contributing their wedding bands to be sold to make money to fight the corporate giants, saying they'd rather live without them than have their community destroyed. I'm planning to give my grandmother's wedding ring. I know she'd approve— she loved this beautiful valley with a passion.

Propaganda for the mine has the same old ring of ads and videos I saw about strip mining in southeast Ohio, where I lived in the sixties and seventies. They showed pictures of cows grazing with contentment on the reclaimed land. The picture didn't match the views of miles and miles of back roads where I often saw huge gouges in the earth where nothing would grow and nearby lakes so polluted by chemicals that they were bright aqua. Yesterday on the radio I heard the same old phrases coming from the mine company—"Let's not be emotional about this, let's listen to reason." What's wrong with emotion when you're about to have more of the landscape devoured by corporate interests who show no care for the well-being of the community? What's wrong with being upset when the government, yet again, tries to lower the standards for clean air and water to accommodate corporations? Have I just gotten on a soapbox? Perhaps. Forgive me. I have the sense that I and many others live with chronic grief for the loss of a healthy environment and the beauty of the natural world.

It is the grief one bears for being conscious. It also challenges us to get into big-mind thinking and see this as part of evolution. A young women in her twenties commented recently, "I hope that people die off first so at least the animals can remain." What a sad yet poignant thought to carry in one's heart—to wish for your own demise so that the natural world might survive.

In *Ishmael*, Daniel Quin explores the role of the human species and the earth. "Man is not alone on this planet. He is part of a community, upon which he depends absolutely." He goes on to say that we are subject to the same laws of nature that govern the mollusks, birds, snails, and rabbits. *"The world doesn't belong to us, we belong to the world."*

To create a soul connection with another person is to know, love, and to experience wonder in all its forms. Our lovers don't belong to us any more than the earth belongs to us, rather, we become part of each other, separate yet deeply intertwined. We cannot fully love other people and be oblivious to the habitat in which we live. Likewise, we need to preserve the habitat without making people the enemy. Some people get involved in working to preserve the earth and the animals and see people as the enemy, crowding out the animals and building ugly houses on remote lands. Other people see preservationists as the enemy, wanting to take their jobs away by limiting timber harvests, stopping mining projects, and preventing construction. The real enemy is ignorance and lack of ability to see the big picture—the ultimate effect of our lifestyles on the habitat, and the people who currently suffer to make it possible. A friend recently commented that most of us in the United States have about twenty-five people slaving for us in other countries to support our lifestyle.

In truth, we need to see the survival of our habitat and of humankind as one big concern—how do we live together on this finite planet, caring for people and the earth? How do we protect the water, air, and earth, and how do we love each other and give safety and care for all? To be a truly loving person, we can't compartmentalize our love and create some faction as the enemy. Our love for each other and for the earth become our love of creation. Which leads to the question of procreation.

95

THE BIG COMMUNITY QUESTION, OR, WHATEVER HAPPENED TO ZERO POPULATION GROWTH?

*I*magine this scenario: Fifty years from now an older person is talking with a young child who has an old picture book about tigers. Imagine that that older person is you—even if that means you are 110.

The little boy asks, "Where do tigers live?"

And you respond, "There are no more tigers."

And the little boy says, "Why?"

What do you say? How do you explain a world in which we let thousands of wondrous animals and plants become extinct?

If thinking about animals becoming extinct feels remote, shift your mind to the place where you live. Have you been caught in traffic lately, felt your eyes and throat affected by polluted air? Has it been hard to find a place to park? Have you seen houses, discount stores, and gas stations being built where there was once grass, trees, and open spaces? Are the parks so crowded it hardly seems worth the trouble to go there? Yesterday I went to take a walk on some old roads "out in the country" and ended up on Dove Court, the center of a huge housing development under construction. All winter long I watched with an ache in my heart as logging trucks carried thousands of logs/trees from the mountains behind us, leaving the land looking forlorn and barren. In the sixties and seventies, there was a big movement for zero population growth. It is a concept we rarely hear about in the United States anymore. We need to bring our attention back to this idea—soon.

Overpopulation affects our ability to create healthy communities. As the population grows, we have more crowding and more sense of scarcity, which often leads to fear. As a result, people retreat to self-protection as they scramble to get what they need to survive. This results in a breakdown of community, of working together, of remembering to care for each other. It often results in people in power maneuvering to maintain their wealth at the expense of others who become poorer and more excluded from mainstream privilege. Fear prevails. The resulting alienation and depersonalization leads to violence. In our isolation and loneliness, we seek more material goods to quell the inner emptiness. This leads to more devastation of the natural world. And on and on it goes.

A deeply spiritual contribution we can all make to community is to become aware of the connection between population and the problems in the world. This is where our willingness to sacrifice in the interest of a sustainable world is tested. *We need to limit the number of children we bring into the world in order to protect the world we leave our children.* As a global community we need to take action, not getting caught in red-herring issues that block us from seeing the big picture. There is almost no problem than cannot be related to population growth, our emphasis on material goods, and a growth-oriented economy that depends on the depletion of the habitat and an increase in consumerism.

While it seems simpleminded to say this, it's a concept we don't yet seem to grasp. *We live on a finite planet with a limited amount of resources. The more people we have, the more we deplete the resources. The more we live unconscious, consumer-oriented lifestyles, the faster this will happen.*

While some European countries have achieved zero population growth, worldwide the population has close to tripled since I was a child—nearly fifty years ago. While population control has become an unpopular subject, calling into question the issues of abortion, birth control, and individual rights, overpopulation is one of the greatest causes of our troubles on the planet.

Think for a minute of the resources one person in Western culture uses in a lifetime in terms of food, electricity, clothing, water, wood, paper, magazines, gas, oil, time on the highways wearing out the pavement, etc. Think of how the things you own were made in factories that pollute the air. As I write this, the town of Alberton, Montana—less than twenty miles away—is being evacuated because of a train derailment that caused 170,000 pounds of chlorine gas to escape. We are praying that the wind won't blow our way. We are praying for the health of the people who have breathed this deadly gas into their lungs.

And speaking of gas in people's lungs, the collective immune system of people is disintegrating in direct parallel to the pollution of the earth and the toxins we have in our food, air, and water. The ecological system on the outside is affecting the ecological system inside of us. Our departure from natural foods and the introduction of food additives and toxins are leading many people to become allergic to numerous foods and to themselves. We see a great increase in diseases of the immune system—where the body literally turns on itself.

Only through the heart will we solve the problems of coexistence on the planet. Our indigenous brothers and sisters historically have managed to maintain a balance because they are conscious of being interrelated with the earth and the animals. In *Mutant Message Down Under*, the indigenous tribe who call themselves the Real People believe that whatever you take from the earth you should give back. Marlo Morgan writes: "It is truly amazing that after 50,000 years they have destroyed no forests, polluted no water, endangered no species, caused no contamination, and all the while they have received abundant food and shelter."

Their philosophy of living centers around the the sense of divine oneness—all life in interrelated. It is encapsulated in the thought, *If you hurt someone, you hurt self. If you help someone, you help self.* Nothing is separate. I would add, *If you hurt the earth and sentient beings, you hurt yourself. If you care for the earth and all sentient life, you care for yourself.* There is no I and other. There is no separation between people, earth, and wildlife. The Real

People refer to Caucasians as "mutants"—those who evolved from natural people and forgot the true meaning of life and their connection with the earth. In the words of Ooota, in his blessing to Marlo Morgan as they said farewell,

> It seems mutants have something in their life called gravy. They know truth but it is buried under thickening and spices of convenience, materialism, insecurity and fear. They also have something in their lives called frosting. It seems to represent that they spend almost all the seconds of their existence in doing superficial, artificial, temporary, pleasant tasting, nice appearing projects, and spend very few actual seconds of their lives developing their eternal beingness.

It takes no materials to create beingness and deepen our spirituality. It takes quiet time, connection, and simplicity. It costs nothing but the release of our grief so we can open our hearts to each other, and feast on the delight of true connection and intimacy. These are the things that will heal us, help us be content with few material possessions, and raise our consciousness so that we become willing to limit population.

We need to move beyond the narcissistic stance that we are keepers and stewards of the earth, and stop referring to natural resources as if they are resources for us. If we think in terms of habitat, we will think of resources being shared equally with people, animals, trees, and flowers. In the words of Ron Erickson, a professor at the University of Montana who has taught courses on population:

> While it is possible to imagine a planet with more people getting food through better distribution, this vision always leaves out the survival of other species. If we look in the areas of the biggest population growth such as Africa, we see the least richness of animals and other species.

While population control is a complex question that has many ramifications, one thing is simple: If we keep having so many children, we will destroy much of the life on the planet. Even if we slow down population growth but continue our materialistic lifestyles, we are on a collision course with the extinction of much of the habitat and human species.

We need to remember that we are dependent on the earth and her bounty. When the food, air, water, trees and plants, and animals are gone, diminished, or polluted, as a species we will die off from cancer, other diseases, and starvation. There are already hints of this—breast cancer rates for women have gone from one in thirty in 1960 to one in eight in 1996. The male sperm count has dropped nearly 20 percent in the last twenty years, possibly from the proliferation of dioxins in the air, which come from manufacturing things like plastic. This is a remarkably rapid change in the big picture of human evolution. In less than 150 years it is estimated that all the gas and oil on the planet will be used up. Gone. It's as if we're living in the path of a tornado, but we're too drunk to notice. I hope to live to be very old, because I am curious as to what we as a species will do.

Time for a sense of humor! A few days ago, two delightful men came to do an energy audit on the house. When I spoke of trying to keep the heat down to help prevent the depletion of gas, one laughed, "Use it, use it, the quicker it's gone, the faster they'll find alternatives that don't pollute the air." He laughed. To survive all this, we need to reach for big mind and big heart and see this as part of evolution.

To create a home for the heart we need to take all life into our hearts and see that we have been given paradise—an awesome, wondrous place with an extraordinary collection of plants, animals, forests, rivers, and oceans, all interconnected, creating a habitable place for us to share.

If ever there was a time for big-mind community thinking it is in the area of human population and the protection of the habitat. We are of the earth, part of all life, and subject to the basic laws of nature.

96

GOOD LOVERS, GOOD BOSSES

*T*he concept of being a good lover extends to bosses, work-ers—everyone. If people with power would live by the underly-ing question, "How much am I bringing respect and love to all people in my life," they would be living in the heart of spirit and would be creating a home in the workplace for all hearts. Instead of thinking, "These workers belong to me," the attitude needs to be, "I belong to these workers, we are in this together." Unfortunately, when we are out of touch with our humanity, numerous policies are put into practice in the work-place that keep a lot of psychotherapists, medical professionals, and rehabilitation counselors in jobs that help people to cope with stress.

As an example, my dear friend Ann called me from Minneapolis this morning, wanting counsel. She was struggling between staying in a good-paying, highly stressful job, or quit-ting, which would provide relief tinged with financial insecurity. Let me give you some history. Ann had overcome tremendous deficits in her upbringing through psychotherapy and personal growth work. Even with severe depression and learning disabil-ities, she had completed nurse's training but had found most jobs too fast-paced and stressful. It was a tremendous victory when she found a niche for herself in home care nursing, work-ing three-quarters' time and receiving benefits. Along with her work success, she had stopped using antidepressants, had improved her network of friendships, and had become active in the Jewish community. In short, she had created a balance in her life—you might say that she was a healthy cell in the com-munity.

Then, suddenly, a new policy was handed down at work: All staff were to increase "productivity"—which meant carrying a bigger caseload. As she read the list of additional clients, her stomach churned, her heart got heavy, and depression rolled in like a storm cloud. Two days later she seriously strained her back and ended up at home for three weeks. "It was as if my whole body said, 'No. I won't do that. I have a good life and they are asking me to go faster, faster, faster, when I am wanting to go slower, slower, slower.'"

She continued talking about the effects of the new policy. "We could just manage what we had to do. Now everyone is under so much stress that it's crazy to work there. People are unhappy and upset. They're talking about joining the nurses' union to fight back because no one is listening." Ann is one of millions of people feeling unduly stressed by inhumane work policies.

Translating this situation into the concept of community as a living organism, it is as if a virus—the inhuman policies—had attacked a huge number of cells—the nurses—who were being stressed in ways that affected all the cells around them—the people they were caring for. It's at a time like this that the human system draws on its surplus resources and friends. But what happens when everyone is overstretched and has little to give?

Stress becomes like a cancer of the spirit seeping into people's lives and setting off a chain reaction. For example, Margo, one of the overworked nurses, came home exhausted, was abrupt with her child, scarfed down a hasty supper, and left for an organizing meeting, leaving her child in tears and her husband upset because he felt overwhelmed and needed support as well. Within a few days, Margo was having headaches and taking aspirin constantly, her son had a fight at school and started wetting his bed, and Margo's sexual relationship with her huband went on hold as the worries about work superceded time for lovemaking. And on it went, stress leading to more stress and disconnection from friends and family, one cell after another breaking down, creating a weakened immune system. The choices Margo faced all had harmful consequences. Quitting her job put her family in a financial bind. Union organizing took time, but at least it brought the hope of something better and felt highly preferable to knuckling under and feeling like a victim. The group of nurses bonding together were like a group of cells mobilizing to fight off the virus that was threatening their health—body, mind, and spirit. But it was a little like chemotherapy—the possible cure had no guarantee and a lot of harmful side effects. That's what happens when community policies do not care for people. It not only affects individuals, but the whole community is weakened.

As I thought of Ann applying for workmen's compensation or possibly unemployment for her stress-related accident, I wondered if the increased workload would accomplish its intent of saving money. I pictured the people receiving home care sitting in chairs on an assembly line, with the line being speeded up as the nurses hurried to keep up: Get to the house faster, give them their meds faster, talk less, get out of the house faster, drive to the next house faster. Any chance for intimate connections that feed the spirit disintegrate as people are treated like products that must produce on a tight schedule—a schedule that goes against the laws of human dignity and balance. And, as with any law of nature, if you push too hard, something pushes back: with Ann, it was literally, her back. If you put people in high-stress jobs, you end up with more illness, alcoholism, absenteeism, need for counseling, troubles at home, and turnover—costs that come out of the community pocket. The owner of the business might possibly make more money, but the community would pay with increased health insurance costs, unemployment benefits, and community mental health centers, not to mention the spiritual cost to human relationships. It would be like draining the immune system of the community to benefit a few business owners.

The sudden jarring of the nurses' lives reflects a scenario happening all over the world as people are seen as objects to exploit for the benefit of a few. Everyone loses, because the one who exploits others for personal gain is torn from spirit and compassion, derailed from a path toward love and spirit. The people who are overworked live under great stress, leading to depression, illness, anger, and frustration. It keeps a cycle of abuse and anger firing through the system, blocking everyone's path toward love.

If we operate on the principles of love and compassion, the concept of productivity would not be measured in work per hours, rather, it would be measured in quality of relationships, the well-being of all people, the well-being of the earth, as well as the quality of the product. The energy flow of an organization would resemble the energy flow of a healthy person with all systems connected and sharing information—an interdependent system in which the good of the whole depends on all systems working well together. A good boss would see him or herself as *part* of the organization, rather than the head, yet would realize that a position of power is a sacred trust. The goal would be to create a stable, respectful work environment rather than to amass great riches, stay in control, or inflate one's ego by taking all the credit. It would probably be more productive for all in the long run because people who feel cared for and respected are healthier, have fewer accidents, and, in the long run, are often more productive.

When I go around the country giving workshops, often sponsored by mental health agencies or other groups, it is easy to see which groups of people feel cared about in their jobs. They come in smiling, are very supportive of me, and shine with excitement. Recently I talked to a woman who loved her job and the organization she worked for. "We're cared about, respected, and our input is important. I have so much energy and feel creative on my job." For the most part, people want to get along, to feel loyal to the company or organization they work for, and to feel included.

Honesty and integrity have been tried in business with great success. Early on, in New England, Quakers were known as good businesspeople. It was often said, "Go to a Quaker. They won't bargain and they won't cheat you. They'll charge a fair price and do a good job." Recently some used car dealerships decided to have salesmen work on salary, and have a return policy on cars. When one organization first decided to be completely honest with customers, sales fell off, but as their reputation grew, they ended up doing an excellent business. We need to have faith in the belief that through care and respect we can create a win-win situation in the workplace. We would do well to remember the words of Jesus: "It's as difficult for a rich man to find the kingdom of heaven as it is for a camel to go through the eye of a needle." People gain satisfaction and pleasure from their jobs and feel empowered when they know that they matter in their community. Truly, our riches are in our hearts and in the joy of working well together.

97
FIT THE POLICIES TO THE GOALS: SEVEN-GENERATION THINKING

*I*t is said that Native Americans made decisions with careful consideration of the seven generations to follow. The decisions took into account humans, animals, and habitat.

As a planetary community we need to agree on the *essence* of what we want to accomplish as a human species. What values do we want to maintain? How do we want to feel? The seven-generation approach brings a spiritual context to problem solving—we think of the big picture and have consideration for all the children who will follow us in the next two hundred years. Unfortunately, most policies being made by corporations and politicians are based on how to make more money faster or how to get reelected.

In the long run, care for people is economical. Current policies limiting the quality of education, safety, day care, and medical care for children will cost us more in the long run. Nearly always, when we look into the past of children who grow up to vandalize and commit murder and mayhem, we see a bleak picture of hurt, loss, and doors of opportunity being slammed in their faces. We see people being marginalized, excluded from the center of community. It is highly unlikely that people who have been loved and cared for will commit drive-by shootings.

Over twenty years ago, I adopted a child who had been abused and had gone through many separations—although at the time no one told me much about her history. She was unable to attach to me, to friends, and, years later, to her three children. Her teenage years, spent in and out of group homes and treatment programs, cost the taxpayers hundreds of thousands of dollars. It turned out that her mother was a fourteen-year-old victim of incest by a stepfather who routinely beat her and her mother. Protecting the mother and grandmother, who often called the police to no avail, would have cost a fraction of the price, not to mention the immense human suffering for all involved, including a new generation of children who have felt the pain of abandonment.

When we assess human values, we begin to ask, What is the human and spiritual cost of poverty, despair, and alienation? Where do we stand in terms of creating a huge class of people living in poverty while others amass great wealth? What is our belief about increased stress in job situations where people feel overworked and unappreciated? If we were thinking of the next seven generations to follow, what policies would we institute? Sometimes it's overwhelming to think of the changes we need to make. It's easy to slip into denial, feel overwhelmed, and let the foundations of our society erode.

This makes me think of a scene with my mom and dad many years ago. My father never liked to admit that anything was wrong, as if it somehow reflected on his worth. One day my mother spotted what looked like a termite in the basement.

She said, "Kenneth, I think we have termites."

He immediately replied, "No, we don't." (His scientific research-oriented mind didn't seem to function on a personal level.)

My mother said, "I've seen them in the basement."

"We don't have termites!" my father said again, adamantly.

My mother went down to the basement, got a jar, put the bugs in it, and showed it to him.

"Those aren't termites," he said.

Then my mother went and got a book with pictures of termites and brought it to him and said, "See these pictures of termites. See these things in the bottle. I think we have termites."

And finally my father agreed that they had termites and did the hard work of digging around the house to rid it of termites. Fortunately, he did it before the foundation collapsed. I think most of us can relate to this type of conversation—either flatly denying there is a problem, or getting frustrated in trying to convince someone to look at the evidence and do something.

The metaphor of the termite conversation is going on with a million variations all over the planet. Groups of people are trying to prevail upon others to see that we have termites chewing away at the foundation of our culture. The others don't want to see it. Seeing termites in the basement is difficult because it reminds us of our imperfections—our house is flawed, we are flawed, and we can't control nature or our destiny. We don't want to see the termites because it means we have to do something that takes time, money, and effort. We have to break our routine, spend money, dig trenches around the house. On the other hand, like my mother, many feel desperate to persuade others to see that we've got termites while there's still time to prevent the house from collapsing around us. The termite conversation encapsulates much of the inner struggle of being human—the part of us that sees the termites and the part of us that lives in blind denial and doesn't want to be bothered. It demonstrates the difference between looking at the big picture of the next seven generations, or blithely hanging on to momentary comfort.

What does it take for us to see? It takes a path toward love. Opening up our vision means opening up our hearts, being willing to see all gradations of good and bad within us and around us. If we take the termites as a personal metaphor, it suggests that we need to shake loose our denial and see the termites within us—our personal shadow side and our role in eating away at the foundation of society. On any given day termites look so little and benign, but, like cancer cells, they eventually wreak havoc and cause collapse. It's up to all of us to get involved and to elect people who are concerned with the welfare of the community.

I feel lucky to live in a town with a mayor who has a holistic concept of community. I spoke with Mayor Daniel Kemmis, who wrote *Community and the Politics of Place*, about his view of community.

"In dealing with the everyday issues of working with a city, I've become more and more focused on thinking about community in physical terms. A city is a living thing with overlapping systems, very much like our body. We have the roads, the sewer system, phone lines, water, air, and electricity, which connect all of us. We are also interconnected through the quality of schools, housing, and parks, although we don't experience that link as directly.

"I believe people used to talk about the body politic not just as a metaphor. It's about understanding the system we share together. It makes me think of the words about body language you find in St. Paul's 'Letter to the Corinthians'—where he imagines a body in which the right hand doesn't know what the left hand is doing. We need to have both hands working together."

"How did people get so separated from this consciousness?" I asked.

"We were settled by people who survived because they were tremendously hardy and worked hard. They did it on their own. There came to be so much emphasis on individualism that we lost track of what it would really mean to be part of one body. It's a way of thinking that is hard for people because it means giving up some piece of individualism."

His thoughts struck me as similar to the struggle people face in forming intimate relationships—the challenge of being ourselves yet creating an "us." Continuing our conversation, I brought up a hot topic in our community related to the concept of "us," namely that many people living on the edge of the city don't want to be annexed because it would mean having a sewer system installed at personal cost to them.

"Here's where individual and community interests collide," Mayor Kemmis continued, "but it's not fair to let your sewage go into the aquifer that affects everyone. It's not fair to use the services of the city without contributing. If you start thinking about community in organic terms, one thing that is clear is that it's not one-dimensional—it's an economic organism, and an ecosystem. In order for the body to be healthy it needs to be fully integrated, including the spiritual connection. The same is true with community."

I asked him what he meant by spiritual connection in community.

"I talk about it gingerly," he said. "I'm more interested in listening to others talking about it. When I ask people how they feel about living here, the conversation invariably moves into spiritual language. People try to find words to express how important the landscape is to them. It's clear that the community extends beyond people and physical systems to the mountains, rivers, and animals as an integral part of people's relationship to this place. For many, it seems impossible to speak about this without saying that it feels like a sacred place. Our relationships to one another are rooted in a love for this particular place and the joy people feel in living here. This unites us in community."

"What do people have to do as individuals to have a community consciousness?" I asked.

"We have to let go of a certain type of hubris. You might call it arrogance or pride, which leaves us operating alone, feeling that the weight of the world rests on our individual shoulders. Even so, one of the hardest things for people to give up is personal, individual control. *Community happens when we share control.* One of the blessings of community is that you come to the awareness that it has a life force of its own. To maintain it and make it prosper, we are each called on to do our part. The minute we throw people out on their own and push them into a survival mode, community breaks down. Ideally, the responsibility and the prosperity of the community are shared with all its members."

98

ONE SIZE NEVER FITS ALL— ESPECIALLY WITH CHILDREN

*T*he other day my partner, Jessie, and I were in an import store trying on clothing. I picked up a jacket and found that it was too big for me. I handed it to Jessie, who tried it on, and found it to be too small.

She looked at the label and read out loud, "One size fits all."

"Except you and me," I said, laughing.

How easy it would be if we could figure out one-size-fits-all policies, apply them to everyone, follow them, and have good results. The problem is that one size never fits all—it never did and it never will. The solutions to our problems will come through the wisdom of the heart, not through theories that lead to blanket policies to be followed in robot fashion. I will tell you about one alarming policy that has resulted in untold harm and sometimes death for children. It created considerable pain in my life.

When I lived in Minnesota, the Hennepin County policy for children was that "all children would be better off with their biological parents." Period. No exceptions. This theory was supported by Richard Gelles, a university professor who wrote books on child abuse and asserted that with the proper education, all parents could become nurturing to their children. As I repeatedly heard this over the years, I wondered if we were living on the same planet. As a therapist seeing the results of children being sent back over and over again to abusive parents, I wondered what kind of research they were doing. Again, we see the hubris of believing that we have total control, of being so invested in a theory that we can't see reality. Whenever we take a one-size-fits-all stance, our ability to process new data is severely limited. This unrealistic, inhumane theory that was affecting a child I dearly wanted to protect was often glibly mouthed by a social worker as, "All mothers should get a chance to fail."

"But what about the children?" I said to a social-service worker.

She hedged. "It's our policy that all children are better off with their biological parent," she repeated in her singsong voice.

"But are they? What kind of data do you have about that?"

"I don't know. That's our policy."

"But what kind of a sentence is that for the child? They don't just get over incest and abuse and neglect. They lose their ability to trust when they are shifted around all the time. That's what leads to delinquency."

I spoke with another social worker dealing with a legal case that involved placing a child back with a mother who was living on the streets, had a sociopathic history, and no evidence of being able to bond. The social worker told me confidentially that she thought the child would be in danger if placed back with her biological mother, but said, "I can't say this in court. I have to recommend that the child go back to the biological mother."

"But why can't you say what you believe?" I implored her.

"Because it's our policy. If you quote me as saying that she is in danger, I will deny it."

I was aghast. I felt a mixture of anger and despair rising inside. We have had attachment studies going back over thirty years that document the long-term damage that results from repeated separations in early childhood. Yet with all this information, we are still jerking children around as if they were objects, ripping their bonds and destroying their trust. That's because we get into one-size-fits-all thinking, which really means no thinking at all.

As part of community, we all have the responsibility of caring for our children. Our treatment of children often mirrors how we treat the vulnerable, tender, dependent parts of ourselves. Part of male socialization is to armor the heart against hurt and sadness—big boys don't cry, they're tough and unafraid.

This makes it difficult for some men to bond with children or empathize with their feelings. This self-rejection often becomes the rejection of care for children. If we are in a policy-making position, our inner denial of our vulnerability ends up in policies that neglect the needs of children. Women are more likely to deny their power, to see the problems but lack the courage and power to stand up for their beliefs. Mercifully, many people have broken the mold and become outspoken about the need to protect children.

We all have the responsibility to stand up against harmful policies. Any person can dream up a theory, but it takes many people in collusion to inflict them on innocent people. To leave a child with a parent until the parent fails puts a child at high risk for lacking trust, being able to bond, or living within the parameters of society.

One definition of insanity: when we keep doing the same thing and expect different results. The one rule for all children is an example of such insanity. Interestingly, or tragically, Dr. Gelles has since recanted and come up with an equally extreme and rigid suggestion. In an article in the *Minneapolis Star and Tribune*, he says that any child who has a broken bone or severe abuse should be removed immediately from the family/parent, with no chance of reunification. He was also quoted as saying that, formerly, he wanted to believe his theory so much that he only looked at the positive results, he wouldn't see that the policy cost the lives of hundreds of children. To go to the opposite extreme is equally "insane."

When we make rigid one-size-fits-all rules in dealing with human life, we end up swinging back and forth from one extreme policy to another, harming people over and over again. What is it in human nature that makes us want such rigid rules to cling to?

Flexible policies challenge us to take personal responsibility, think, feel, and look at a situation from many perspectives. We need to weigh many variables and make a decision that isn't always easy or clear. If we are wrong, we have a personal connection to the outcome that we will feel deeply. This challenges us to grow rather than abdicating responsibility by saying, "I was just following the rules." It requires great courage and integrity to treat each case on its own merits. To do this, we need to be in tune with our own complexity, to transcend rote rules with considered judgments on a daily basis in our own lives. It requires the ability to think, to love, and risk being wrong. Creating healthy community is a challenge, but it is a challenge that will lead us to our wisdom and humanity. When we stop hiding behind a one-size-fits-all type of decision making, whether it be in regard to learning methods, prison sentences, or policies for children, we will meet ourselves head-on in a way that will increase our humanity and help us function at a much higher level of consciousness in community.

99

THE HANDS OF GOD: SERVICE

It is well to give when asked, but it is better to give unasked through understanding.

—Kahlil Gibran

When we join together to benefit others, we are lifted beyond our own daily concerns into the spirit of community. We accomplish things together that we could never do alone. Our internal harmony rests upon living in a community in harmony. We can't have individual happiness in a chaotic, violent community.

In *Upon This Rock* by Samuel G. Freedman, we hear the story of a pastor, Reverend Johnny Ray Youngblood, who became the minister of a church in a devastated area in New York—and created a vital center for the community that resulted in 5,000 members and 52 staff people. Prior to the revitalization of the church, a visiting mayor had called the neighborhood "the beginning of the end of our civilization." What jumps off every page of this book is practicality, creativity, humility, and the deep sense of a man following his calling. In one sermon Reverend Youngblood says, "I'm just another beggar, tellin' other beggars where to find bread." His warmth, immediacy, passion, vision, and vitality help him draw out the best in others. He constantly spoke to the heart of others, building self-esteem and helping people feel special. He did this in myriad ways, from announcing people's birthdays to reading children's good report cards from the pulpit, often with humorous remarks. He helped build a youth center, asking people to reach deep and contribute to the financial needs of the church—the living church that ministers to the need of the people.

His vision was grounded in understanding the essence of what was needed. It was as if his will merged with the aching heart of the community, and instead of being paralyzed by it, he became an instrument of transformation. He combined power with humanity, strength with love.

I spoke with numerous people who are often of service to others. No matter what their faith, they see service as an integral part of life, or, in the words of my cousin Janet, "If we don't do it, who's going to do it? Helping others is the reason for life." She said this as if it were the most obvious thought on the planet. "We're the physical evidence that God is living. God works through our thoughts and our love. We're God's hands."

One of my first experiences with "giving" was when our girl scout troop did a Christmas sing for "shut-ins." I remember standing together in the cold, our little group of sixth-graders wanting to be noble, picturing some helpless person inside being deeply moved by our singing. This act of giving was both sentimental and had a vast separation between the givers and the receivers. Even so, it struck a cord in my heart—I started wondering what it was like to be the person inside and if I'd end up being a "shut-in" one day.

True service is different from sentimental acts that make us feel noble, or clear out a guilty conscience. Part of true giving is that the giver stays connected to his or her own inner experience, which allows the boundaries of giving and receiving to melt away. In other words, it taps into a form of spiritual intimacy—love in action. I'll give you an example from my high school days when I was about sixteen years old. It was a definite improvement over the "shut-in" sing.

Frequently, service organizations would call Ann Arbor High School, where I was a student, and ask for music groups to come and perform. One day, the choral teacher asked me if I was interested in playing piano for a Saturday afternoon coffee hour for "mental patients" in the veterans hospital in Ann Arbor. My immediate response was curiosity—"I wonder what it would be like." My second thought was, "I don't play well by ear and would have to use music." My third thought was, "I don't know if I could give them what they want." My last thought was, "Yes. Why not?"

Later, during a phone call from a hospital staff member, I was reassured that there was not a big agenda and that any kind of pop music or even classical music would be appreciated. I showed up with a sense of anticipation, carrying a stack of music, and started playing.

As I looked out on the huge room full of men sitting around tables, talking and smoking, I was struck by how normal everyone looked. I don't know what I expected, but my first image of mental patients was that people would look different. The playing was warmly received, and during a break an attractive man in his early twenties invited me to sit down with him and his friend. I felt uneasy, not because I didn't want to sit with them but because I wasn't sure it was okay with the staff.

I was transformed by the conversation. It was the first real, feeling-level exchange I had ever had with a man. I became a person with a life and he became a person with a life—I don't remember much of the content, but I remember the look in his eyes when he talked about being on the battlefield. I remember feeling something stirring deep inside me. I told him I often felt lonely. I remember feeling a profound sense of human connection that forty years later still triggers a sense of warmth and brings a tear to my eye.

I became the monthly regular at the coffee get-togethers and the conversations continued. It was like my secret world of Real People. I never told anyone of my experience because I didn't have anyone in my life who would understand. I was definitely struck by the paradox that my first genuine conversation happened in a mental hospital with a patient. I remember thinking, "Why are the people in here called sick and the ones on the outside called well?"

The veterans hospital experience strikes me as more in the nature of true service. I wasn't rescuing anyone, I didn't feel separate or superior, and I was deeply aware of my own feelings and reactions. It wasn't so much about doing something for others, it was like answering an invitation and immersing myself in an experience. We were both learning from each other. The piano playing was almost incidental, but it was the vehicle that got me there.

Whatever you love to do, wherever your heart lives—let that lead you into some form of service. If you already have too much to do, let someone be of service to you so that you will one day be filled up and able to pass it on.

100

PARENTS AND CHILDREN IN COMMUNITY: HELP ON A SATURDAY NIGHT

When my daughter was young, I had the blessing of being part of a group of parents who were bonded together through an alternative elementary school—the White Oak School, near

Athens, Ohio. Many of us were single parents, which increased our need to be of help to each other. I remember one chilly, rainy Saturday night when I was looking forward to a cozy evening at home with a book, while my daughter, then age six, played in the back room with a friend. As I nestled into my chair near the fire, the doorbell rang. I could feel a chill as I opened the side door and saw Margie, a fellow mother from the White Oak School, peering out from her plastic raincoat with two kids in tow. There was a big, sheepish grin on her face.

"I was going to stay home with Matt and take care of Jeffrey tonight, but . . . there's a party I really want to go to."

"And you'd like me to take the kids?" I said, laughing.

"Yes," she said, smiling.

"Sure," I said. "Janel's in the back room with Amy and I'm totally happy to be home tonight."

Without a word, the two children came in, dumped their boots on the boot heap, put their coats on the hooks, and charged toward the back room.

"Do you want to get them tonight, or in the morning?" I asked.

"It would be nice if they could spend the night."

"That's fine. I need to be gone by ten-thirty in the morning," I told her. "Could you come by ten?"

"Great," she said. "Thanks."

She zipped back to her car and reappeared with two sleeping bags and little overnight bags. The sheepish grin was replaced by the wide smile of a woman about to go out and have some fun. She waved to the kids, and told them she'd pick them up in the morning.

I again settled into my living-room retreat. I had one or two visits from the kids that evening, and I got up once to make popcorn for them. When I was about to head up to bed, I checked in with the kids and said it was about time to turn in. I asked if they needed anything, and they all seemed to be fine. I went to sleep. In the morning, I got up and made breakfast as they all played in the back room. I could hear a little bickering at times, but it always subsided without my intervention.

Does this sound all too easy? It was easy, but not by accident. We were part of a community. The ease and flow of Margie dropping off the kids, their playing together in the back room with little conflict, sleeping in a friend's house as if it were home, sprang from our connection as a community of parents who worked together to support and help each other. It was as if the cells of our individual homes were interconnected. The kids went from one house to another with barely a blink. They knew the different house rules, and generally accepted the directions of the presiding parent. Along with being our separate families, there was also a group sense of "the parents" and "the kids." It was our form of having a village to raise our children.

We connected in myriad ways: In the summer there was the Wednesday potluck at a park followed by volleyball games, camping trips to music festivals, school meetings, parties, and last-minute kid swaps. On several occasions we gathered together to talk about ways to help kids handle conflict. For example, our steadfast response to one child "telling" on another was, "Have you told him what you feel/need?" and "I'm sure you can work it out." Over time, the kids stopped trying to engage us in their arguments. It was fascinating watching new children learn the ropes. One time when I was sitting in the kitchen having coffee with David—one of the fathers—we overheard a newcomer, Mike, threatening Allis with the age-old phrase, "I'm going to go tell your dad on you."

Allis replied with complete equanimity, "All they'll say is, 'I'm sure you can work it out.'" She knew she was completely safe from the blame and shame of parents jumping into the middle of kids' arguments. Mike, stunned at the response, shifted tactics, and the children continued playing. David and I went on chatting.

On another occasion, someone called a meeting to talk about sexuality in relationship to children. What about touch, asking for kisses, kids being nude together, having a lover stay with you? What about taking pictures of the kids, naked in the bathtub? We also talked about limiting TV, discouraging war toys, and ways to forestall power struggles. Several of us who had adopted children compared notes about some of the troubles we were experiencing. This resource of people, so able and willing to talk about the often taboo subjects of child rearing, was a rich experience that eased the burdens of single parenting. I almost never hired anyone for child care. I took care of a lot of children and I had a lot of time off.

I sorely missed this group of people and community spirit when I moved to Minneapolis and was unable to establish such warm and flexible ties. While some people did help out early on by swapping child care on occasion, I never found the same sense of community. People often said things like, "We need to spend time just with our family."

Bonding and connection reflect the most primitive yearning of the human heart. From the moment of our birth, if we are welcomed into the world, warmly cradled, looked at with adoration, fed with care, and allowed our creativity, a warm sense of belonging will infuse our very being. Rich or poor, if eyes light up when we toddle into a room, people radiate excitement with us as we discover the wonders of creation, we are rich in that which we can never buy—trust and a feeling of safety. It is a lot easier to have light in our eyes for our children when we have support and time off. In our highly stressed lives, most of us need each other to help parent our children.

In a healthy community, *the* children become *our* children—a shared commitment to protect and provide opportunity for all young people and their families.

In my image of healthy community, we would have organizations that help bring families together to have fun and help each other out. Some communities have drop-in centers for children in crisis, but I'm thinking of the average overstressed parents who need help and need a break. Even if people aren't overstressed, they need connections. Child care coops have been around a long time, but it would be great to see it go deeper—to have community agencies provide networks and services for people with children.

Community mental health organizations, YMCAs, YWCAs, religious organizations, schools, and other social service agencies would be ideal for organizing such groups. There could be some introductory sessions to help people get acquainted—both the parents and the children. There could be arrangements for afternoons of child swapping and Saturday/Sunday afternoon outings. The adult who likes to hike could take a group of children hiking. The adult who likes to cook could have them over for an afternoon of cookie-baking or preparing a meal and inviting the parents in. By giving to several children at a time, parents would have time off and the children would enjoy a broader range of experiences. I remember in New York City being part of such a group organized by an agency for adoptive parents. The particular group for single adoptive parents had monthly gatherings that eventually led to several warm and supportive friendships.

The care we show for children reflects the soul of our society. And the care for children must be reflected in our care for their parents. The two are inseparable. In the United States we are not doing well by many of our children. Quality education for all, arts, sports, good affordable child care, medical care, subsidized lunches, and access to college loans are being reduced as we spend more and more money on prisons. This inverse relationship is no surprise. For a society to spend more on prisons than education suggests that we have a great problem with cause-and-effect thinking.

We have no right to be surprised when children who are given little access to care, respect, and safety become angry, violent, and so emotionally detached that they can pull a gun and kill someone without remorse. We have no right to be surprised when addictive behavior escalates and teenage girls/young women increasingly have babies they can't care for. We would be far better off to put money back into education, the arts, sports, creating summer jobs, creating places for teenagers to have fun, and supporting vocational training and college education. It would also be economically wise, as every dollar spent to help young children saves many dollars later on. Children are an image of creation happening before our eyes. Our relationship to them is the measure of our humanity. The homes we create for children reflect how much we are at home with our hearts.

101

COMMUNITY LIVING IN YOU

*C*ommunity consciousness is grounded in an "us" mentality. No matter where we go or what we do, a part of us stays tuned into the good of the whole. It doesn't mean we cease taking care of ourselves, it means that our consciousness extends beyond our personal needs to a sense of being part of a circle. We know deep within that by supporting the integrity of the circle, we feel richer in spirit and heart.

I had a touching experience with people well grounded in community thinking on a late autumn day–hike to Pilot Knob, a spectacular lookout on the Idaho border. Two women friends—Rene and Sallie—and I saw the hike listed in the "Montana Mountain Ears" newsletter and decided to join them. Everyone met exactly at 8:30 in the K-Mart parking lot as planned. (This is community behavior number one—be on time—keep agreements.) There were the three of us, two men—Dick and Greg, and a beautiful woman named Jean who had just moved to Missoula and had come by herself. She joined us in my van and we headed off behind the truck with Dick and Greg. Within minutes the four of us were like a gaggle of gals chatting away, having the sense of being kindred spirits.

When we got onto the back roads leading us to the trail head, Dick slowed down at every juncture to make sure we were together. (This is another example of community thinking: Keep track of each other.) Before we started up the trail,

Dick asked if we had the right clothes because there would be snow higher up. Dick and Greg had both brought extra gators (waterproof wraps for the ankles), which they gave to Jean and Rene. (Another example of community thinking: Bring your expertise to a situation to help others out.) There was total concern that everyone be okay and have what they needed.

Because I've been on hikes where people got separated and I am slower than average in hiking up hill, I was concerned that I would be a drag on the others; I also didn't want to be alone on what would easily be a seven-hour hike. My fears were quickly relieved when Dick said that at each juncture in the trail they would stop and make sure everyone was together. When I said I was a bit slow, he seemed totally unconcerned.

When we started, Dick asked if the pace was okay with everyone. If someone wanted to go ahead, he asked that they wait periodically so that we could meet up. I fell behind at a steep place and told people to go ahead. Then, when I knew I could keep up with them because it wasn't so steep, I asked them to wait for me. They all stopped, smiled, and waited. I wasn't treated like a nuisance. It was easy to keep up after that.

When Jean started getting wet as the snow got deeper, Greg brought out his Gore-Tex pants and gave them to her. He gently volunteered that cotton jeans aren't such a good idea on a hike in snow. At lunch, we huddled together on a circle of logs in the deep-pine forest as the snow started falling. An abundance of sandwiches and little bags of raisins, nuts, and fruit were pulled out of our respective day packs. Immediately people started passing their food around. There was a feeling of comraderie, abundance, and generosity. (Community thinking: Share what you have with each other—there's enough.)

As the hike progressed we realized that we had underestimated the amount of snow and ended up tromping through fourteen- to eighteen-inch-deep snow on the trail. Greg and Dick were in the lead most of the time, cutting the trail. My cotton pants were soaked and I scolded myself for not putting on my waterproof pants in the first place. (I had brought them but was afraid of being too warm.) Sallie offered to loan me her extra pair of longies but I didn't want to hold up the group so I hiked a bit farther. When I realized I was getting very cold, I finally said, "I need to stop and change." My inner embarrassment and fear of being chastised was quickly alleviated. Without prompting, groaning, or rolling their eyes, everyone circled around me to help with the task of changing clothes in deep snow without getting wet. Together they stomped out a flat place in the snow beside a log where I could sit to take off my boots. Then, as if people were opening the packs to have a picnic, orange vests and extra jackets popped out of day packs and were laid down on the snow to make a floor so I could take off my boots and socks without getting wet. Hands reached out to hold my gloves and socks as I peeled them off. It was sheer pleasure putting on those dry longies over my cold pink legs and then pulling up my rainproof pants. I moaned with joy and said, "This is as good as sex." Everyone laughed, and Sallie said, "I wouldn't know."

What felt remarkable to me was the complete lack of judgment or impatience and the goodwill of everyone helping out. It was like being bonded together, with a total sense of goodwill. I wasn't made to feel bad or stupid for my poor judgment in what to wear. Being treated with such kindness helped me remember in the future to dress more carefully.

At one point Rene let it be known that she was getting very tired and that her leg hurt. Everyone wanted to continue, but they showed concern for Rene. Someone offered to go back with her if need be but said that they preferred to continue. She agreed to go another half hour and check in again. (Community thinking: Talk things over, everyone say what they want, and come to an agreement that includes everyone.) We lost track of time, and when the subject came up again Dick said we were 95 percent of the way to the peak. Soon after that we climbed up to the lookout place to enjoy a breathtaking panoramic view of mountains stretching for miles on all sides. I felt that sense of elation that comes from reaching a destination powered by my own effort and the company of friends.

In a short while, after the chill started to settle in, we headed back. On the way down, when Rene's pain became acute, Jean asked if a song would help. We circled around her and sang some songs, which helped Rene's pain subside a great deal. (Community thinking: Care for each other and be creative.) When we arrived together at the bottom, nearly seven hours after we'd started, I was glad to reach for the thermos of hot cider. I was both tired and invigorated, but most of all, I felt a warm stirring in my heart. In this single day, with several people I had never met before, I witnessed more genuine kindness, caring, and true community than I had on numerous other trips. I kept thinking of the story of the loaves and fishes, which is about love and abundance. Every time someone needed something, someone reached into a day pack and brought it out. It was like having magic purses that operated like genies' lamps. Say what you need, and out it comes.

The next morning Sallie, Rene, and Jean all appeared, glowing, at Quaker meeting. It was Jean's first time. It was wonderful to see each other again after feeling so connected and close from our snow hike. At the close of meeting when we were invited to share a joy or a concern, Sallie spoke beautifully and lovingly of how much she valued our connection. It brought tears to my eyes.

I learned so much from these people about the warm bonds we create when people have a community consciousness. Every time I remember this trip I feel a warmth and happiness stirring inside. I've often felt lonely hiking with people who are more interested in charging ahead than in having an experience together. I also learned a valuable lesson about bringing extra things along for others. On the next hike, I came equipped with extra wool socks and gloves that other people ended up using.

This is one small story, but it epitomizes the small pieces of the mosaic that go into creating community consciousness. It's easy to get overwhelmed, wondering what we can do to be of help in the world. The answer is to do little things often. It's not usually big, heroic deeds so much as a daily commitment to consciously living from the center of your heart, knowing how much your kindness and care mean to others.

102

JOY IN THE HEART OF COMMUNITY: CELEBRATION

*S*ome synonyms for celebrate are "intensify," "observe," "praise," "bliss," "honor," "sanctify," "respect," and "consecrate." Celebration invites us to open our creative, wild, spontaneous inner world and feel the pulse of our being connect to others, the natural world, and the passages in our lives. On New Year's Day, 1995, I awoke after a sound sleep with a sense of energy pulsing in my belly, and a warm glow in my heart. I felt a heightened sense of pleasure and awareness, as if I were buoyed up by the joy I had felt the night before.

That wonderful charge of energy came from a celebration called "First Night Missoula," our own community's version of a nationwide movement to provide a drug-free New Year's Eve celebration for everyone, created by a wide range of people and organizations in the community. As I went around Missoula, going to everything from Celtic harp and cello music in St. Francis Church, to African and Native Americans drumming, to watching a chess master called "the Octopus" play twelve people at once (including our mayor), to dancing in a huge hall to the Montana Mud Flaps, numerous thoughts danced through my mind: What a great party, everyone's invited, no one's left out, no one has to buy fancy clothes, no one has to have a partner, no one is drinking, and there's something for everyone— adults, children, old and young. Here we were together, everyone seemed happy. In that moment, I felt a great hope for the future of the world.

Shortly before midnight, we went to the courthouse lawn to join a group of drummers and a mass of people congregating to dance, chant, and welcome in the New Year with a song of peace for world unity. I had been in constant motion to a steady beat for nearly two hours. The high was the natural high of spirit and joy, of dancing and caring about each other, a high that would not leave a morning hangover.

The energy one gets from healthy celebration goes far beyond the notion of having enough energy to get through the day. It's like an earth spirit energy that goes to the heart, belly, mind, and soul, nourishing our creativity, health, mental capacity, and sense of well-being. It brings a heightened state of joy and awareness, enabling us to experience all of life more truly.

Another form of community celebration I encourage people to experience are the "Dances of Universal Peace." Created with the intention of providing a means for personal and planetary transformation, the dances are being done in many places all over the world. They include secular and sacred songs and chants from all major spiritual traditions and cultures, using movements and steps that emanate from the spirit and feeling of the words. Most of them are simple and easily learned. There are groups doing the dances on a regular basis in many cities and towns throughout the United States and other parts of the world. (The address for the national organization is listed in the back.)

Performed in a circle, sometimes concentric circles, often with ever changing partners, the dances are flowing, beautiful, and healing. Sometimes when I am dancing, I have a profound sense of connecting with people in other cultures who have sung these words millions of times throughout the years. It's a way to tap into the essence of other cultures through their traditions.

At one point, when feeling bogged down in writing this book, I took a weekend break to attend a three-day Peace Dance gathering in Pocatello, Idaho. As testament to the power of the dances, I came back with renewed energy and creativity and the writing poured out of me for days. It was as if the dancing had unblocked my inner voice and channels for creativity. Here are the encouraging words to one of my favorite dances of universal peace (the words to the first verse come from a poem by Rumi; the second verse is one used frequently in the Peace Dances):

> Come, come whoever you are
> Even though you've broken your vows
> a thousand times
> Come, come, again.

> Ya Mevlana Ruh Allah
> La illaha illa 'llah.
> Oh Guide of the Spirit of God
> There is no reality except for the One.

However we choose to celebrate in our communities, we find the greatest power when our gatherings are inclusive, creative, and include some form of spiritual consciousness—a sense of being tied to something bigger, an awareness that our community is a wheel in a bigger wheel. This is not contrary to having a good time, rather, it keeps us mindful that the joy of celebration comes from opening to a wider consciousness and connecting to the hearts of each other. Going back to the synonyms for celebrate, we observe, intensify, feel bliss, and as our joy overflows, we send our prayers and warm wishes out into the world.

103
COME RIDE THE MISSOULA CAROUSEL

We've done the work, now let's go play!

Nestled at the edge of Caras Park by the Clark Fork River, in the middle of Missoula, stands a wondrous, hand-carved carousel—the first of its kind since the thirties. The opening celebration in May 1995 was one of the most festive, spirited gatherings Missoula has ever seen. It was hard to tell the gleaming eyes of the children from those of the adults as they looked with wonder at the beauty, playfulness, and perfection of the carousel. There was an eruption of happiness and wonder when the grand organ began to play and the carousel started going around.

Born of Chuck Kaparich's dream to build a carousel, its creation became a community event that took nearly five years, drawing people together to raise money, design, carve, sand, and paint. According to the book, *The Missoula Carousel*, adapted from an extensive article in *The Missoulian* (ordering information in the back), in Kaparich's mind it was a project that would help him earn his place as an American, the same way his grandfather had worked hard to become an American and create opportunities for his children.

No one was paid a penny for their work, but everyone was rewarded by becoming part of something wonderful, something that helped them stretch, feel connected, and have a sense of pride. One woman said she "was intrigued by the 'pure communism' of the project—everyone working for the good of the community, without financial gain, without prima donnas."

When you start adding up the time it took—each of the 40 horses took between 400 and 800 hours to carve—you get a small idea of people's dedication to make the carousel come alive. And that was just part of the picture. People raised money, sold buttons, created a newsletter and, eventually, a foundation for the Missoula carousel.

The horses on the Missoula carousel were not designed from a recipe. Each horse represents a story or interest of a person or group of people who adopted (funded) the horse. Many represent aspects of local history. For example, one of my favorite horses is Orchard Belle, wearing a straw hat and carrying fresh vegetables behind her saddle. Adopted and designed by the Several Orchard Homes groups, it commemorates the truck farmers who settled in Orchard Homes, west of Missoula. My father was among these people. His poor but proud college-educated parents left a tiny railroad town in northern Montana over eighty years ago to truck farm in Orchard Homes so their children could go to college in Missoula.

People were invited to adopt a horse and be part of the design. While it cost $2,500 to adopt a horse, which gave you the right to contribute to the design, many horses were the result of groups of people working together. Twenty-five women—Moms for a Carousel—each contributed $100, which went to the creation of Star Boy. A schoolteacher started a "pennies for ponies" project that resulted in children collecting nearly one million pennies for the carousel, which gave four different classrooms the right to participate in designing a pony. Snapples, for example, is a black-and-white pinto with apples— some partially eaten—on the bridle and saddle. It was named affectionately for their teacher who loved apples—Sally Nelson's apples—and has pennies lodged in the design.

Genius is born of dreams and passion, which ignite our spirit and allows us to say, *Why not me? Maybe I could do that.* Kaparich had always loved carousels. As a child, Carousel Gardens in Butte, Montana, had been a welcome escape from the dullness of the drab mining town. His was awakened to his vision to create a carousel after visiting the Spokane carousel with his wife. When he realized that they were hand-carved of wood, he touched them with a sense of awe, thinking, "What a piece of work; who would do that?" When he read that the horses were carved by a Danish immigrant—just like his grand-father, whom he deeply admired—he got swept away learning and reading about carousels. He called a carousel historian, hoping to buy one for himself and was chastised for wanting to be a "carousel vulture." That night, with thoughts about Carousel Gardens, his grandfather, and the Spokane carousel churning in his head, he had a sudden awakening: "You know, if they could do this a hundred years ago, why couldn't some-one do it today?" And he vowed to build a carousel if it took him the rest of his life.

Passion and dedication give us courage. Kaparich walked

into the mayor's office carrying one of the first carved horses and said that he'd like to build a carousel for Missoula and have it located on the riverfront in Caras Park. Could they save that land for the carousel? He didn't want money, he just wanted the carousel built in a place where it would be preserved. That was the beginning of many visits to fairs and shopping centers—carrying horses and raising money. Kaparich's passion for creating a carousel was magnetic. People volunteered, raised money, sold carousel calendars, and joined him nightly in his garage to carve horses. People brought cookies, contributed expertise, learned, and worked together.

Kaparich's passion and humble desire to create something wondrous for Missoula brought many people together. He marveled at the synchronicity of people appearing with the needed expertise at just the right moment. That's what happens when we live from the heart for a greater purpose. We tap into an energy field that connects us to others and draws them to us. People become led by some force beyond their grasp to create, join in, and contribute, not out of some altruistic belief but because it's fun, it feels good.

At its best, healthy community helps us reach for our wildest dreams and stretch beyond ourselves, coming together to create something beautiful, something for everyone to enjoy. While it was initially Kaparich's dream and passion to build a carousel, and he set standards of the highest possible quality, everyone was welcome to join in the venture—it wasn't so much *his* project, although he became known as "the carousel man"—it was a project for Missoula and a way to honor his grandfather. He was incredulous as people contributed money or came to help and take part. "Everyone I dealt with was one of the nicest people in the world."

It's easy to see the creation of the Missoula carousel as an unusual, magical event. But maybe it's not magic at all. Or maybe it's the magic we all have within us when we dare to live our dreams. For me, the Missoula carousel symbolizes the potential that lies in any group of people who bring passion, determination, creativity, and generous hearts together. The more people's basic needs are met, the more we become free to create something of wonder and beauty for all of us to enjoy, not because of reward or fame, but simply because there is nothing that brings us greater happiness than joining together in the wonder of our shared creativity and joy.

So listen to the music, pick out your favorite horse, feel the wind in your hair, and ride the Missoula carousel.

Blessings and joy in abundance to you and all people.

Sources

INFORMATION ON CHARLOTTE KASL'S WORKSHOPS AND TRAINING AND MARATHON PSYCHOTHERAPY SESSIONS

Workshops and Training Sessions

Charlotte Kasl presents talks, workshops, and training sessions on intimacy, relationships, empowerment, sexuality, spirituality, addictions, and healing.

Marathon Psychotherapy

Dr. Kasl is available for marathon psychotherapy sessions—lasting one to three days—for couples and individuals needing interventions in destructive behavior patterns, wanting to improve their sexuality and intimacy, or seeking deep levels of healing. She also does phone consultations. Dr. Kasl is a licensed psychologist in Minnesota, a licensed clinical counselor in Montana, and a certified addiction specialist. She has twenty years' experience in working with survivors of abuse, individuals, and couples.

Letters/Workshop Information

I love to receive letters and I read them all. Unfortunately, I do not have references for therapists around the country and I am not always able to respond personally. If you would like to be on my mailing list or receive a list of workshops, send a self-addressed, stamped envelope (preferably legal size) to the address below.

Book Orders

In addition to books published by HarperCollins (listed in the front of this book), which can be bought in most bookstores, Charlotte Kasl has self-published *Yes, You Can! A Guide to Empowerment Groups* (based on *Many Roads, One Journey: Moving Beyond the 12 Steps*), which can be ordered by sending $16.00 to the address below. I also have a videotape on overcoming addiction empowerment and the sixteen steps for doing this for $25.00. Please send orders and don't phone unless you are a bookstore.

Charlotte Kasl
P.O. Box 1302
Lolo, Montana 59847
Phone: (406) 273–6080

FOR INFORMATION ON THE DANCES OF UNIVERSAL PEACE, WRITE:

Peaceworks
International Center for the Dances of Universal Peace
444 N.E. Ravenna Blvd., Suite 306
Seattle, WA 98115-6467
Phone (206) 522–4353

To order a copy of *A Carousel for Missoula,* a picture book telling the story of the creation of the Missoula Carousel, send your order to either:

A Carousel for Missoula
1 Caras Park
Missoula, MT 59802
or
The Missoulian
500 S. Higgins
Missoula, MT 59801

Softcover: $15.95 + 3.95 Shipping = $19.90
Hardcover: $24.95 + 4.95 Shipping = $29.90

BIBLIOGRAPHY

Bach, George R., M.D., and Peter Wyden. *The Intimate Enemy: How to Fight Fair in Love and Marriage.* New York: William Morrow & Company, Inc., 1968.

Barks, Coleman. *Rumi: Like This.* Athens, GA: Maypop Books, 1990.

Bly, Robert. *The Kabir Book: Forty-four of the Ecstatic Poems of Kabir.* Boston: Beacon Press, 1971.

Buber, Martin. *I and Thou.* New York: Charles Scribner and Sons, 1958.

Caldicott, Helen, M.D. *If You Love This Planet: A Plan to Heal the Earth.* New York: W.W. Norton & Company, 1992.

Csikszentmihalyi, Mihaly. *The Evolving Self.* New York: HarperCollins*Publishers,* 1993.

———. *Flow—The Pyschology of Optimal Experience.* New York: HarperCollins*Publishers,* 1990.

Dass, Ram. *Journey of Awakening: A Meditator's Guidebook.* New York: Bantam Books, 1990.

Edinger, Edward F. *Ego and Archetype.* New York: Penguin Books, 1985.

Freedman, Samuel G. *Upon This Rock: The Miracles of a Black Church.* New York: HarperCollins*Publishers,* 1993.

Fromm, Erich. *The Art of Loving.* New York: Harper & Row, Publishers, 1956.

Gibran, Kahlil. *The Prophet.* New York: Alfred A. Knopf, 1923.

Goodenough Community. *A Goodenough Story, A Goodenough Life: An Experiment in Community Formation and Self-Governance.* Goodenough Community, 1993.

Harris, Thomas A., M.D. *I'm OK—You're OK.* New York: Harper & Row, Publishers, 1969.

Hendrix, Harville, M.D. *Getting the Love You Want: A Guide for Couples.* New York: HarperCollins*Publishers,* 1988.

Imber-Black, Evan, Ph.D., and Janine Roberts, Ed.D. *Rituals for Our Times: Celebrating, Healing, and Changing Our Lives and Our Relationships.* New York: HarperCollins*Publishers,* 1992.

Johnson, Catherine, Ph.D. *Lucky in Love: The Secrets of Happy Couples and How Their Marriages Thrive.* New York: Viking, 1992.

Judith, Anodea. *Wheels of Life: A User's Guide to the Chakra System.* St. Paul, MN: Llewellyn Publications, 1989.

Kasl, Charlotte Davis, Ph.D. *Finding Joy: 101 Ways to Free Your Spirit and Dance with Life*. New York: HarperCollins*Publishers*, 1994.

———. *Women, Sex, and Addiction: A Search for Love and Power*. New York: Harper & Row, Publishers, 1989.

———. *Yes, You Can! A Guide to Empowerment Groups*. Lolo, MT: Many Roads, One Journey, 1995.

Keyes, Ken, Jr. *Handbook to Higher Consciousness*. Coos Bay, OR: Love Line Books, 1988.

Levine, Stephen, and Ondrea Levine. *Embracing the Beloved: Relationship as a Path of Awakening*. New York: Doubleday, 1995.

Morgan, Marlo. *Mutant Message Down Under*. New York: HarperCollins*Publishers*, 1991.

Quinn, Daniel. *Ishmael*. New York: A Bantam/Turner Book, 1992.

Scarf, Maggie. *Intimate Partners: Patterns in Love and Marriage*. New York: Random House, 1987.

Tannen, Deborah, Ph.D. *You Just Don't Understand: Women and Men in Conversation*. New York: Random House, Inc., 1990.

Wachtel, Paul L. *The Poverty of Affluence: A Psychological Portrait of the American Way of Life*. Santa Cruz, CA: New Society Publishers, 1989.

Welwood, John, Ph.D. *Journey of the Heart: Intimate Relationship and the Path of Love*. New York: HarperCollins*Publishers*, 1990.